Teaching Kids with Mental Health & Learning Disorders in the Regular Classroom

Teaching Kids with Mental Health & Learning Disorders in the Regular Classroom

How to Recognize, Understand, and Help Challenged (and Challenging) Students Succeed

Myles L. Cooley, Ph.D.

Library of Congress Cataloging-in-Publication Data
Cooley, Myles L.
Teaching kids with mental health and learning disorders in the regular classroom : how to recognize, understand, and help challenged (and challenging) students succeed / Myles L. Cooley.
p. cm.
Includes bibliographical references.
ISBN-13: 978-1-57542-242-8
ISBN-10: 1-57542-242-5
1. Children with mental disabilities—Education—United States. 2. Learning disabled children—Education—United States. 3. Inclusive education—United States. I. Title.
LC4031.C663 2006
371.9'046—dc22 2006101754

Edited by Douglas J. Fehlen
Cover design by Marieka Heinlen
Interior design by Percolator

10 9 8 7 6 5 4 3 2 1
Printed in the United States of America

Free Spirit Publishing Inc.
217 Fifth Avenue North, Suite 200
Minneapolis, MN 55401-1299
(612) 338-2068
help4kids@freespirit.com
www.freespirit.com

Dedication

To my wife who, without any complaints, endured the hundreds of hours I spent in my office researching and writing over the past two years.

To my daughters who have chosen careers in counseling psychology and school counseling. They will continue the mission of helping young people and make the world a better place.

To the thousands of children and adolescents I've seen over the years who have taught me more than all the books on my bookshelves.

Acknowledgments

I want to thank the following individuals for assistance with various aspects of this book:

Rabbi Richard Address, Director, Department of Family Concerns, Union for Reform Judaism, for providing initial enthusiasm and encouragement for this book

Judy Galbraith, founder and president of Free Spirit Publishing, for sharing the vision of educating teachers about mental health disorders

Douglas Fehlen, my editor at Free Spirit who helped me learn to write in the style and language of educators. Douglas's mellow demeanor provided stability through the ups and downs of this project. He may have a potential career as a psychotherapist!

Lynn Welton for help with word processing and formatting tasks

Eleni Savvides for being the best office assistant I've ever worked with

Regina Appleby, M.Ed., Joanne Byron, S.S.P., NCSP, and Denise Guadagnino, B.S., for their assistance with educational accommodations and interventions

Russ Feldman, Ed.S., Executive Director, Exceptional Student Education and Bob Templeton, Ed.S., Manager, Psychological Services, Palm Beach County School District, for consultation regarding Response to Intervention and IDEA

Suzette Gingold, M.S., CCC-SLP, and Donna Wexler, M.A., CCC-SLP, for assistance with Communication Disorders

Johanna Kandel, founder and director of The Alliance for Eating Disorders Awareness for help with Eating Disorders

Susan Sentell, M.Ed., for consultation regarding Reading Disabilities

A special thanks to Dr. Alvin Rosen for over 25 years of intangibles

Contents

Introduction

"Why did I choose this profession? Why am I here?
Simply put, I'm here to make a difference."

—Tommie Lindsey, educator and author of *It Doesn't Take a Genius*

How many hats are you wearing today? As an educator, of course, you have many. It's your job to teach a diverse population of students—many who have difficulties with learning. Add to this the fact that children come to you with a wide variety of social and emotional issues and your job becomes considerably more difficult. Some students may have problems with self-control, mood, or socializing that interfere not only with their learning but also with your ability to teach.

You've got a tough job—one of the toughest there is. That you're reading this book shows your deep concern for students' learning and mental health. In my work with children and their families, I've come to know and admire many dedicated teachers. Like you, they are hungry for information they can use to help students who struggle with various problems. That's why I wrote this book. I wanted to provide practical classroom strategies that teachers can use to best teach and support all students—especially those with mental health and learning disorders.

TODAY'S MAINSTREAMED CLASSROOMS

What is it that makes your job so demanding? Without a doubt, you are expected to teach a wide spectrum of students. Some of your students come to you with academic and behavioral difficulties. This is, in part, the result of the practice of mainstreaming children with special needs. Gone are many of the special education classes of the past, in favor of keeping these students in the regular classroom.

While good intentions underlie mainstreaming, you can imagine, or may have experienced, some major challenges: How can I help all kids succeed academically? How do I deal with children's social and emotional development? What about training for me? How can I respond to children with mental health problems?

SOMETHING TO THINK ABOUT . . .

Only about 25 percent of children needing mental health care receive necessary professional attention, and 70 to 80 percent of those children receive that attention in a school setting.

The task of helping students with mental health, behavioral, and learning problems may seem daunting. The good news is that there are many strategies you can use to support students. *Teaching Kids with Mental Health & Learning Disorders in the Regular Classroom* provides interventions for the regular classroom teacher as well as advice for determining when students may need the help of other school staff or outside professionals.

HOW COMMON ARE MENTAL HEALTH AND LEARNING DISORDERS?

The number of children being diagnosed with learning and mental health disorders is increasing. Up to 10 percent of students have a learning disability. About 20 percent have a mental health problem that interferes with daily life—and half of those children meet the criteria for a diagnosable mental disorder. Add these numbers and you have up to 10 million young people with challenges that can make it difficult for them to learn or behave properly in the classroom. Many of these students have more than one area of difficulty.

More and more it's being acknowledged that academic problems are often grounded in significant differences in *how* students learn, as well as in social and emotional difficulties they may be facing. Multiple learning approaches and innovative instructional techniques are being used to engage learners. Rather than simply penalizing students for misbehavior or low achievement, educators are looking more deeply into what might be causing problems. They're finding that when psychological or learning problems are identified and addressed, students not only feel and behave better, but achieve at a higher academic level.

Providing attention to students' differences can seem to be a great challenge when, at the same time, you're accountable for the performance of your entire class. You might fear that giving too much attention to certain children will keep you from helping the majority of your class achieve state standards and reach grade-level proficiency. The information and strategies presented in this book are meant to allow you to provide individual attention to those students who need it with minimum negative impact on the rest of the class. You will also learn ways to address problems with student behavior that can interfere with teaching.

HOW TO USE THIS BOOK

My goals in writing this book are to provide current information on mental health and learning disorders and make it easy for you to apply this knowledge in the regular classroom. Here's what you'll find:

Part I. The Role of Schools in Addressing Mental Health and Learning Disorders

The first part of the book provides background to help you meet the needs of students with mental health and learning disorders. "The Changing Nature of Special Education" features a discussion of the recently revised Individuals with Disabilities Education Act (IDEA) and how it continues to change special education services in schools. You can use the section titled "Assessing Student Needs" to identify students who may need academic help, emotional support, or behavioral interventions. "Effective Classroom Policies and Procedures" offers classroom management guidelines—including recommendations for setting consistent rules and positive, proactive disciplinary measures. You can use "Effective Teaching Strategies for Meeting Diverse Student Needs" to incorporate into your school day best practices for motivating all students to learn. "Establishing a Safe and Caring Classroom" gives you suggestions for making your classroom a place where students feel respected, valued, and safe. The last section of Part I, "Building Social Skills in Students," provides ideas for fostering social development in children—an area of growth often affected by mental health and learning disorders.

Part II. Mental Health and Learning Disorders

The second part of the book opens with "Terms Used in This Book"—a section with general information on disorders and terminology used by different professionals to describe these problems.

Next you'll find detailed information on mental health and learning disorders. All of the sections are laid out in a consistent way so you can easily reference the information you need. Each section defines the disorder with its symptoms, and then it gives helpful strategies for working with students. Also included are statistics on how common disorders are among children, in-the-trenches stories, treatments professionals may use, and other information that can be helpful in your work with children.

The book concludes with sections you can use to find out more about conditions. "Resources" are organized by disorder and include information on related books, organizations, and Web sites. The "Notes" section provides sources for statistics and information that appear throughout the book.

This book can be used whether or not you know a child who has a disorder. In cases where you already know what disorder a student has, you can find relevant information by referencing it in the contents. When you're not sure about the existence of a disorder, you can identify potentially helpful strategies by consulting the index and referencing behaviors you have observed. A child who is always disorganized, for example, may benefit from some of the strategies that you'll find for helping students who have ADHD—even though other symptoms might not match up.

I have written this book with regular classroom teachers in mind, but the information can be helpful to many personnel at school. School counselors and psychologists will learn techniques they can use with students in guidance settings. Classroom aides and special educators who work in pull-out settings will find strategies they can use with students to improve academic performance and promote appropriate classroom behaviors. Administrators can benefit from the information on legal responsibilities a school has in the education and care of students with certain problems. Parents and others involved in the care and education of children can also gain insight into the difficulties that may underlie a child's behavior.

THE POWER OF LABELS

Throughout this book, labels are used in a way that accounts for a child being more than a mental health or learning disorder. This means that children are not called "ADHD," "autistic," or "obsessive-compulsive." Instead those affected by disorders are referred to, for example, as "children with ADHD," "students with autism," or "young people with Obsessive-Compulsive Disorder." Labeling children ("He's learning disabled," for example) may seem more convenient, but it does a disservice to human beings who are complex individuals with specific strengths and weaknesses. In short, calling people by labels implies that their entire being is characterized by a condition and doesn't allow for the complex nature of their being.

YOUR POWER TO MAKE A DIFFERENCE

Our youngest daughter was about seven years old when a teacher told us she was concerned because she thought Lisa looked sad. The teacher suggested that maybe Lisa was depressed. Another teacher asked us if Lisa was afraid of teachers. When we asked why, she said that Lisa didn't talk to her as much as other students did.

These comments came as quite a surprise to us—we were used to a bubbling chatterbox at home. As it turns out, we found out that Lisa had considerable anxiety in the classroom. Her anxiety was showing up as shyness. While this story demonstrates the importance of avoiding diagnosing students (Lisa was not depressed), we benefited from knowing that something was not "right." A school counselor helped Lisa with her shyness and anxiety, and Lisa was able to be more comfortable and successful in school.

This story highlights the important role you play in the lives of students. As an educator you may spend as much waking time with children as their parents do. As a result, you'll often be among the first to observe potential problems. While it's important to avoid rushing to judgment, your ability and willingness to share concerns with parents is crucial. Early intervention in mental health and learning disorders can mean fewer and less severe academic, emotional, or behavior problems.

Like most teachers, you probably came to this job knowing that it wouldn't always be easy. Instead, you probably knew about teaching's challenges but chose it because you recognized its importance and couldn't pass up the opportunity to enrich children's lives. Along the way, you've probably realized another truth of the trade: Teaching is one of the most rewarding professions there is. Your work with children makes you a very influential person in a child's future. Lisa can attest to this—she recently received her master's degree in school counseling and is employed at an elementary school.

I hope this book helps make your work even more rewarding. I'd enjoy hearing about how you're using the strategies in your classroom with challenged (and challenging) students. I'd also like to learn about any other methods you have found effective. You may share your thoughts in care of my publisher:

Free Spirit Publishing Inc.
217 Fifth Avenue North, Suite 200
Minneapolis, MN 55401-1299
help4kids@freespirit.com

Keep up your important work.

Myles L. Cooley, Ph.D.

Part I

The Role of Schools in Addressing Mental Health and Learning Disorders

The Changing Nature of Special Education

"The most universal quality is diversity."

—Michel de Montaigne, author

In recent years, regular classroom teachers have been increasingly responsible for educating students with mental health and learning disorders. This section offers a snapshot of special education and how it has evolved. A look at these changes can provide you with insight into this trend of mainstreaming students—and give you an idea of what to expect in the future.

Special education has existed in our schools for over 30 years. In 1975, the U.S. Congress passed a law called the Education of All Handicapped Children Act, which guaranteed students with disabilities the right to a "free and appropriate public education" in the "least restrictive environment." In 1990, the title of the special education law was changed (with substantive updates) to the Individuals with Disabilities Education Act (IDEA).

As you know, the name of this legislation is not all that has changed in over three decades of special education. Shifting instructional philosophies and best practices—including those represented in the latest reauthorization of IDEA in 2004—have led to innovations in the education of students with special needs. You've probably become familiar with many of these changes as your school seeks to meet federal, state, and local school district requirements.

While many improvements have been made to IDEA over the years, some areas of contention remain. For example, many believe that the law fails to respond adequately to some of those most in need of special education. The vast majority of students in special education have traditionally qualified under the categories of "specific learning disability (SLD)" and "speech and language impairment." Many other students—including those with behavioral or psychological disorders—have been underserved by IDEA. In the past, these students have traditionally made up only 1 percent of all children in special education programs.

SECTION 504 OF THE REHABILITATION ACT OF 1973

For children with special needs who do not qualify for services under IDEA, there is another law that enables you to offer additional support and services. *Section 504 of the Rehabilitation Act of 1973* is a civil rights law that requires schools to give students with disabilities or "handicapping conditions"—including mental health and learning disorders—equal opportunity to succeed in the classroom. If a student's handicapping condition "substantially limits" his ability to learn, he might be eligible for a *504 plan.*

You can request a child be evaluated for Section 504 eligibility if you observe poor performance in your classroom. (Parents may also request assessment.) A student's 504 plan can provide a wide array of accommodations. A child with Attention Deficit Hyperactivity Disorder might be given frequent reminders to stay on task and allowed to move about the classroom more than other students. Children with anxiety that makes them reluctant to speak might not be graded on class participation. A student with Obsessive-Compulsive Disorder who is a perfectionist and continually erases his answers might have written work requirements reduced.

PRIVATE EDUCATION

Many private schools (sectarian and nonsectarian) are also accountable to respond to Section 504 if they receive any federal funding. Private schools may be held to a lesser standard of response to students eligible for 504 plans. The law requires private schools to provide "minor adjustments" compared to public schools, which must provide "reasonable accommodations." It's important to be aware of your school's responsibilities and the role you play in meeting them.

DEFINING LEARNING DISABILITIES

A learning disability is officially recognized in IDEA as "a disorder in one or more of the basic psychological processes involved in understanding or in using language, spoken or written, which disorder may manifest itself in imperfect ability to listen, think, speak, read, write, spell or do mathematical calculations." This includes "such conditions as perceptual disabilities, brain injury, minimal brain dysfunction, dyslexia, and developmental aphasia." Not included in this definition are "children who have learning problems that are primarily the result of visual, hearing, or motor disabilities, of mental retardation or emotional disturbance, or of environmental, cultural, or economic disadvantage."

You may be aware of one of the most intense debates in special education—that of how to determine which students are eligible for services under this definition. Identification in the past has been based largely on the discrepancy between a child's ability and academic achievement. The assumption has been that a student achieving at a lower level than his ability indicates a learning disability.

The federal government left it to individual states to determine how this discrepancy between ability and achievement should be measured. Many chose to compare academic performance to a child's intelligence, usually measured by an IQ test. This is a simplistic approach to determining disabilities. It does not provide any information about the "disorder in psychological processing" that IDEA cites in its definition of a learning disability. Educators and researchers have pointed out other shortfalls of the discrepancy model:

1. The model determines *eligibility for special education services*—not the existence of a learning disability. Eligibility is largely determined by scores from tests. If students' scores meet the criteria for a significant discrepancy, the students may qualify for special education in the SLD category. If scores don't fit the criteria, students will not likely qualify and parents may be told that no learning disability exists. These students may actually have significant problems processing information and learning that should be addressed.

2. The discrepancy formula has been called a "wait to fail" model. In order to qualify for services, students' achievement levels have to fall very low. This may not happen until at least the middle of elementary school or—for many students—until middle or high school. The longer interventions are delayed, the less chance there is for effective remediation. In addition, a student's self-esteem and motivation may be negatively affected for years while she struggles academically.

The formula also penalizes students with learning problems who have worked for hours and hours with parents or tutors to maintain adequate academic performance. Despite their difficulty with learning academic skills, these students may have achieved at too high a level to qualify for special education.

3. The model has over-identified students with high IQs and under-identified students with low IQs. Over-identification occurs when students with high IQs score in the average or below-average range on achievement tests. This discrepancy may qualify them for special education. A learning disability, however, is only one possible reason for this discrepancy. Underachievement might be another reason. Under-identification occurs when a student with a low IQ also has low achievement scores.

4. The model may over-identify students from culturally and linguistically diverse backgrounds. Nonnative speakers have been referred for special education services despite the fact that difficulties with English, not a learning disability, are responsible for low achievement.

5. Research indicates that a student's IQ (above a level of generalized mental deficiency) may not make a significant difference in his ability to respond to academic interventions. A student's intelligence level may have little to do with the choice or likely success of academic interventions. With research-based interventions, both high- and low-IQ students benefit.

6. A discrepancy formula doesn't provide any information about why a child is having difficulty in an academic area. Interventions may be generic and not necessarily relevant for different students with weaknesses in the same academic subject. For example, students with reading problems may have difficulties with phonological awareness, phonetic decoding, comprehension, fluency, vocabulary, or a combination of these. Only by performing a detailed analysis of each student's particular difficulties with reading can a plan be developed that targets specific problems and implements relevant interventions.

What does all of this mean for you? In a word, change. Following years of effort from educators, researchers, and parents, Congress revised IDEA in 2004 to address concerns with identification of students with learning disabilities. The new law makes the ability-achievement discrepancy *optional* during identification and will lead to an increased number of students with learning difficulties being taught in the regular classroom.

INCLUDING STUDENTS IN THE REGULAR CLASSROOM

In 1986, Madeleine Will, the assistant secretary of the U.S. Office of Special Education and Rehabilitation Services, proposed that all attempts should be made to include students with mild disabilities in regular, instead of separate, classrooms. This new philosophy led to the Regular Education Initiative, the goal of which was to educate as many children with disabilities as possible in regular classrooms.

The 1997 reauthorization of IDEA validated this commitment to inclusion. The language in that legislative update required that children with disabilities be educated "to the maximum extent" in the least restrictive environment. In addition, general education teachers were now included as part of the team that developed Individualized Education Programs (IEPs) for special education students.

The diversity of your classroom probably reflects these philosophical and legislative changes. You likely have been increasingly responsible for the education of students with disabilities. The numbers bear this out: In 2000–2001, almost one-half of public school students with disabilities were spending at least 80 percent of their day in general education classes—an increase of 16 percent from 1988–1989.

A NEW MODEL FOR HELPING STUDENTS WITH LEARNING DIFFICULTIES

The latest reauthorization of IDEA in 2004 again affirmed a commitment to inclusion. The legislation also sought to address controversial issues in the identification process and intervention procedures for students with learning disabilities. A new approach suggested by IDEA 2004 is called the *Response to Intervention (RTI)* model. It's a model that places less importance on labeling disabilities and more on providing sound instruction for *all* students.

The RTI model turns around the approach to identifying students with learning disabilities. Rather than waiting for a small group of students to fail academically (and then providing a small number of them with educational interventions), this new approach is much more proactive and preventive. It recommends evaluating all children in early grades and providing interventions to those having difficulties. Students are chosen for additional instruction based on norms established by individual school districts. The end result: There will likely be a further increase in the number of special needs students educated in the regular classroom.

In the RTI model, students with learning difficulties receive high-quality instruction or interventions in the regular classroom. State and local education administrators most often choose these interventions. A student's response to intervention is then evaluated and necessary instructional adjustments are made. Interventions occur in three tiers, with a student's progress determining the intensity of instruction. Students can move back and forth among tiers based on their progress over time.

Tier 1: All students receive high-quality instruction and behavioral support in general education classrooms. At this level, teachers implement a variety of teaching strategies based on individual students' needs.

Tier 2: Students whose skills and rate of progress lag behind those of peers based on norms derived within individual school districts receive more specialized instruction or remediation within the general education setting. More intensive, short-term instruction will be involved at this level, and general education teachers may collaborate with more specifically trained educators to design interventions. Parents are notified and included in the planning at this level.

Tier 3: Students who have not progressed adequately with Tier 2 interventions are given more-intensive individual interventions. More-intensive small group or individual long-term interventions may be implemented. Special education personnel are likely to be consulted and involved in planning at this level. Only those students who fail to respond to the most-intensive levels of intervention may be identified as needing special education. This determination will continue to be based on the student's qualifying for a disability as defined by IDEA criteria and the student's need for special education.

These are significant changes, but there is optimism surrounding the RTI model because it serves not only students with learning problems, but all children. Each student receives instruction that is guided by frequent assessments of his ability and academic progress. RTI has been called a proactive, preventive approach that will address students' difficulties before they fail and become demoralized, and before interventions are too late. Some researchers have predicted that this type of early identification and intervention could ultimately reduce the number of students with reading problems by 70 percent.

IMPLEMENTING RESPONSE TO INTERVENTION

The RTI model signifies a substantial change in the way students with learning difficulties are identified and educated. Individual states may choose to permit or prohibit the use of the discrepancy formula until the RTI model is fully implemented. This process is expected to take several years as states and local norms for student performance are developed and teachers are trained in assessment and interventions. Implementation will likely be a constantly changing process so it's important to stay up-to-date with your state and school district policies.

How will all of this affect your classroom? You—the teacher in the trenches—will be expected to assess all students and provide much of the additional instruction required by children who fall behind. If this worries you, you're not alone. Critics of the RTI model have raised several concerns including questions about who will provide training and whether regular classroom teachers have time to assume these new responsibilities.

Concerned educators have also cited a lack of scientifically based interventions in areas other than reading, as well as the RTI model's inability to identify the causes for learning difficulties. Some opponents of the model fear that students with learning disabilities will not be identified because all struggling learners and underachievers will be grouped together and provided the same interventions. In particular, students with above-average abilities who have processing or learning difficulties may be missed because they may not score poorly on tests measuring academic progress.

While less than perfect, the RTI model represents a start toward closely monitoring all student needs and offering individualized interventions that can help all students succeed. Students with special needs will increasingly be taught in regular classrooms and you'll be responsible for implementing interventions for them. That is where this book can aid you. It can help you respond to the needs of students with learning difficulties as well as mental health problems. Regardless of how education policy or procedures change over the years, the important work of meeting the individual needs of students will remain with dedicated educators like you.

Assessing Student Needs

"This is at the heart of all good education, where the teacher asks students to think and engages them in encouraging dialogues, constantly checking for understanding and growth."

—William Glasser, psychiatrist and author

There are a number of ways in which you may learn a student has a mental health or learning disorder. With some children, you will be informed of their difficulties. You might be asked to pick up where another teacher has left off in providing accommodations or special services to help a student who has a learning disability or a condition such as depression. Other children might come to the classroom with parents reporting a disorder for the first time.

In situations where you have been informed of a problem, it can help a great deal to make yourself familiar with any student data already collected by the school. This might include a student's academic history, past IEPs, 504 plans, and information on behavior and social skills. You can also gather anecdotal background by talking to other staff members who have taught or counseled a student in the past.

Whether or not you have prior information about a student's disability or disorder, early intervention can make a significant difference in the progress that child makes during the school year. A prompt change in instructional approach might allow you to engage a student in a new way that prevents the need for special services. In other instances, a referral for special education assessment might be necessary. The more quickly students are provided with instructional strategies or accommodations that best respond to their needs, the better chance they'll have to be successful.

SCHOOL REGISTRATION FORMS

Your school's registration form is a great first opportunity to gather important information about a student. Registration forms are most often standard throughout school districts. These forms query general information about students and any mental health, behavioral, speech, or learning problems that may affect their education. It's important that a confidentiality statement is included on forms.

To minimize the possibility that a parent forgets to note a child's condition, it's best if the form lists common problems like learning disabilities, Attention Deficit Hyperactivity Disorder, mood and anxiety disorders, tics, seizures, and speech/language difficulties. There should also be space for parents to list physical illnesses, such as allergies and diabetes, as well as an "other" space where conditions can be listed. Allow for plenty of space for parents to provide relevant comments about problems.

If students are not required to register yearly, distribute a form annually that asks parents to alert the school to any changes in medical history or special circumstances about a child. Also be sure an emergency contact form is on file.

Early intervention is just as important (perhaps even more so) in regard to mental health disorders. Students who are experiencing emotional distress due to a mood disorder or another condition are affected in multiple ways. Academic performance can suffer, as can self-concept and relationships with others. Inappropriate behavior can jeopardize a student's placement in a classroom or school. Some educators may be reluctant to intervene in the issues related to a child's emotional well-being. It does require good judgment to make this decision. Remember, however, that a student's difficulties seldom are resolved without intervention from a caring adult. Your role is important.

IMPORTANT! When speaking with a child (or his parents) about behaviors, avoid diagnosing disorders. This is going beyond your qualifications as a teacher. Your responsibility is to report behavior you observe—not to diagnose a condition that may be causing it. As necessary, involve counselors, school psychologists, and other specialists in your conversations with parents.

What should you do if you observe a child having difficulties? If problems are minor, you alone might be able to resolve an issue with a student. For more serious problems, it's important to consult with colleagues. Counselors, school psychologists, other specialists, and administrators can all provide significant insight. Often they will have background information on a child that you simply could not be privy to. These people are also responsible for knowing the ins and outs of school procedures and important legal considerations that will likely determine the best next steps for helping a child.

It's best if the policies for reporting behavior problems (and any forms used) are uniform within your school or district. If your school does not have guidelines for responding to these issues, collaboration with other school staff in a team approach is even more crucial.

WORKING WITH COUNSELORS AND SCHOOL PSYCHOLOGISTS

Make it a matter of routine to check in with counselors, school psychologists, and other specialists before deciding on interventions for students. There are many ways in which you can reach out for this help:

- If you don't completely understand a child's behavior, consider asking a counselor, school psychologist, or special educator to sit in on your class. This person may be able to offer insight into why a child is acting a certain way, or could conduct additional assessments to help determine what's happening.
- Sometimes a child's difficulties won't present you with an obvious strategy for intervening. Rely on counselors, school psychologists, and other specialists to provide suggestions for interventions.
- For students facing certain sensitive problems, request that one of these specialists intervene. Particularly in elementary schools, counselors conduct groups for students who may be experiencing social problems or difficulties dealing with divorce, the loss of a loved one, or other major life changes.
- Call on school psychologists, counselors, and other specially trained staff to manage crises with students. Consider including in any student coping plan (see page 24) a provision where students can get the help of a specialist to talk to and calm down during emotional times.
- A counselor, school psychologist, and other specialists can be a great resource during parent meetings in which you are discussing a child's problem.

Also remember to make full use of any other specialists in your school—the school nurse, speech/language pathologists, occupational therapists, aides, and any others who may be able to offer help with a child's behavior. Consult these staff members when their areas of specialty correspond with needs you observe in students.

IMPORTANT! Although it's essential to communicate about a student with other staff, be cautious about revealing information a student may have told you in confidence. A high school girl may tell you a certain boy has been calling her a lot. A fifth grader might confide to you that he dislikes another teacher at school. By sharing too much, you could damage student trust and jeopardize a relationship. However, in some situations—such as in the case of abuse or self-injury—you are legally obligated to report information.

COMMUNICATING WITH PARENTS

Sharing sensitive information with parents may be one of the most challenging parts of your job. A helpful suggestion to keep in mind when speaking with parents is to keep your reporting limited to the way in which problems are negatively affecting the child academically, emotionally, or socially. In this way, you'll avoid saying anything that may sound like a value judgment against the student or a parent's childrearing. Hopefully a parent will respond to your comments with something like, "Thank you for sharing this information. I've noticed this behavior, too, and I'm concerned about it. I appreciate how much you care about my child and her education."

Even when you've made your best efforts to show sensitivity, parents may not react favorably. A parent may disagree with what you have to say ("Are you saying that my child has a problem?!") or blame you for the child's difficulty ("If school were more interesting and you were a better teacher, my child wouldn't behave this way!"). If any of the remarks sound familiar, you're not alone. During these difficult times, another member of the school staff can be especially helpful. He can verify what you are saying about a child and serve as a witness to the conversation that you—and by extension, your school—are having with a parent.

What can you do if a parent becomes defensive or even confrontational? Stop and take a deep breath. It's your responsibility to stay calm and listen to what she has to say. It's possible that a parent's claims are true—that a child doesn't show a behavior at home. Acknowledge this and say you're glad to hear that she hasn't observed the child showing this behavior outside of school. You may want to add, however, that for whatever reason, the child is choosing *your* classroom to show certain behaviors that are affecting learning—her child's and that of other students.

In some situations, you may know that a child also behaves in a certain way outside of school. Don't dispute a parent who tells you otherwise, as this may only cause greater tension. Remember that a child's behavior is an obviously sensitive topic for parents. They may struggle to come to terms with a child behaving in an inappropriate way or having an emotional problem. It may take more than you (or other school staff) sharing information about a child for parents to acknowledge certain realities about their children. In some cases, parents simply do not want to acknowledge that a problem exists.

In times of difficulty, remember why you have brought up concerns with parents. You're looking out for the welfare and successful education of a student. The sooner any issues are raised, the sooner that child might receive some assistance—and early response is the best way to decrease the long-term effects of any problems. Also, remember that in your interactions with a parent you will be working with him to address a child's problem. The best approaches for helping students will involve a team approach with you, other school staff, parents, and any outside professionals working as allies to address difficulties.

HOW TO SAY IT . . .

Following are some examples of inappropriate and appropriate suggestions for speaking to parents.

Instead of . . .	Try . . .
"I think your child is depressed."	"I'm a little concerned about Sally. She doesn't laugh or get excited anymore when all the other students are having a good time in class. Have you noticed anything different about her behavior lately?"
"Janie's a shy little girl. Is she afraid of people?"	"I've noticed that Janie sometimes has trouble joining others at playtime. She also looks down at the floor much of the time. Have you noticed any of these behaviors when Janie is with others outside of school?"
"Eric never stops running around. He must have ADHD."	"Sometimes Eric seems to have a hard time paying attention and staying still. I notice that he also forgets instructions much of time and often seems distracted. Have you ever noticed behavior like this at home?"

CHILD ABUSE AND NEGLECT

There may be times when you suspect parent mistreatment as a cause for a child's difficulties. Teachers are legally obligated to report suspicion of child abuse or neglect. Statutes for all 50 states (and reporting information) are available at www.smith-lawfirm.com/mandatory_reporting.htm.

The laws only require the reporting of a suspicion. Your state agency will conduct an inquiry to determine the validity of a suspicion. Informants are kept anonymous. Make sure you or your school administrator has checked the applicable law in your state. If you do not report suspected child abuse or neglect, you and your school could be held liable for harm a child experiences.

MEDICATION

It's important that school officials are aware of any medications children are taking. Side effects (such as stomachaches, mood changes, headaches, agitation, and changes in appetite) of these medications can affect them at school. When reporting potential side effects to parents, follow guidelines similar to those for discussing behavior. At first it's best to make behavioral observations. ("Sam was very sleepy today." "Luis keeps complaining of headaches.") Let the parent respond with an explanation that may or may not mention medication. If the parent does not mention a connection with medication, it may then be appropriate for you to ask whether a medication the child is taking may be causing the problem. You may want to involve a school specialist in these conversations.

Even when you are very tactful, some parents misinterpret teacher comments about medication. They may interpret teachers as being in favor of or opposed to its use. Remember that your job is to manage students in the classroom as effectively as you can, regardless of other treatments or interventions parents pursue. Medical treatment is the parents' responsibility and choice.

Effective Classroom Policies and Procedures

"True educational reform will only come about when we make our education appropriate to children's individual growth rates and levels of mental development."

—David Elkind, educator and author

Children with mental health and learning disorders often have challenges at school that extend beyond academics. You know that much of the time they need accommodations and additional supports to help them function in the classroom. Depending upon the disorder and its severity, you may need to teach these children even basic classroom expectations and reinforce them consistently. Otherwise, a student's behavioral or learning difficulties can interfere with your teaching—and test your patience.

It's important to remember that inappropriate behaviors are often not the result of a child consciously disregarding rules. Instead, these students are experiencing effects of disorders that make it difficult for them to comply with classroom expectations. A child with ADHD may understand rules and try to obey them but find it very hard to control impulsive urges. A student with language deficits might have difficulty understanding or remembering rules. There are many possible ways a student's disorder can affect her ability to show appropriate behavior and academic skills.

It's important to acknowledge a student's difficulties, but to also remain proactive in helping him develop strategies to comply with expectations. This section includes some basic classroom management information to keep in mind with these children. Specific supports and interventions are also included throughout the book within respective disorder sections.

IMPORTANT! All students benefit from structure and predictability in the classroom. This is especially true of those who have mental health and learning disorders. Strive to create consistency in your classroom to help children establish routines. Posting daily schedules and classroom rules prominently can serve to strengthen students' understanding of daily events, transitions, and expectations for behavior.

SCHOOL RULES

Rules should be developed in conjunction with a mission statement that clarifies your school's purpose and goals. Teachers, counselors, administrators, and other school staff should be involved in the development of rules and disciplinary policies. When all staff members are involved in creating a policy, they will more likely carry it out consistently.

Many schools and districts also involve parents and children when creating student codes of conduct. Recent initiatives to address bullying, in particular, have brought school staff, students, and parents together in efforts to build respectful school communities. This collaborative approach can increase staff and student buy-in and ensure that expectations regarding appropriate behavior are clear to the entire school population.

While conduct guidelines will vary between schools, there are some important things to keep in mind when establishing school rules:

Rules should be realistic. It's important that behavior expectations are appropriate given a child's age and development.

Rules should be consistent. Rules are most effective when they can be consistently applied to multiple settings in school. When teachers have very different expectations and standards for behavior, children do not receive a clear message about expected behavior. Expectations for behavior in some settings, such as the lunchroom or playground, need to allow more flexibility to accommodate non-classroom activities; however, even these rules should be consistent with the school's general behavior code.

Rules should be concise. Students with mental health and learning disorders often have difficulty understanding and remembering rules. The more straightforward and concise rules are, the better students will be able to remember and follow them.

Rules should be explicit. Rules should refer to concrete behaviors, not abstract ideas. For example, "speak in a respectful way" is a directive that must be interpreted by a student. Instead you might say, "Raise your hand if you would like to speak during class. If you are called on, speak in a calm voice." Other similarly specific rules may be required for different settings, such as small group work.

Rules should be stated in the positive. Telling a student what she *shouldn't* do doesn't indicate how you would like her to act. For example, instead of stating, "No hitting," a rule might read, "Always keep your hands and feet to yourself."

Rules should be discussed and agreed upon. Rules should be posted in all areas. Teachers should go over rules with students and ensure they are understood. Consider providing handouts with classroom rules (or a school "code of conduct") when discussing them. Ask children to bring this handout home, discuss rules with a parent, and return the sheet to you with a parent's signature. Also provide space for a student to sign to indicate that he understands the rules.

BEHAVIORAL SUPPORTS

Even when positive, concise, and explicit rules are clearly communicated and reinforced, students may continue to have difficulty behaving appropriately at school. Children with mental health and learning disorders face a variety of challenges that can make it difficult for them to remember, understand, and comply with rules. Many will require ongoing supportive strategies.

Accommodations and behavior management efforts should ideally involve a counselor or school psychologist and be made, if applicable, in conjunction with a child's IEP, 504 plan, functional behavioral assessment (FBA), or other behavior plan. All staff involved in a child's education, as well as parents, should be familiar with and adhere to academic and behavioral plans; students benefit from consistent rules and a uniform system of consequences. Following are some other ways to help students display positive behavior.

Sample Certificate of Respectful Behavior

Certificate of Respectful Behavior

On this 8th (date) day of May (month),

Jonas (student's name) has earned this Certificate of Respectful Behavior.

Jonas has earned this certificate for terrific behavior on the playground during lunch recess. When a disagreement came up in the baseball game, Jonas talked it out with the other player without raising his voice or getting physical.

Keep up the respectful behavior Jonas!

Mr. Alvarez (Teacher signature)

Provide positive reinforcement. One of the most powerful ways to encourage desired behavior is to regularly praise students when they behave in appropriate ways. "Catch them being good" is one of the most simple, yet effective, ways a teacher can help students follow rules. Be specific in your praise so that the student knows exactly what she did that earned your praise. You might also reward students for positive behaviors by granting them a privilege or some other tangible form of acknowledgment. A reproducible certificate of respectful behavior can be found on page 26.

Keep parents informed. Parents should know about their children's behavior—the good as well as the bad. Passing along positive comments to parents about their children is a nice way to let them know that you're balanced in your approach to behavior. You'll give credit when credit is due yet also hold students accountable when their behavior is unacceptable. One of the simplest ways to do this is to call or send positive notes or emails to four students' parents each week. Not only do parents appreciate positive information about their children, but it increases your credibility when you have to send negative information home. Remember—even when reporting on a student's difficulties—to also include some positive information. ("Xiang has always been an excellent all-around student—and he continues to read and write at a very high level. I'm concerned, however, about his poor performance recently in math. I'd like for us to work together in helping Xiang do as well in math as he does in reading and writing.")

Sample Behavior Contract

Behavior Contract

This behavior contract between Cheryl (student's name) and Mrs. Jacobson (teacher's name),

is for the period of March 1 (start date) through March 5 (end date).

The behavior(s) Cheryl agrees to show:

1. Standing in line quietly before lunch.

2. Keeping her hands to herself in the lunch line.

If Cheryl is able to show these behavior(s), she will earn:

1. The chance to decide what game the class plays on Friday, March 5.

Date: March 1

Student signature: Cheryl Hawkins

Guardian signature: LaDonna Hawkins

Teacher signature: Mrs. Jacobson

Make students aware they are responsible for behavior. A behavior contract can be an effective approach for helping students focus on one or more inappropriate behaviors they are exhibiting at school. When children feel they play a role in how they are treated (as opposed to simply being disciplined by an authority figure), they are more likely to take personal responsibility for behavior. Appropriate behaviors should be tied to rewards so that they are reinforced. Parents and other school staff should be aware of and involved in these behavior modification efforts. A reproducible behavior contract can be found on page 27.

Teach children to monitor their own behavior. Having students monitor their actions is another way to give them responsibility and teach them self-control. Ask a student to focus on decreasing one negative behavior. Develop a silent signal you can use during class to let him know when he has committed the behavior so that he can mark it down on his form. Set weekly goals with him and tie rewards to progress. This can be done in conjunction with a behavior contract. A reproducible self-monitoring checklist can be found on page 28.

Sample Self-Monitoring Checklist

Self-Monitoring Checklist

Ron's Self-Monitoring Checklist
(student's name)

The behavior I am trying to stop is speaking without being called on in class.

I will make a checkmark each time I make a mistake.

Monday 9/17 ✓✓✓✓
Tuesday 9/18 ✓✓✓✓✓✓
Wednesday 9/19 ✓✓✓
Thursday 9/20 ✓✓✓
Friday 9/21 ✓

Notes: If I make a mistake and speak without raising my hand, Mr. Mouhasha will touch his earlobe to remind me to make a checkmark.

Sample Behavior Modification Plan

Behavior Modification Plan

melinda's Behavior Modification Plan
(student's name)

What did I do that is against the rules? I hit Tom in the arm.

What rule did I break? Keep your hands and feet to yourself.

Why did I break this rule? Tom would not let me have a turn on the computer.

How did my behavior affect others? I hurt Tom.

What will I do next time I face a similar situation? If I want to play on the computer, I will wait for my turn.

How can my teacher help me do this? Mr. Lofflin can listen to me when I have a problem and try to help me.

Date: November 17

Student signature: melinda martinez

Parent signature: Elias Fernandez

Teacher signature: Mr. Lofflin

Make students aware of why rules are in place. Children often fail to see the reasons for rules or understand why they are important. Ask students to think about how negative behavior affects them as well as others. Help them come up with constructive strategies for times they are frustrated or need to solve a problem. A reproducible behavior modification plan can be found on page 29.

Conduct a behavior assessment. Some children who have behavior difficulties require a functional behavioral assessment (FBA). This process involves extensive data collection on difficult behaviors, when they are shown, what preceded them, consequences, and possible alternative behaviors. Student patterns are analyzed with the intention of creating effective behavioral supports. This process (and its forms) vary between states, schools, and districts.

Build specific skills. Students often need to develop specific skills before they are able to follow rules. For example, a child with Asperger's Syndrome may have great difficulty understanding basic social skills such as sharing and turn-taking. When forced to do these things without proper instruction or practice, the child may become confused and frustrated. There are many areas in which children may need to be taught skills before they can be expected to comply with rules.

Sample Student Coping Plan

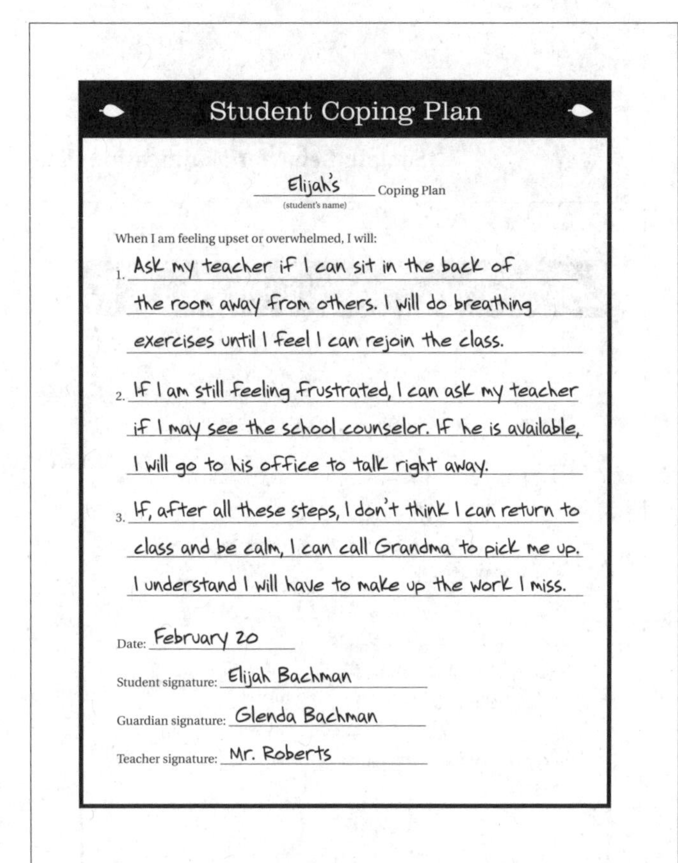

Student Coping Plan

Elijah's Coping Plan
(student's name)

When I am feeling upset or overwhelmed, I will:

1. Ask my teacher if I can sit in the back of the room away from others. I will do breathing exercises until I feel I can rejoin the class.
2. If I am still feeling frustrated, I can ask my teacher if I may see the school counselor. If he is available, I will go to his office to talk right away.
3. If, after all these steps, I don't think I can return to class and be calm, I can call Grandma to pick me up. I understand I will have to make up the work I miss.

Date: February 20

Student signature: Elijah Bachman

Guardian signature: Glenda Bachman

Teacher signature: Mr. Roberts

Establish provisions for times when students feel overwhelmed. Set up a quiet place in or near your classroom where students can go to calm down when they are upset or explosive. Allow students to visit a counselor if one is available. Consider setting up a coping plan for students who feel overwhelmed. A reproducible coping plan can be found on page 30.

Address misbehavior with a minimum of attention. Keep comments to a minimum and try to give feedback in nonverbal ways (such as a look or a hand gesture). This can help you minimize the behavior's impact upon other students and prevent a child seeking attention from getting it.

Stay calm. It's important to remember not to take behavior personally. These children have problems that greatly influence their behavior. It's your responsibility to stay calm, positive, and proactive in addressing student behavior.

SOMETHING TO THINK ABOUT . . .

Ross Greene, in *The Explosive Child,* describes four important qualities educators should possess when teaching students with mental health and learning disorders.

1. Teachers have a clear understanding of students' unique difficulties.
2. Educators know how to reduce specific demands on certain students and identify, in advance, specific triggers that may cause a student to react with negative behavior.
3. Teachers should have some understanding about appropriate interventions or responses for students.
4. Educators are able to identify any of their own actions that might be contributing to or making a student's difficulties worse in the classroom.

CONSEQUENCES

After behavioral plans are implemented, children need to be accountable for their behavior. As a rule, penalties for behavior should usually be combined with opportunities that reward positive behavior.

It's best if all staff members who are involved with a child use the same rewards and penalties. This type of consistency and the following discipline plan is most effectively used in a self-contained elementary school class. This plan follows a hierarchy of increasing penalties for violations. The first violation represents a warning. Rule violations can add up over the course of a day, a week, or another period of time, depending upon what the behavioral supports call for. Following is an example of a discipline plan for mild misbehavior. Remember that it's important to be sure students know and understand rules before administering negative consequences for infractions.

1st violation of a rule: Student's name is written on board. No verbal comment is made to the student when the name is written. This prevents disruption of teaching and reinforcement of (through attention) a negative behavior.

2nd violation: Student gets a checkmark by his name on the board and loses a privilege (free time after lunch).

3rd violation: Student gets another checkmark next to her name and a note is sent home with student that must be signed by a parent and returned.

4th violation: Student gets another checkmark by his name. A parent is called the same day to discuss the student's difficulty following rules.

A modification of this plan is necessary for students in upper grades who have multiple classes and teachers. These students can carry clipboards with behavior plans that can be marked throughout the day. One teacher or counselor needs to be responsible for dispensing the total penalties at the end of the day.

These behavior plans are typically effective for most students if implemented consistently. Severe rules violations often require more severe consequences. Work with school counselors, administrators, and other staff to determine appropriate disciplinary actions for these students. Additional strategies for addressing severe behaviors can be found in the section on disruptive behavior disorders (see pages 147–154).

Certificate of Respectful Behavior

On this ________ day of _________________________,
(date) (month)

_________________________ has earned this Certificate of Respectful Behavior.
(student's name)

_________________________ has earned this certificate for

____

____

____

Keep up the respectful behavior_______________!

____
(Teacher signature)

Behavior Contract

This behavior contract between ________________ and ______________________ ,
(student's name) (teacher's name)

is for the period of _______________________ through ______________________ .
(start date) (end date)

The behavior(s)_______________________ agrees to show:

____

____

____

If _______________________ is able to show these behavior(s), _________will earn:

____

____

____

Date: ______________________

Student signature: _______________________________

Guardian signature: ______________________________

Teacher signature: _______________________________

Self-Monitoring Checklist

_________________ Self-Monitoring Checklist
(student's name)

The behavior I am trying to stop is _______________________________________

____

____

I will make a checkmark each time I make a mistake.

Monday __________

Tuesday __________

Wednesday __________

Thursday __________

Friday __________

Notes: ____

____

____

____

Behavior Modification Plan

____________________ Behavior Modification Plan
(student's name)

What did I do that is against the rules? ________________________________

____

What rule did I break? ____

____

Why did I break this rule? ____

____

How did my behavior affect others? ____________________________________

____

What will I do next time I face a similar situation? _______________________

____

How can my teacher help me do this? __________________________________

____

Date: ________________________

Student signature: __________________________________

Guardian signature: _________________________________

Teacher signature: __________________________________

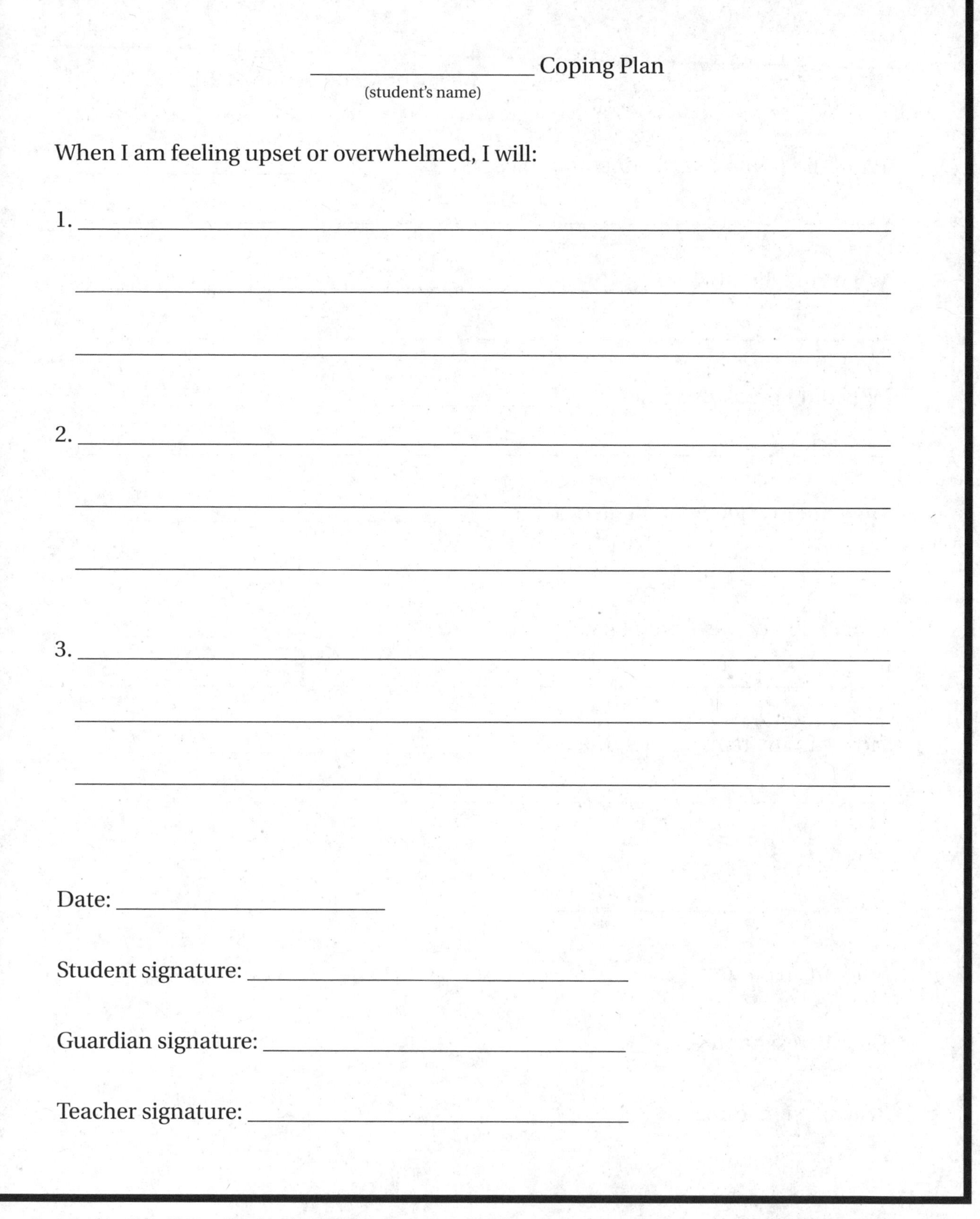

Student Coping Plan

_______________ Coping Plan
(student's name)

When I am feeling upset or overwhelmed, I will:

1. ______________________________

____

____

2. ______________________________

____

____

3. ______________________________

____

____

Date: ______________

Student signature: ______________________

Guardian signature: ______________________

Teacher signature: ______________________

Effective Teaching Strategies for Meeting Diverse Student Needs

"Because all *students are capable learners, you as a teacher must demonstrate that* all *students are expected to fully participate in all activities. Sometimes you will want to offer options for students to choose from, but everyone should be involved in learning."*

—Susan Winebrenner, author of *Teaching Kids with Learning Difficulties in the Regular Classroom*

Mental health and learning disorders can create many challenges. You probably know some students who, because of difficulties, don't like school. Learning and psychological problems can make them feel worried, frustrated, and unable to succeed. Maybe you have struggled to motivate children who have become demoralized—doing so when you are accountable for raising the achievement of *all* students can seem impossible. You might wonder, "How can I address all of these needs while at the same time meeting state and federal requirements?"

This section includes some creative teaching strategies you can use to teach students with different needs in the ways they learn best. It summarizes some of these methods that help to better understand and respond to these students. You can incorporate these instructional efforts, when applicable, with supports and accommodations spelled out in a student's IEP or 504 plan.

Differentiate instruction. It's important to recognize that "fairness" in education doesn't mean that all children are taught in the exact same way. Instead it means accounting for the needs of individual students and adjusting the curriculum accordingly. Differentiation allows you to provide individualized instruction by changing the pace, level, or style of teaching to engage student strengths and interests. Students with mental health and learning disorders are not the only children who benefit from this instructional philosophy—all children in your classroom can achieve at higher levels when you are conscientious about providing instruction that fits how they learn best. Differentiating instruction includes, when appropriate, reducing assignments or extending deadlines to accommodate a child's abilities.

Capitalize on learning styles. Students learn in a number of different ways. *Visual learners* learn most effectively from visual information, while *auditory learners* learn best from verbal or audio presentations. *Tactile-kinesthetic* learners do well when touching or moving in some way as they take in information (experiential learning). While students can often learn to some degree in all of these different ways, many excel in one area so that instruction based on a particular style is much more effective than that of another. Deficits in one or more areas of learning can be particularly common in students with learning disabilities.

Incorporate multiple intelligences into curriculum. Students often have areas of learning in which they are particularly strong. These learning strengths can be engaged to help students succeed in the classroom and reach their full potential. The multiple intelligences are a framework of strengths outlined by Harvard psychologist Howard Gardner. They are linguistic, logical-mathematical, visual-spatial, musical-rythmic, bodily-kinesthetic, interpersonal, intrapersonal, and naturalist. Most students have strengths in one or two of these areas.

Capitalize on student interests. One of the best ways to motivate students is to incorporate their interests into the curriculum. As much as possible, allow students to choose the topics they'll report on in a paper or project. Also look to include interests in other smaller ways—such as in math word problems. Tying learning to interests is a potentially powerful way to reinforce core curriculum concepts.

Involve students in educational goals. Students perform best when they feel they are active participants, as opposed to passive subjects, in learning. Try to involve students in creating goals related to learning activities. Children with mental health and learning disorders may have a negative attitude toward schoolwork so incentives are required at the outset. Your goal ultimately should be to have students genuinely engaged in learning so that rewards become less important.

Use computerized instruction. Most students enjoy working with computers, which can stimulate their interest in schoolwork. A wide assortment of available programs—from reading instruction to voice-recognition software—makes computerized instruction very relevant in helping students with special needs. Activities and games that incorporate material from content themes can reinforce concepts for visual and tactile learners.

Group students effectively. Group projects provide great opportunities for you to put together the talents of students in complementary ways. A child who struggles in one aspect of a subject may excel in another. Group students so that they can both showcase strengths and learn from peers. Also give careful consideration to the social dynamics of groups. Children who have mental health and learning disorders benefit from working with students who are especially kind, patient, and empathetic.

Consider outside placement options. Some children may have needs you simply cannot meet in the regular classroom. At these times, work with your school's specialists to ensure skills are developed in other settings. A child with a communication disorder might require intensive work with a speech-language pathologist. An extremely disruptive student may need to spend part of the day in a program set up for children with serious emotional disorders.

Establishing a Safe and Caring Classroom

"We think of efficient teachers with a sense of recognition, but those who have touched our humanity we remember with gratitude. Learning is the less essential mineral, but warmth is the life-element for the child's soul, no less than for the growing plant."

—Carl Gustav Jung, psychotherapist

All kids need to feel safe and supported at school. Students with mental health and learning disorders often struggle with problems that cause them to be seen as "different" from others. As a result, these children are often targets of teasing, physical aggression, exclusion, and other forms of mistreatment. These behaviors often escalate so that harassment becomes more severe over time.

You, no doubt, strive to immediately stop any mistreatment that you observe. It's also important to be *proactive* in your efforts to create an environment where students are respected and able to learn. You can take advantage of any schoolwide anti-bullying or character education programs that are in place. Following are some other ideas you can use to promote a positive environment.

Create a welcoming environment. Greet students by name as they enter your classroom and express pleasure in seeing them. Open the day or period with opportunities for students to share stories from their lives that make them proud or excited. If students are reluctant, take the lead in sharing something from your own life. Tell children that you are happy to have them as a class. Work to make students feel comfortable and important in your classroom.

Arrange activities that build rapport among students. Structured activities designed to help students get to know one another can be very helpful—particularly if they are instituted throughout the school year. Consider opening with welcoming activities and periodically arranging group activities during the school months.

Talk in a positive way about our differences. Discuss the ways in which people differ—from cultural backgrounds to body types, and from physical talents to learning strengths. Highlight individual students' strengths and talk about how our diversity makes the world a beautiful and exciting place.

Talk openly about bullying and other forms of mistreatment. Addressing teasing and other mistreatment with your students is an important part of getting them to think about their behavior. You might ask students to tell about times when they have been put down and how they felt. Work to build empathy in students. Emphasize that everyone deserves to be respected and has a right to learn.

Emphasize the importance of speaking out against bullying. Educate students about what they should do if they observe bullying. In situations where they are not in danger, you can recommend they step in and help the child being bullied. If they don't feel safe intervening, they should get the help of an adult right away.

Monitor unstructured times. Teasing and other mistreatment often occur during recess and other unstructured times—often just out of the range of teachers. Do your best to watch over students who you know may be targets for bullying.

Be cautious about asking students to participate in class. It's important to show sensitivity when asking a student to contribute during class. Try not to ask her to perform a task you know she will struggle with. For example, you might not want to ask a child who is nervous around others to read a paragraph in front of the class. Encourage classroom participation by preparing students for requests.

Avoid using labels when referring to students. Students often do not feel good about their mental health and learning disorders, and labels tend to have connotations that make them feel worse. Even if a child is not present, do not apply a label to him; labels can cause peers to perceive him as more different.

Consider educating your whole class about a disorder. This is a step you should take very carefully and only after full consultation with a student and her family. Collect written permission and involve a school counselor or psychologist in class discussions. This can be particularly effective when a child's condition is obvious (such as tics) and observed by others students. When a child's classmates understand why he acts as he does, they are less likely to tease him about the behavior.

Building Social Skills in Students

"Theories and goals of education don't matter a whit if you do not consider your students to be human beings."

—Lou Ann Walker, author of *A Loss for Words*

You've probably observed that students with mental health and learning differences often have poor social skills. These difficulties, of course, can differ a great deal, depending on a child's specific disorder. A student with Social Anxiety Disorder may feel intense fear at the idea of joining a group. Another with Asperger's Syndrome might readily join others but promptly redirect the conversation away from group tasks to his love of trains, for example.

Do what you can to identify your students' key social skills deficits and foster their development. It can be very helpful to build skills in classroom settings because it develops rapport and a sense of community among students. Some students, however, will likely need greater help with social skills than you're able to provide in the regular classroom. You might work with these students outside of class time or refer them for placement for social skills development in a counseling setting.

Remember that some students may need to be taught very basic social behaviors in specific detail. It is children in need of this intensive help, in particular, who can benefit from working with a counselor—either individually or in a group setting. It's important that whoever works with children models these behaviors, offers step-by-step instruction, and gives the children opportunities to practice social skills. Following are more suggestions for building social skills.

Teach listening skills. Help students master basic listening skills. Have them practice maintaining focus on you as a speaker. Talk about how eye contact, posture, and facial expression can all be used to show attention. Also teach students strategies for understanding others, such as keying in on main ideas.

Build conversation skills. Students with mental health and learning disorders often struggle with basic conversation skills. Difficulties can range from basic turn-taking to a very literal interpretation of speech. Role-play conversations with students to help them improve conversational skills. Model appropriate voice volume, tone, and inflection. Some students—especially those with communication disorders—may need to build basic skills with a speech-language pathologist.

Teach nonverbal communication skills. While most children learn nonverbal communication naturally through social interaction, students with certain disorders may need very specific instruction to understand body language and facial expressions. Many social skills programs feature illustrations and photos that can help a student learn the significance of gestures and expressions.

Help students show kindness. Show students the importance of kind words and actions. Talk about how sincere compliments can make others feel good and also more likely to also be kind. You can also encourage acts of kindness. Ask students about times when others said or did something nice for them and how they felt. Reinforce kind acts with praise or another form of recognition.

Help students empathize with others. Some students speak or behave insensitively, often without understanding the effect their actions have on others. Do your best to make students aware of how inappropriate words or actions make others feel. Ask questions about times when someone upset them. Using books and movies with compelling narratives is another way to help students recognize the feelings of others.

Teach anger management skills. Show children that there are respectful, positive ways to deal with anger and other strong feelings. Teach students basic calming techniques like deep breathing and counting down from 10. Also talk about the importance of expressing feelings, and volunteer yourself as someone the student can talk with when feeling upset or overwhelmed. Consider putting into place a coping plan for times when students feel on the verge of losing control.

Help students develop conflict resolution skills. Often children have difficulty staying in control of their emotions when something does not go their way. This may include episodes during games and other activities. Show children that there are constructive ways to end disagreements. You may need to reinforce basic concepts of sharing and compromise with some students. Affirm the benefits of peacefully resolving differences and provide students with specific tools and language (such as I-messages) they can use to get along with others.

Foster friendships through classroom activities. Group students with children you know to be especially kind, empathetic, and helpful. These students will be more likely to forgive a child's inappropriate actions and aid her during class. They can also be helpful allies outside of class for a student who draws negative attention to his behavior.

Help children resist peer pressure. Children with mental health and learning disorders are often immature for their age. This may cause some students to take advantage of a child's naïveté and suggest she engage in activities that are dangerous or wrong. Other students are at greater risk for behaviors such as cutting or drug abuse. Teach children skills they can use to resist peer pressure and make positive personal choices.

Build student self-esteem. Students with mental health and learning disorders often have low self-esteem. These children may recognize and feel embarrassed by the ways they are different from others—whether it's their poor academic performance or difficulty controlling feelings and behavior. Do your best to build self-concept in these students by offering consistent praise of their strengths. Also reinforce positive social actions. Students who feel good about themselves are more likely to be able to put a positive foot forward when interacting with others.

Part II

Mental Health and Learning Disorders

Terms Used in This Book

"Unless someone like you cares a whole awful lot,
nothing is going to get better. It's not."
—Dr. Seuss (Theodore Seuss Geisel), author

The conditions in this book are referred to by the formal terms under which they are classified in the *Diagnostic and Statistical Manual-IV-TR.* Published by the American Psychiatric Association (APA), this classification system is the most universally used system for categorizing mental disorders. While the APA's classification is not perfect due to the complexity of human behavior and overlap among disorders, it is the best tool available to diagnose disorders.

WHAT CAUSES DISORDERS?

Mental health and learning disorders can be the result of nature (biology) and nurture (environment). Evidence for a biological basis comes from research on structural, chemical, and electrical differences in the brains of people with certain disorders. Other research suggests genetic links as many disorders occur more often in families and twins. We also know that environmental influences can have as powerful an effect as biology. Negative environmental factors (like abuse, sustained stress, trauma, and low socioeconomic status) can lead to the onset of disorders. On the positive side, some people who are predisposed to certain disorders may not develop them because positive environmental factors (such as a parent or peer influence) create a resiliency. This is one of the reasons why a teacher can be so critical in the lives of children.

Unlike mental health professionals whose goal is to diagnose and treat disorders, educators seek to identify and qualify students for special services or accommodations. Consequently, the terms used by these professionals are usually different. For example, think of a student who has severe difficulties reading. He might be diagnosed *dyslexic* by a psychologist working outside of a school district but labeled SLD (Specific Learning Disability) by a school district. Another student might be diagnosed with multiple psychological disorders by an outside mental health professional but labeled ED (Emotionally Disturbed) by a school district.

The potential problem with different terminology is that sometimes students don't get the help they need. An outside psychologist may diagnose a child with dyslexia but the school district may not provide services because the student's test scores and other information do not meet the district's definition or criteria for SLD. In this situation, parents may not believe there is reason to pursue outside interventions (such as tutoring) and the child may not receive necessary help.

THE CONFUSING WORLD OF A LEARNING DISABILITY

School psychologist: "Mrs. Gomez, Juan has a processing problem that causes some of his reading difficulties."

Mrs. Gomez: "But a psychologist who evaluated him told me he had a learning disability called dyslexia."

School psychologist: "Well, the problem is that people inside and outside school districts don't necessarily use the same language to describe similar problems."

Mrs. Gomez: "I'm confused. What is Juan's problem, then?"

School psychologist: "I can understand your confusion. The problem is that in school districts, a student's scores on IQ and achievement tests are required to fall in a very specific range in order for us to call him 'learning disabled.' Outside a school district, a child can be called reading disabled or dyslexic if they show a certain pattern of weaknesses in reading. Scores don't necessarily have to fit the 'formula' required by school districts. So the psychologist you went to can call Juan learning disabled or dyslexic but we can't because his scores don't meet the criteria for this designation that are required by school districts."

With the RTI model of special education (see pages 10–12), this confusion will hopefully diminish—less emphasis will be placed on qualifying, diagnosing, and labeling students with learning difficulties and more emphasis will be placed on providing all students with individualized attention to improve specific academic skill deficits.

Anxiety Disorders

"Teachers possess the power to create conditions that can help students learn a great deal—or keep them from learning much at all. Teaching is the intentional act of creating those conditions, and good teaching requires that we understand the inner sources of both the intent and the act."

—Parker Palmer, educator and author

Students with anxiety disorders experience excessive and irrational fears. While it is normal for every child to feel anxious at times, students experiencing anxiety disorders have worries that can last for long periods of time. This anxiety can affect a child's ability to learn as well as his ability to get along with other children.

About 13% of young people experience an anxiety disorder at some point during childhood or adolescence. Up to one-half of these children may have at least one additional mental disorder.

Some students' anxiety may be obvious. A young child might cry and resist being separated from a parent when she is dropped off at school. A student who excessively worries about following classroom instructions may repeatedly ask you for assurance that he is doing an assignment correctly. An extremely shy student might refuse to participate in classroom activities. Each of these behaviors might be possible signs of excessive anxiety.

Other students may not outwardly show that they are anxious or afraid. A child who obsessively worries about performing well on tests often won't share these feelings with you or ask questions. An extremely shy student may be well behaved so as not to draw attention. If a child's behavior appears normal and doesn't obviously interfere with learning, it may be difficult to notice problems with anxiety.

This section provides information you can use to better identify and understand students who experience anxiety disorders. It also offers many strategies you can use to help these children succeed in school.

DISORDERS COVERED IN THIS SECTION

Generalized Anxiety Disorder (GAD)

Students with GAD have persistent and unrealistic fears about everyday life activities. While these students may appear to be doing well at school, they may have exaggerated concerns about schoolwork. Anxiety can cause them to feel constant tension, self-consciousness, and pains (like headaches) that do not seem to have a physical cause.

Most students struggle at times with new experiences that can cause them to feel anxious, but children with General Anxiety Disorder seem to worry about anything and everything. They may have daily fears about grades, friends, parents, sports, health, schedules, appearance, and other aspects of school and life. Students often have worries even when there does not seem to be a reason for them.

General Anxiety Disorder is not the only way anxiety affects children. *Adjustment Disorder with Anxiety* describes more brief periods of excessive anxiety that is an overreaction to a real-life event. For example, the transition from elementary to middle school might cause a student to experience excessive fear or worry while adjusting to a new school and increased teacher expectations but eventually acclimate to the situation.

About 3% of children and adolescents experience Generalized Anxiety Disorder (GAD). Younger children with GAD also are more likely to have Separation Anxiety Disorder (pages 72–73) and Attention Deficit Hyperactivity Disorder (pages 135–146). Older students may be more likely to experience Depressive Disorders (pages 79–84).

Behaviors and Symptoms to Look For

Students with General Anxiety Disorder may be especially difficult to spot within your classroom. They often are the quietest and best-behaved children. Here are some signs to watch for.

Children with GAD may:

Express apprehension about tests, assignments, and grades. Concerns may center on the difficulty of material ("This is too hard"), workload ("I'll never be able to get all of this done"), or evaluation ("If I don't get a B, my mom will kill me").

Feel fatigued or restless. Excessive worries often keep children and adolescents from getting enough sleep. These students may appear to be exhausted or fidgety.

Have trouble concentrating. Anxiety can make it difficult for students to concentrate. They may be inattentive or easily distracted by noises or other students.

Be overly emotional. Fatigue and long-term anxiety often cause children to be very sensitive. Crying and tantrums are common in younger students. Older students may be irritable and easily frustrated.

Experience frequent headaches, stomachaches, and other pains. The stress of constant worry often leads to muscle tension and physical pains. A young student may experience a stomachache on the first day of school. This is common and needn't be cause for concern. Aches and pains that continue may indicate an anxiety disorder.

Avoid participating in school activities. Students with GAD often will try to get out of class activities, fearing they won't perform well. Such situations may include being asked to respond to questions, reading aloud, or solving problems on the board. Children also may be afraid to try a new activity. Participation in extracurricular activities often is avoided.

Be absent frequently. Frequent absences not related to medical problems may suggest ongoing anxiety. Students (especially younger children) may feign sickness to stay at home. Older students—with or without parent consent—simply may not show up for school (see "School Refusal" on pages 70–75). Absences often occur on test days and at other times when students are overwhelmed by the demands of school.

Abuse alcohol and other drugs. Some students—especially those in middle school and high school—may use alcohol, tobacco, and other drugs in an effort to lessen anxiety.

Classroom Strategies and Interventions

You'll likely observe a wide range of behaviors from students with GAD depending upon children's ages and the severity of the disorder. These factors often will determine your response. Student accommodations also will depend on class size, your everyday activities, and other aspects specific to your classroom.

Following are some suggestions for helping students with General Anxiety Disorder succeed at school:

Give lots of reassurance and genuine, specific praise. Provide students with ongoing reassurance to diminish their anxiety. Compliment them on specific areas in which they excel or are showing improvement. Sincere compliments are an effective way to promote desired behaviors. Be aware that students with GAD often deflect compliments and instead focus on what they feel are weaknesses. Do your best to emphasize students' positive qualities and accomplishments.

Carefully monitor students. Because children with GAD often do not act in ways that attract attention, a student's worry may not be obvious. Pay special attention to students who seem especially shy or timid.

Empathize with a student's anxiety. Respond to an anxious student's concerns with an empathic response. Show concern while at the same time suggesting a more rational way for the student to think about her worries. ("I understand that you feel the speech wasn't your best, but I thought it was excellent. I learned a lot about black bears.")

Establish routines and clarify expectations. Students with anxiety benefit from consistency and clear expectations. Consider posting a daily schedule and behavior guidelines so students know what to expect (and what is expected of them) in the classroom. For more information on establishing consistent classroom routines and expectations, see "Effective Classroom Policies and Procedures" on pages 19–25.

Allow for flexibility in workload. Because students with GAD are often anxious about meeting a teacher's or parent's expectations, they may excessively worry about getting assignments or projects in on time. As appropriate, relax deadlines and give full credit for work that is turned in late.

Establish curricula check-in points. Checking in with students enables you to verify that they are on schedule with an assignment or project. Check-in points also are opportunities to provide guidance and encouragement. Emphasize progress students have made on given assignments.

Modify instruction for diverse learning styles. Motivating students with anxiety using different learning strategies can be a powerful antidote to anxiety. Consider curriculum that incorporates a student's learning styles and interests. For more information on strategies for motivating learners, see "Effective Teaching Strategies for Meeting Diverse Student Needs" on pages 31–33.

Establish provisions for times when students feel overwhelmed. You may choose to set up a "safe" or "quiet" place in your classroom (or one nearby) where students can calm down. Also allow students to visit the office or a school counselor as necessary. Consider setting up a coping plan for students who feel overwhelmed. The "Student Coping Plan" on page 30 can help you do this.

Speak with the school counselor, parents, and outside professionals working with the child. General Anxiety Disorder also affects children in the home. Parents and mental health professionals can be valuable sources of information for anxiety-reducing strategies that you might also use in the classroom. Consulting a school counselor or psychologist also can provide you with ideas for your classroom.

HOW TO SAY IT . . .

How you speak with students who have Generalized Anxiety Disorder is very important. These scenarios show how you can acknowledge while helping to diminish fears:

Elementary school student (starting to cry toward the end of school): "I'm scared my mommy's going to forget me."

You (kneeling to his level and taking his hand): "That must be awfully scary to think that your mom would forget you. But no mommy has ever forgotten her child at our school. And I have my cell phone right here. If she's late, I'll call her."

Middle school student: "I'm afraid I'll get car sick on that long field trip."

You: "I don't blame you for worrying about getting car sick. That's an awful feeling. Would it be helpful if we made sure you could sit up front? Can we ask your mom what she's done in the past to make sure you don't get sick?"

High school student (with a worried look): "I don't know if I can memorize all of those algebra equations."

You: "Sounds like you're not sure you can do well on the math test. You know what? You've always done well before. What's the worst that can happen if you miss a couple of problems?"

WHAT NOT TO SAY . . .

With students who have GAD, it's best not to say what you might be thinking. Asking a question like, "Why in the world would you be worried about something like that?" could make a student feel *more* different or anxious because of your astonishment at his fear. Keep in mind anxiety often is not rational, but the feelings kids have are real.

It's important to avoid discounting or criticizing a student's concerns. ("There's nothing to worry about," "That's silly," "That will never happen.") These responses can cause a student to believe you aren't taking her seriously. She may choose to keep future concerns private.

PROFESSIONAL TREATMENTS

Cognitive-behavioral therapy is an effective treatment for General Anxiety Disorder. This therapy helps children become aware of exaggerated or unrealistic fears and teaches them to be more objective. Relaxation training, breathing exercises, and the use of imagery also are used to help decrease anxiety. Young children who cannot fully verbalize their thoughts and feelings may find success working with a play therapist.

Medication also is a helpful treatment for anxiety disorders in children. It may be prescribed by a psychiatrist or another physician when anxiety is severe. The most common medications used for anxiety disorders are *selective serotonin reuptake inhibitors (SSRIs)*. Children must be monitored closely during the initial days and weeks when taking these medications. A small percentage may experience heightened symptoms or depression. Other possible side effects of medication can include drowsiness, insomnia, stomachaches, headaches, nervousness, and weight gain. Any troubling symptoms you observe in a child taking medication should immediately be shared with the school nurse and parents.

Obsessive-Compulsive Disorder (OCD)

Students with OCD experience unwanted, intrusive thoughts or images (obsessions) that can cause them to engage in repetitive behaviors (compulsions). These compulsions often are elaborate and time consuming, interfere with children's routines at home, and affect their performance at school.

Obsessions usually include exaggerated or imagined thoughts or images. A student may worry excessively about being contaminated by germs or that she (or loved ones) will be harmed in some way. When a child is unable to ignore these thoughts, she may perform a compulsive behavior, believing it can prevent what she fears. A child who imagines a parent being harmed in an accident may tap his pencil a certain number of times when he writes or repeat a string of numbers or words to himself. In his mind, this behavior is preventing the event from taking place. Other children with OCD do not have a specific obsessive fear. They may instead feel like "something just isn't right" and engage in compulsions to make things "feel right."

Between 1% and 3% of children have Obsessive-Compulsive Disorder (OCD). Those with OCD are more likely to have other anxiety disorders and mood disorders (pages 72–88) as well as disruptive behavior disorders (pages 147–154).

Obsessions and compulsions may wax, wane, and change throughout childhood and life. A student who feels she must go through the contents of her backpack three times an hour may eventually replace that compulsion with the need to check a clock every minute. In both cases she fears something "bad" will happen if she does not perform the behavior.

COMMON OBSESSIONS AND COMPULSIONS

Obsessions

- Fear of illness, death, or contamination
- Fear or image of harm to oneself or others

- Fear of doing or saying something evil or sinful
- Fear that "something bad might happen":
  - if something is not done "correctly"
  - in association with particular numbers
  - if something important is thrown away
  - if something is asymmetrical or out of order

Compulsions

- Avoidance of germs or dirt (including excessive hand washing or showering)
- Repeated requests for reassurance
- Frequent prayer or confessions
- Repeated checking of locks or appliances
- Extreme perfectionism
- Seeking balance by ordering, straightening, or arranging objects
- Doing activities in certain sets of numbers
- Excessive collecting or hoarding (including items of no value)

Behaviors and Symptoms to Look For

Students with OCD can have many obsessions and compulsions. Some of these may be very obvious (like frequent requests to wash hands in the bathroom). Others (such as frequent mental images of being harmed or always having to choose items with an even number) may be difficult for you to observe in the classroom.

Children with Obsessive-Compulsive Disorder may:

Be indecisive and slow to accomplish tasks. Students may believe they cannot be absolutely "sure" of a correct answer or decision. As a result of this doubt, they get stuck trying to complete tests or work, erase excessively, count and re-count items, or check and re-check written answers.

Avoid some classroom materials. Children who obsessively worry about their health and safety may refuse to use scissors (and other sharp objects), paint, glue, paste, clay, tape, ink, or other classroom materials they perceive as dangerous.

Wash hands excessively. Students who frequently request to use the bathroom may be fulfilling a compulsion to wash their hands. Red, chapped fingers and hands may be signs of excessive hand washing.

Be stubborn, argumentative, and demanding. Defiance may often result from a student's need to get something "just right." When others interfere with this need, students often will feel anxious and react with a negative or hostile attitude.

Act in a distracted or an inattentive way. Students' intense preoccupation with obsessions can make it difficult for them to focus on work or classroom activities. These students may miss instructions and be inefficient in completing work.

Repeat particular sounds, words, or music. Students may make repetitive sounds, say certain words, numbers, or phrases, or sing in an attempt to relieve anxiety.

Excessively request reassurance or explanations. Students may doubt their perception or recollection of something you have said. In order to make sure they've heard or done something correctly, they may repeatedly ask for reassurance or clarification.

Be irritable or have erratic mood swings. Constant anxiety related to an obsession can make students very emotionally sensitive. Impatience, a quick temper, and outbursts can result.

Be ostracized by peers. Children whose compulsive behaviors are obvious and "strange" may be bullied or ostracized by their peers. Pay close attention to students who are teased or excluded by others.

Classroom Strategies and Interventions

Your reaction to obsessive and compulsive behaviors will vary depending on a given situation. There will be times when a student's compulsive behavior has little impact on others and may be acceptable in class. In other situations, compulsions may interfere with your ability to teach and need to be addressed.

The general approach to helping students with Obsessive-Compulsive Disorder is to minimize their anxiety while not enabling their OCD behaviors, which can be a difficult balance. It's helpful to work with parents, outside mental health professionals, and school staff in a team approach to address a student's needs.

Following are suggestions for helping children with Obsessive-Compulsive Disorder in the classroom:

Provide student with consistent reassurance. When appropriate, assure students it isn't necessary (or expected) for every aspect of a project, assignment, or test to be exactly correct. Talk about how it is acceptable to make mistakes and that fear of making them (including repeatedly erasing answers) can slow progress. In situations where students are struggling, reinforce positive steps they've accomplished to encourage continued progress. Finally, model a healthy attitude toward uncertainty and talk about how perfectionism is an impossible goal.

Empathize with student's difficulties. It's important to avoid dismissing or ignoring a student's questions, especially questions that are repeated. Provide an empathic response while simultaneously trying to communicate a realistic perspective on classroom expectations. Rather than punishing a student for minor rule infractions that her compulsions might cause, be flexible with classroom rules.

Consider decreasing a student's overall workload. OCD can substantially interfere with schoolwork. Think about ways in which you can address this while still allowing students to show what they know. For example, for the student who compulsively checks and re-checks his work, assign fewer problems on a math or reading assignment.

Allow for flexibility in deadlines and testing. Students with OCD often obsess about completing assignments, tests, and projects perfectly. They also may procrastinate due to uncertainty about the "right way" to complete an assignment. To accommodate these students, relax deadlines, give full credit for work that is turned in late, and allow additional time to take tests.

Closely monitor student's progress with class work. Watch a student to ensure she is consistently progressing (not erasing, checking and re-checking, or starting over on work). When reviewing a student's progress, reinforce the importance of moving ahead instead of making sure the work is perfect.

Avoid grading students on the neatness of work. Students can become obsessed with writing perfectly and become stalled as they write and rewrite answers. Reiterate when neatness will not be part of student's grade and place emphasis on completion of the work.

Create a place where students can calm down when frustrated. Students who are upset might sit on a beanbag chair in the back of the classroom until they feel ready to rejoin the class. A visit to the office or school counselor also may help. Page 30 has a "Student Coping Plan" you can use to establish provisions for students who are overwhelmed.

Eliminate teasing. Children may have "strange" compulsions that draw negative attention from peers. Institute anti-bullying interventions to protect children with OCD from abuse or exclusion by peers. "Establishing a Safe and Caring Classroom" (pages 35–36) provides ways you can address bullying behavior.

If student and family approve, educate your whole class about OCD. Classmates are less likely to tease (and more likely to befriend or help) a student when they understand why she acts the way she does. In taking this step, ensure written student and parent permission and involve a guidance counselor or school psychologist if possible.

TRICHOTILLOMANIA

Trichotillomania is a disorder that causes people to compulsively pull hair from their scalp, eyebrows, and eyelashes. Many consider it to be a specific kind of Obsessive-Compulsive Disorder. A person feels a tension or need to pull out hair and the pulling relieves the tension.

Between 1% and 4% of people have this disorder; one-half of them show symptoms before age thirteen. Many more girls than boys are affected.

With children who have Trichotillomania, you may see them compulsively pulling hair in your classroom—or only see evidence of thinning eyelashes, eyebrows, or hair on the scalp. If you observe hair pulling, privately ask a student if she's aware she pulls her hair and whether there's anything you can do to help reduce any stress related to pulling. Also speak with a student's parents. For students with thinning hair or bald patches, it's possible a physical illness is responsible for hair loss.

If students are involved in therapy for Trichotillomania, it can be helpful to speak with the involved professional so that strategies are consistent across settings. Some students take medication to address compulsive hair pulling.

COMMON TYPES OF OBSESSIVE-COMPULSIVE DISORDER

These are not formal diagnostic categories but informal labels that can be used to describe how OCD might look in different students:

The Reassurance Seeker

A student might worry that the topic he chose for a paper is not the "right" one. He may question you repeatedly. After reassuring him a couple of times, it's probably best to say something like, "I told you the topic you chose will be okay. I wouldn't have said it if I didn't mean it. Please stay with that topic and it will be just fine." Another student might worry that she won't get a good enough grade on a paper because she didn't finish it in class. This student spends too much time perfecting her work and takes much too long to complete it. You urge her to turn in her work and she may resist or reluctantly comply. She may express concern multiple times during the remainder of class that her work was "bad." After your second reassuring response, tell this student her work was definitely good enough and it's not worth worrying or talking about anymore.

The Bathroom's Best Friend

Many young people with OCD may ask for excessive trips to the bathroom to perform a cleaning or washing ritual. When you first notice this behavior, it's best to check with parents to find out if the child has a medical problem. If there is no medical problem and you have reason to suspect the child is washing his hands excessively, it's important to inform the parents.

The Eraser/Cross-Out Queen

A student whose written work or drawing has to be "just right" may erase and cross out letters and words excessively. This student may also be very cautious, careful, and slow completing work. Emphasize to this student that she won't be penalized for penmanship or artwork as long as it's legible and understood. You might also consider providing a copy of another student's notes. This will allow a student who struggles with note-taking to reference and stay on top of information presented during class. Reducing the quantity of required writing and offering alternative methods of evaluation in place of written tests also might help.

The King of Questions

This student asks many questions for clarification in an attempt to be reassured he's heard something correctly. His questions are a form of a checking compulsion in response to his doubt that he understands directions. Reassuring this student more than once will only perpetuate the problem. Privately, tell this student you'll repeat something for him once, then he's to do the best he can with what he thinks he's supposed to do. If he continues to ask, arrange a hand signal such as putting up your index finger to indicate he's already used his one request for assurance. This acknowledges that you see him, but you are sticking to the one-time plan. Don't penalize this student for making an error after you've repeated an instruction. This will only increase his anxiety about the consequences of being wrong.

The Snail

Imagine the student whose work has to be perfect, who doubts if it's perfect, who has to re-check to see if it's perfect, who has to correct the "imperfections," who has to start over on the paper because it's not perfect. . . . The teacher and class are moving on while this student is stuck. This is a student who'll be perceived as very slow and nonproductive. Until progress can be made in reducing this student's anxiety you may decide to shorten her assignments or allow her extended time on tests.

PROFESSIONAL TREATMENTS

The most effective treatment for OCD is a behavioral therapy called *response prevention*. Response prevention attempts to show people with OCD that compulsions do not benefit them and are not necessary. The therapy requires a person to gradually stop engaging in the compulsive behavior. In the early stages of treatment, children feel more anxiety but are taught strategies to manage it. If they can withstand anxiety long enough to realize that whatever they're worried about won't occur, they are likely to realize the compulsive behavior isn't necessary and give it up.

Depending upon the severity of OCD, medication may be used to complement behavior therapy. Medications in the family of *selective serotonin reuptake inhibitors (SSRIs)* are commonly used for OCD. Children should be carefully monitored during the initial stages of starting medication since there can be side effects. These include drowsiness, insomnia, nervousness, stomachaches, headaches, nausea, agitation, and weight gain. A very small percentage of children may become depressed when beginning medication. If you observe any troublesome behavior in a student on medication, notify the school nurse and a parent right away.

JOHANN

Thirteen-year-old Johann had been homeschooled for a year because of a severe fear of germs. His parents wanted to reenroll him in school so he would have more interaction with peers. Johann's parents met with the school psychologist. They worried that even getting Johann to enter the school would be difficult.

The school psychologist and Johann's parents developed a plan. Johann entered the school after classes began and when not many students were in the hallways. Johann's parents opened all doors and the psychologist waited in her office with anti-bacterial wipes on her desk. Johann saw that staff at the school understood his problem. The plan also included the following accommodations:

- Johann came to school 15 minutes after it started and entered through a side door.
- His school day was shortened.
- He had his own desk and chair slightly set apart from other students.
- He received extra time for class work with frequent check-ins from the teacher.
- Teachers did not touch him or his desk.
- Johann's mother brought his lunch to school and ate with him.

These accommodations may appear to have enabled Johann to continue his obsessions and compulsions. But with the slow realization that he was not in danger, Johann grew more comfortable at school so that fewer accommodations became necessary. After getting Johann back into school—which represented major progress—continued collaboration with the school psychologist and an outside mental health professional allowed Johann to be a successful student.

This set of accommodations happened to work well for Johann and his school. Your own plan will depend on school or district policies and a child's needs.

Social Anxiety Disorder (SAD)

SAD, sometimes called *Social Phobia,* affects students in social or performance settings. Children with SAD may be very shy and resist playing and working with other students. They may also fear situations in which they are expected to perform—whether it's providing an answer in class or playing in the school band. These students worry they will act or perform in a way that embarrasses or humiliates them.

While some shyness or performance anxiety isn't necessarily unusual or bad, extreme anxiety can lead to avoidance of many situations which can negatively impact a child's life. Children who feel anxious around others may avoid social situations. Fear of performing in front of others may cause them to resist joining school activities. Social Anxiety Disorder is one of the most common reasons why students refuse to attend school (see "School Refusal" on pages 70–75).

Unfortunately, Social Anxiety Disorder frequently goes unrecognized and untreated. Young people who are affected often keep their anxiety private and behave in ways that do not draw attention. A small percentage of younger children have such severe anxiety that they don't speak to anyone outside of the immediate family. This anxiety disorder is called *Selective Mutism.*

> Social Anxiety Disorder (SAD) affects about 11% of children and adolescents. Up to 60% of these young people may have an additional mental health disorder. Most commonly these disorders include a specific phobia, Panic Disorder (pages 67–69), or Depressive Disorder (pages 79–84).

Behaviors and Symptoms to Look For

Many students feel anxious in new social situations. It's also common for children to worry in advance of a performance—whether a concert, class speech, or sporting event. In most cases, students are able to overcome their fears and perform capably. With repetition, they gain confidence in their growing abilities.

Other children feel overwhelming dread at the thought of socializing with or performing in front of others. This fear is not always obvious. Students with social anxiety may be among the best behaved in your classroom. They appear to be doing well but privately feel fearful and anxious. For this reason, it's important to carefully monitor extremely shy or quiet students.

Children with Social Anxiety Disorder may:

Act in an extremely shy manner. Interacting with peers, particularly in new situations, can cause socially anxious children great anxiety. Because they fear humiliation, students often will isolate themselves and speak as little as possible. The importance of social relationships in adolescence makes this a particular problem for older students. Students with SAD may respond to social overtures by blushing, sweating profusely, looking away, or stuttering.

Avoid participating in school activities. Students with SAD often fear making mistakes and feeling embarrassed. These students are unlikely to respond to questions you ask the class. Reading aloud or solving math problems in front of others may terrify them. During group work, students with SAD may stay on the periphery of the activity. These students may also limit their participation in extracurricular activities.

Act in a distracted or confused way. Social anxiety can be all consuming. Students frequently are very self-conscious and may appear distracted or inattentive.

Be overly emotional. Constant social anxiety can cause students to be emotionally sensitive. Fits of crying and tantrums (especially in younger students) are common. Older students can be moody, irritable, or oppositional.

Experience frequent headaches, stomachaches, and other physical pains. Social anxiety may lead to dizziness, "butterflies" in the stomach, and muscle tension. While many people experience these feelings at times, students with SAD experience them often.

Frequently miss school. Frequent absences may suggest that a student feels social anxiety. Students (especially younger children) pretend to be sick so they can stay home. Children who feel performance anxiety are often absent on days when there is testing or another important event.

ASSESSING YOUNG CHILDREN'S SOCIAL COMPETENCE

While the pace of social development varies among students, it's important to evaluate children's progress on key social abilities. The following list of skills comes from the ERIC Clearinghouse on Elementary and Early Childhood Education.

Individual Qualities

- Is usually in a positive mood.
- Is not excessively dependent on adults.

- Usually comes to the program willingly.
- Usually copes with rebuffs adequately.
- Shows the capacity to empathize.
- Has positive relationships with one or two peers; shows the capacity to really care about them and miss them if they are absent.
- Displays the capacity for humor.
- Does not seem to be acutely lonely.

Social Skills

- Approaches others positively.
- Expresses wishes and preferences clearly; gives reasons for actions and positions.
- Asserts own rights and needs appropriately.
- Is not easily intimidated by bullies.
- Expresses frustrations and anger effectively and without escalating disagreements or harming others.
- Gains access to ongoing groups at play and schoolwork.
- Enters ongoing discussion on the subject; makes relevant contributions to ongoing activities.
- Takes turns fairly easily.
- Shows interest in others; exchanges information with and requests information from others appropriately.
- Negotiates and compromises with others appropriately.
- Does not draw inappropriate attention to self.
- Accepts and enjoys peers and adults of ethnic groups other than his or her own.
- Interacts nonverbally with other children with smiles, waves, nods, etc.

Peer Relationship Qualities

- Is usually accepted versus neglected or rejected by other children.
- Is sometimes invited by other children to join them in play, friendship, and schoolwork.
- Is named by other children as someone they are friends with or like to play and work with.

Classroom Strategies and Interventions

Symptoms of social anxiety often vary among students. Some children may approach unfamiliar situations with obvious signs of fear or apprehension. Others will not be visibly affected. Some students overcome anxiety as an activity progresses while others do not. Young people who experience extreme fear may refuse to participate at all. The strategies you use to help students will depend in part upon the severity of their social anxiety and a given classroom situation.

Following are some suggestions for helping students with Social Anxiety Disorder in the classroom:

Provide a warm and encouraging environment. Show students, especially those who are socially anxious, consistent empathy and support. Do not tolerate bullying or teasing and promote positive behavior in peers. Strategies for creating supportive school environments can be found in "Establishing a Safe and Caring Classroom" on pages 35–36.

Work to improve children's social skills. The primary emotion affecting socially anxious students is fear. Help to diminish fears by providing socials skills instruction at a pace comfortable to the student. Some social skills activities and resources can be found in "Building Social Skills in Students" on pages 37–39.

Foster friendships and joint activities through curriculum. Pair up a socially anxious student with another student who is kind and pleasant. When students choose partners, make sure a shy student is chosen (or facilitate an appropriate choice for her). Keep in mind that socially anxious students may need coaching even on very basic conversation skills.

Give high, genuine praise for social behaviors. Compliment students on specific social skills they show. If a student gives the wrong answer after raising her hand, you might say, "That's an interesting idea and thanks for answering the question." For the child who reluctantly joins a small group project for the first time, say, "It was terrific to see you join the group!"

Show sensitivity when speaking about a socially anxious student. Avoid referring to a student by using a label such as "shy." Students with SAD do not feel good about their social fears, and labels tend to have connotations that make them feel worse. Instead use phrases like, "Sometimes Sam doesn't feel like talking" or, "Michelle is just feeling quiet today."

Create a place where overwhelmed students can go to avoid large groups. You may choose to establish an "alone place" where a student with Social Anxiety Disorder can go to calm herself when anxiety overwhelms her. She might also visit the school counselor. Page 30 has a "Student Coping Plan" you can use to set up accommodations for students with SAD.

Give students plenty of time to prepare for class discussion questions. Prepare socially anxious students so they know you intend to call on them. ("I'd like to call on you in class today. Do you mind answering a question about the Civil War?")

Share or talk about a student's work or contribution. Make a point to acknowledge a student's work before the entire class. Be sure to seek the permission of the student before you do this. ("I really like your project on Iceland. Do you mind if I share it with the class tomorrow?") If a child resists, talk about how much you like his work and why you'd like to show it to the class.

Minimize students' oral reading requirements and oral reports. Depending upon the severity of a student's social anxiety, consider assigning written work or projects to replace oral reports. Modify curriculum in any other appropriate ways. For additional accommodations you might make for students, see "Effective Teaching Strategies for Meeting Diverse Student Needs" on pages 31–33.

Speak with others involved in the care and development of a student. Consult parents and mental health professionals working with the child to learn interventions that work well with a student outside of school. Meet a student's needs at school by working with school counselors and other staff.

CAUTION! Some people believe forcing socially anxious students to interact with others will help them overcome anxiety. This doesn't respect the enormous fear children have and may lead them to believe their experience isn't being taken seriously. Instead of being helpful, this can make a student's symptoms worse.

PROFESSIONAL TREATMENTS

Students with social anxiety often worry that their behavior will humiliate them and that others are judging them critically. *Cognitive-behavioral therapy* can help these children be more objective in their thinking. Calming and relaxation techniques may also help students manage anxiety.

Medication may be prescribed to complement therapy, especially when Social Anxiety Disorder is severe. *Selective serotonin reuptake inhibitors (SSRIs)* are typically prescribed in these situations. Possible side effects of these medications include drowsiness, insomnia, nausea, weight gain, stomachaches, headaches, and an increase in anxiety or depression. It's important to carefully monitor students who are on medication—especially in the early weeks—and to inform a school nurse and parents immediately of any side effects you observe.

Post-Traumatic Stress Disorder (PTSD)

Students with PTSD relive traumas through nightmares, flashbacks, and other recurring images. Children often fear the traumatic events will happen again and avoid objects, people, or places that remind them of the trauma. Trauma can be a source of intense emotional pain and can cause insomnia, loss of appetite, and other physiological effects.

Car accidents, natural disasters, violence, terrorism, and abuse are examples of traumatic events children may experience. Effects of these and other events can vary a great deal among children. Fortunately, not all children who experience a trauma will develop PTSD. Some may experience increased anxiety or mood changes for a period of time but eventually overcome much of their emotional difficulties.

Children who experience severe and long-lasting effects of trauma may be diagnosed with PTSD. It can be difficult for these students to function as they did before the traumatic event. They seem to lose interest in friendships. Extreme changes in mood and symptoms of anxiety also are common.

Family and teacher support is essential to help children overcome the effects of a traumatic experience. Even with this support, some students experience long-lasting effects of the trauma, which can influence how you teach and relate to them in the classroom.

Not enough studies have been done to determine the number of children who have PTSD. It is known that children living in inner-city environments are at greater risk for PTSD due to higher rates of violence. Fifty percent of these young people experience a traumatic event and up to one-half develop PTSD. Individuals with PTSD are more likely to have other anxiety disorders and mood disorders (pages 77–88).

RISK AND RESILIENCY FACTORS FOR POST-TRAUMATIC STRESS DISORDER

Risk Factors

- **Severity.** The more serious a trauma, the more likely it is to have long-lasting effects.

- **Physical injury.** A child who is physically injured in an event may feel trauma more intensely.
- **Involvement.** Those directly involved in a traumatic event (as opposed to witnessing it) are more likely to experience PTSD.
- **History.** Children who've experienced trauma in the past are more likely to be severely affected by another traumatic event.
- **Family.** Family instability or dysfunction can make children more susceptible to PTSD.

Resiliency Factors

- **Social and family support.** Positive support from family members and others who care for a student can help reduce an event's effect.
- **Coping mechanisms.** These may include anxiety-reducing strategies a child has learned prior to trauma.

Behaviors and Symptoms to Look For

You may not know whether a student has experienced a traumatic event. Even in situations where you do know what's happened in a child's life, symptoms (and when they occur) can vary widely among students. Most often the effects of Post-Traumatic Stress Disorder occur within a few months of an incident, though it may be months or even years before signs emerge.

Students with Post-Traumatic Stress Disorder may have symptoms that include:

Disorganized and agitated behavior. Children may appear to be extremely confused, upset, or out of control. They may not seem to be aware of or able to explain their behavior.

Separation Anxiety Disorder. Young children who experience trauma may become overly attached to parents or caregivers. Children often fear that once outside of the protection of these people, the traumatic event will recur. See page 72 for more information on Separation Anxiety Disorder.

Stress associated with "triggers." Students may have unexpected reactions to what seem like normal daily routines. Certain objects, places, or people at school may remind them of the trauma. This association also can extend to conversations or ideas from the curriculum. Students most often will attempt to avoid these triggers.

Fatigue and inattention. Sleeplessness due to nightmares or flashbacks can cause children to be tired and distracted in the classroom.

Play reenacting the trauma. Students, especially younger children, may begin to play in ways that include themes of the trauma.

Intense fear and vigilance. Students may experience all-consuming terror and become hypervigilant of their surroundings. They believe constant alertness can help them avoid future trauma, and they are extremely sensitive to environmental cues they believe may signify danger.

Extreme moodiness or depression. Post-Traumatic Stress Disorder can lead to erratic fluctuations in mood and, in some cases, depression. Regardless of a second diagnosis, many symptoms of other anxiety disorders or mood disorders (see pages 77–88) may be observed in students who have experienced a trauma.

Rapid change or drop-off in interests. Children who were once outgoing and had many interests may suddenly become withdrawn and refrain from activities they previously enjoyed. Younger children may stop playing games they like; older students may avoid or limit participation in extracurricular activities.

Private, invisible experiences. Children may experience intrusive, frightening memories or flashbacks of the trauma. Nightmares also are common.

Abuse of alcohol or other drugs. Middle and high school students may use alcohol or other drugs to try to diminish the anxiety they feel.

Classroom Strategies and Interventions

In helping students with PTSD, it's best if you know the trauma they experienced or witnessed. Some families will disclose this information to schools while others will not. Families tend to be secretive about incidents of sexual abuse. Your best antidote to secrecy is to gain the confidence of your students. Showing empathy and genuine interest in a student can help you establish trust. If a student does share his situation with you, work with him and other school staff to provide support.

Although PTSD is an anxiety disorder, it can have a strong effect on mood. In addition to the following suggestions, recommendations for other anxiety disorders and mood disorders (see pages 77–88) can be helpful.

Create a sense of safety and security in students. Children who have experienced a traumatic event can benefit a great deal from positive words of comfort. Empathize with a student and make sure he knows his feelings are not "bad" or "crazy." Emphasize that your classroom is a place where he can feel safe and encourage supportive behavior from other students. More information on creating a welcoming environment can be found in "Establishing a Safe and Caring Classroom" on pages 35–36.

Be especially sensitive to a student's background. Urban youth are more likely to experience trauma than peers from suburban or rural environments. Students whose families have immigrated may be from countries where violence or war are common.

Provide a "safe place" for students who become overwhelmed. It is possible that traumatic memories and associations might be triggered by various stimuli within the classroom. Should this happen, allow the student to visit a previously designated place to escape the troubling stimuli. Calling on a school counselor or school psychologist who is familiar with the student's history might be helpful.

Modify academic requirements. Base curriculum accommodations upon the severity of a student's PTSD. If emotional difficulties are causing her to struggle in the classroom, possible accommodations might include a reduction in her workload, flexible deadlines, or alternative assignments.

Create a calm, predictable environment. Students with PTSD have experienced events outside of their control and may become anxious when variations occur in routines. It is important that your classroom be a place of consistency where students know what to expect. Discuss with students schedule changes, field trips, or other special events well in advance. More information on creating consistent routines can be found in "Effective Classroom Policies and Procedures" on pages 19–25.

Speak with the school counselor, parents, and outside professionals working with the child. Some students' families may not share information about a child's traumatic event. Try to open lines of communication with parents and any mental health professionals treating the child so that all adults are well informed and working together.

EMILY

Emily entered sixth grade far away from home. Her family had been displaced when their home was destroyed by Hurricane Katrina. They were stranded for three days before being rescued. Emily remembered standing on top of furniture to avoid the floodwaters.

She had been in her new school for a couple of months when teachers began to grow concerned. Emily always looked very worried. Changes in routines and ordinary classroom sounds upset her. She frequently daydreamed and often had to be reminded to pay attention. She also asked to be seated away from windows. She was especially anxious on very windy, cloudy, or rainy days.

The guidance counselor requested a meeting with Emily's parents. They had noticed her anxiety when it rained or thundered. She also became upset when she saw footage of the hurricane on television. Emily often awoke to nightmares and would demand to sleep with her parents—something she hadn't done since she was four years old.

The guidance counselor spoke with the school psychologist and the consensus was that Emily was likely experiencing Post-Traumatic Stress Disorder. The family was referred to a local social service agency for counseling and a plan was developed for teachers to respond to Emily's anxiety. These interventions included seating Emily away from windows, preparing her for changes in schedules or activities, notifying her of predictable loud noises (such as fire drills), and repeating any instructions her inattention might cause her to miss.

PROFESSIONAL TREATMENTS

Students who experience Post-Traumatic Stress Disorder may benefit from more than one type of therapy. *Cognitive-behavioral therapy* is a technique that gradually exposes a child to a stimulus associated with the trauma while helping him think in a different way about the event. *Eye Movement Desensitization and Reprocessing (EMDR)* is another treatment shown to be effective.

These therapies may be complemented by the use of medication, especially when PTSD causes severe physiological effects (including insomnia, intense anxiety or panic, loss of appetite, or depression). *Selective serotonin reuptake inhibitors (SSRIs)* are the most common medications prescribed for PTSD. It's important to closely monitor students on these medications, especially in the first several weeks. Possible side effects include drowsiness, agitation, nausea, headaches, weight gain, and increased insomnia or depression. If you observe troubling changes in behavior, you should immediately share this information with a school nurse and parents.

GET HELP! Students with Post-Traumatic Stress Disorder may experience terrifying flashbacks related to a trauma at any time. These children may have other extreme emotional reactions that can frighten them and other students. Teachers should be prepared to get immediate assistance to safely accompany a student out of class to see a counselor or school psychologist.

Panic Disorder

A panic attack is a brief period of sudden, intense fear or discomfort that includes physical symptoms (like chest pain, nausea, sweatiness, and dizziness) as well as mental effects (such as a feeling of unreality or doom). Up to 65% of adolescents may experience isolated panic attacks, but only a small percentage experience Panic Disorder. Students with this disorder may have multiple attacks of panic and begin to fear that more attacks will occur. They may have fears of dying, heart attack, suffocating, or "going crazy." Panic Disorder may cause children to avoid certain places, activities, or objects they fear will cause another attack.

Between 1% and 5% of adolescents experience Panic Disorder. About one-half of these young people also experience another anxiety disorder or Depressive Disorder. It isn't known how many younger children have panic attacks.

Panic attacks are related to the fight-or-flight response experienced when we feel in danger. Adrenalin and other chemicals flood the body in a normal stress response that is meant to help us escape potentially harmful situations. Panic attacks might be thought off as a "false alarm" to this fight-or-flight response. The response occurs even when there is no real danger. The increase of panic attacks in adolescence may be related to hormonal changes occurring at puberty.

The mental and physical effects of panic attacks are frightening, but so is their unpredictability. Much of the fear children experience comes from not knowing when the next attack might occur. Some adolescents can become very isolated. They may be afraid to leave their homes or the company of their parents. These children may have *agoraphobia*—anxiety about not being able to escape or get help in a situation where panic might occur.

Behaviors and Symptoms to Look For

With students who experience panic attacks, it's important for you to be alert to possible attacks as well as to students who fear having them. A child experiencing her first panic attack will be frightened and bewildered by the experience. Students who have Panic Disorder (but are not experiencing an attack) may not be as easily identified. These students may be privately dreading another attack and constantly checking their bodies for signs of anxiety.

Possible signs of panic attacks and Panic Disorder include:

Visible physical changes. Physical symptoms of panic attacks can include sweating, shaking, rapid breathing, shortness of breath, dizziness, or unsteadiness.

Private, invisible sensations. Students may experience heart palpitations, a feeling of choking, nausea, stomachaches, numbness, feelings of unreality, or fears of losing control, "going crazy," or dying.

Avoidance of certain places, activities, and people (agoraphobia). Students may associate panic attacks with certain classrooms, activities, or people. Fear of another attack may cause them to avoid any situation that makes them feel uncomfortable.

Inattention. Students worrying about having a panic attack are constantly monitoring physical sensations. With so much attention focused inwardly, students may not be able to focus on your lessons or instructions. Students may appear distracted and may be unable to remember something that was just said.

Slow, inadequate work production. Constant self-monitoring for signs of anxiety can make it difficult for students to complete work. Students may fail to finish tests, classroom assignments, or homework within expected time frames.

Abuse of alcohol and drugs. Some adolescents attempt to prevent panic attacks by "calming themselves" with chemicals.

Classroom Strategies and Interventions

It's important to respond right away to a student who is experiencing a panic attack. Immediate reassurance is the best way to help calm children's fear. It's also a good idea to work with parents and mental health professionals who are involved with the child. They may be able to offer ideas that you, counselors, and other staff can use to ease a student's fears.

Following are ideas for helping students with panic attacks or Panic Disorder:

Respond to a panic attack with reassurance and calming suggestions. Stay brief, calm, and reassuring in your response to an attack. If you know a student has had panic attacks, tell her that her body is sending those false alarms again and there's no real danger. Suggest slow, deep breaths. Take your lead from the student. If she wants to be alone, let her be alone. If she wants someone to stay with her, make sure someone—whether inside or outside the classroom—stays with her.

Minimize attention from other students. Other students may be startled or frightened by a child experiencing a visible panic attack. Do your best to deflect students' attention toward some other activity. As you help a student, you might calmly say to the class, "I'd like for you all to turn to page 16 and begin reading."

Establish provisions for students experiencing panic. Create a "safe" or "quiet" place in your classroom (or one nearby) where students can calm down, or allow students to visit the office or a school counselor. Consider setting up a coping plan for when students feel panic (see "Student Coping Plan" on page 30).

Allow for accommodations to address panic and constant worries of an attack. A student may require extended time for tests and assignments, a reduction in workload, and other curricular accommodations. If a coping plan allows a student to leave the classroom when he begins to feel panic, you may choose to seat him near the door.

Allow students to be excused from panic-triggering activities and situations. A student may feel panic at the thought of being alone, standing in a crowd, riding on a school bus, or being trapped in enclosed places (like an elevator). When possible, provide alternatives for these situations.

PROFESSIONAL TREATMENTS

Cognitive-behavior therapy can be effective in treating students with Panic Disorder. Children are first taught that the effects of a panic attack—although very frightening—are not dangerous. Therapy focuses on realistic thinking, breathing, and relaxation exercises (including biofeedback). While panic in students is not always set off by a specific situation, a discussion of possible environmental triggers is often part of therapy.

Depending upon the intensity of panic attacks, medication may also be used in treatment. *Selective serotonin reuptake inhibitors (SSRIs)* are commonly used to control panic. SSRIs may take several weeks to take effect so other medications may be used initially to reduce anxiety. Possible side effects of SSRI medications include drowsiness, insomnia, nausea, stomachache, headache, or increased anxiety and depression—particularly in the first several weeks of medication treatment. It's important to monitor students on medication and report any side effects you observe to a school nurse and parents right away.

School Refusal

School refusal (or school avoidance) is not a mental health disorder. Instead, the term refers to a student's fear or unwillingness to attend school. Possible causes for a student's refusal include:

A mental health disorder. Many children afraid to go to school—especially those who are younger—have Separation Anxiety Disorder. Social Anxiety Disorder (see pages 57–61) is another common reason for absences. Up to 75 percent of students with Social Anxiety Disorder may refuse to go to school. Other mental health disorders also can create feelings and behaviors that cause a student to miss school.

Between 1% and 5% of children and adolescents refuse to attend school at some point. Ultimately, about 10% of students over the age of sixteen drop out of school permanently.

Student anxiety about performance. Meeting classroom expectations causes some students great stress and can lead them to miss school. This is especially true for students who have learning difficulties. Up to 40 percent of elementary school students experience test anxiety that can contribute to school refusal. This statistic is likely to grow with the prevalence of standardized testing to measure students' progress as required by the No Child Left Behind Act.

Students fear for their safety and well-being. Many children are teased, bullied, or ostracized by peers. When students don't feel safe or accepted at school, they may choose not to attend. It's estimated that 160,000 students miss school each day due to fear of being teased, attacked, or intimidated by others. Consistent harassment by other children can lead to the development of mental health disorders.

Students experiencing difficulties at home. Some children have a legitimate concern about a family member or a situation at home. They feel more comfortable if they can be there to monitor what is happening.

Children who are disengaged or defiant. There are some children who would simply rather stay home and watch TV or play video games than attend school. These children often struggle with learning difficulties and behavior problems. Students who experience only failure or punishment at school are more likely to avoid school.

Behaviors and Symptoms to Look For

Frequent absence is the most obvious sign that a student is afraid of or unwilling to attend school. Other children make it to school only after some resistance. Young children, especially preschool and kindergarten students, often will protest when they are dropped off in the morning. Older students may oversleep or be tardy for another reason. Some children readily go to school but report sickness or physical complaints once there so they may go home.

Classroom Strategies and Interventions

There are many reasons for school refusal. It's important to understand why a student is missing school. A team approach can help. Talk with the child as well as with the parents. Check in with counselors, other teachers, and administrators for any insight they may have on a student's struggles. A mental health professional should be consulted if a child can't (or won't) say why he doesn't want to go to school. These professionals can be helpful if school refusal continues for more than a few days and collaborative parent and school interventions fail.

In extreme cases of school refusal, you may not be able to do anything to address the problem—a child may simply be absent for long periods of time. When students *are* at school, use these strategies to encourage their continued presence:

Eliminate bullying and create safe learning environments. Many children stay home because they don't feel safe at school. It's important to prevent bullying at the school-wide level (including in classrooms, hallways, gymnasiums, lunchrooms, and locker rooms, and on playgrounds and buses) so students feel safe. Suggestions for creating supportive school environments can be found in "Establishing a Safe and Caring Classroom" on pages 35–36.

Avoid criticizing students' anxiety. Questions like, "You're not a baby, are you?" or "What are your classmates going to think if they see you crying?" can make students feel worse about school. Empathize with a child's feelings and remain positive about her ability to overcome anxiety.

Modify instruction to reach reluctant learners. Motivating "tuned-out" students through learning can be effective in increasing a child's enjoyment of school as well as her motivation to achieve. Consider adapting the curriculum to a student's learning styles and interests. For more information on teaching to learning styles and interests and other strategies for motivating learners, see "Effective Teaching Strategies for Meeting Diverse Student Needs" on pages 31–33.

Adjust classroom expectations. Depending on the reasons (and severity) for a student's school refusal, it may be important to adjust expectations. This could include modifying assignments or relaxing deadlines.

Praise student successes and applaud progress. Compliment students on specific areas in which they excel or are showing improvement. Help them perceive school as a place where they are succeeding and let them know you are glad they are in your classroom.

Build students' social skills. Students who refuse to attend school often feel anxious or overwhelmed by the social expectations there. Help diminish a student's trepidation of other students and school staff by providing socials skills instruction. Some social skills building activities and resources can be found in "Building Social Skills in Students" on pages 37–39.

Speak with a school counselor, parents, and outside professionals working with the child. Speak with other school staff who are addressing attendance issues. Parents and mental health professionals also can provide helpful information. If a student begins experiencing problems after he has initially adjusted to the classroom, a parent may be able to explain the change.

SEPARATION ANXIETY DISORDER

Separation Anxiety Disorder is one of the most common causes of school refusal. Children with this disorder feel intense anxiety when they are separated from parents or caregivers. Approximately 4 percent of all children experience Separation Anxiety Disorder.

Preschool and kindergarten educators are most likely to observe Separation Anxiety Disorder because it is during the early school years that children and caregivers are first separated for long periods of time. Common signs of the disorder are:

Crying, tantrums, and clinging behavior. These can be especially intense when a child is dropped off at school or during other transition times.

Stomachaches, headaches, nausea, and other physical complaints. Aches and pains may be real (caused by anxiety) or feigned (an excuse to return to the parent).

Excessive questioning of parent. Questions might include "Where are you going?" "When will you be back?" "Is your phone going to be on?" "What if something happens to you?"

Excessive fears. Children may refuse to sleep alone or go anywhere without a parent or caregiver. They may ask a lot of questions about the possibility of a parent being severely injured, kidnapped, or killed.

If symptoms of Separation Anxiety Disorder last longer than four weeks and cause significant distress in some important area of functioning, the child may qualify for a diagnosis of Separation Anxiety Disorder. (Briefer disturbances resolved within four weeks—such as the first week of school—might be diagnosed as *Adjustment Disorder with Anxiety.*)

Treatment for Separation Anxiety Disorder usually includes slowly exposing children to graduated increases in separation. Parents learn to separate quickly and confidently from children. This reduces the parents' anxiety, which may have provided the fuel for a child's fears. Treatment is more effective if it begins as soon as possible after symptoms develop.

FELIPE

Seven-year-old Felipe and his mother were in a minor car accident. Although not injured seriously, both were taken to the hospital for observation and then released. Felipe seemed fine upon arriving home. He looked forward to returning to school and telling his friends about the excellent ice cream he had at the hospital.

The following Saturday, Felipe spent the day with his grandparents. Though he knew his mother was working, he tried to call her. When she didn't answer her phone, Felipe began to panic. Even as his grandparents did their best to reassure him that his mother was okay, Felipe grew more and more upset.

It was not until she was on her way to pick up Felipe that his mother received the tearful messages and was able to call the grandparents. When she arrived, she found Felipe asleep after many hours of crying. He woke up briefly and said that he never wanted her to leave again.

Felipe refused to return to school on Monday morning. He cried and protested when his mother tried to force him to go. This persisted for a few days until Felipe's mother took him to a therapist. After a conversation with Felipe, the source of his anxiety became clear. He now associated being separated from his mother with the car accident. The thought of her leaving filled him with terror because he feared she'd be hurt.

After another session with the therapist, Felipe was able to accept being separated from his mother for a shortened day of school. This period of time was incrementally expanded. Within a week Felipe was back in school full time. He still experienced occasional fears about his mother's safety, but reassurance from his teacher helped him realize his fears were not rational.

TWO GRADUATED EXPOSURE PLANS FOR STUDENTS EXHIBITING SCHOOL REFUSAL OR SEPARATION ANXIETY DISORDER

One effective way to help a student who has fears about school is to use a graduated exposure plan. This collaboration between parents and school officials helps children to adjust to separation. A child's time at school is expanded over several days or weeks.

The following steps can be practiced multiple times on the same day depending upon how a child responds. It's important for students to be comfortable with each step prior to moving on to a more difficult one.

PLAN 1

- Step 1. After school has started, the student and parent sit in the parking lot for fifteen minutes. If a bus or train is taken, the student and parent may remain together at the transit stop for fifteen minutes.
- Step 2. Repeat Step 1. Next the parent and student walk ten steps toward the school building and stand for five minutes.
- Step 3. Repeat Step 2. Next the parent and student walk up to the school sidewalk and stand for five minutes.
- Step 4. Next the parent and student walk up to the front door of the school and stand for five minutes.
- Step 5. The parent and student enter the school together and then exit quickly.
- Step 6. The parent accompanies the student to the school entrance. The student enters alone and exits quickly.
- Step 7. The parent accompanies the student to the school entrance. The student enters alone and stands for five minutes.
- Step 8. The parent accompanies the student to the school entrance. The student enters and walks the halls with the school counselor for five minutes. The parent waits at the school entrance.
- Step 9. The parent accompanies the student to the school entrance. The counselor walks the student to the classroom door and they stand there for five minutes. The parent waits at the school entrance.
- Step 10. The student walks into school alone while the parent waits outside. The student walks to class with the counselor and they stand outside of the door for ten minutes.
- Step 11. The student walks into school alone and walks to class with the counselor. Then the student enters the classroom alone.
- Step 12. The student walks into school alone and enters the classroom alone.

PLAN 2

- Step 1. The parent and student meet with the teacher in the classroom after school. This is meant to help the student become more comfortable with the teacher.
- Step 2. The parent and student enter the classroom in the morning. The parent is introduced to the class as "the helper" and assists the teacher with various tasks throughout the day.
- Step 3. The student is required to interact with classmates and to work away from the parent. The parent and student may accompany each other to the restroom.
- Step 4. The parent observes class from the back of the room. The parent and student may accompany each other to the restroom.
- Step 5. The parent observes class and tells the student he will be leaving the room briefly (without the student) to use the restroom. The student must also use the restroom alone.
- Step 6. The parent observes class and stays in the room during recess while the student plays.
- Step 7. The parent gradually leaves the classroom for increasing periods of time. He returns to reassure the student before leaving again—this time for a slightly longer amount of time. This is repeated until a student is comfortable being separated from the parent.

Mood Disorders

"Education is a social process. Education is growth. Education is not preparation for life; education is life itself."

—John Dewey, philosopher and author

Students with mood disorders experience disturbances in their emotions that can negatively affect how they feel about themselves and act around others. The most common mood disorders are Depressive Disorders and Bipolar Disorder. Children with Depressive Disorders experience unhappiness, loss of interest in their usual activities, and irritability. Those with Bipolar Disorder experience depression or irritability that alternates with periods of feeling elation, exaggerated self-esteem, "racing" thoughts, and less need for sleep (manic phases).

About 5% of children and between 10% and 20% of adolescents experience mood disorders. Up to two-thirds of these young people may have at least one additional mental disorder.

Mood disorders have a negative impact on many aspects of a person's life. Children often have low self-esteem and feelings of guilt, worthlessness, and hopelessness. They may become socially withdrawn. Moods that are too "high" may cause problems with peers and family members. Any of these mood changes also can create difficulty doing schoolwork.

Depressive Disorders can be difficult to detect in children. Students may be quiet and experience their feelings privately. Often students are affected by an event or situation outside of school about which you may have no knowledge. The manic moods of children with Bipolar Disorder are most often much easier to observe.

If you suspect a child might have a mood disorder, it is important to tell counselors (and other school staff) as well as parents what you have observed. Sharing information on behaviors that alarm you can be an important step toward getting a student the help he needs.

DISORDERS COVERED IN THIS SECTION

CAUTION! Mood disorders can be very serious. Depression is the most common reason for attempted suicide. In the United States, a young person commits suicide every two hours. For every child who succeeds in taking her own life, twenty-three others make suicide attempts or gestures. It is important to take suicidal wishes and threats seriously and to respond immediately. Any student suspected of being dangerous to himself (or others) should not be left unsupervised. For a full list of suicide warning signs and appropriate responses see Self-Injury on pages 173–177.

Depressive Disorders

Including Adjustment Disorder with Depressed Mood, Dysthymia, and Major Depression

Children with Depressive Disorders experience low mood or loss of interest in usual activities. They may also have strong feelings of sadness, irritability, guilt, or hopelessness. Low self-esteem, lack of energy, difficulties concentrating, and loss of interest in daily activities are common, as are physical symptoms like insomnia, changes in appetite, and body aches and pains.

Children who are depressed are at a greater risk of poor school performance and becoming socially isolated. Most severely, they are at greatest risk to attempt suicide.

Approximately 1% of children and 5% of adolescents experience Dysthymia. About 3% of children and up to 20% of adolescents have Major Depression. Between one-half to two-thirds of young people with Major Depression have at least one other mental disorder.

It is natural for all children at times to feel unhappiness or a decreased interest in activities. Many experiences at home or school can cause these feelings for a brief period of time. Major life changes (like the loss of a loved one) may also cause major changes in mood. Children—with the help of adults—most often are able to overcome challenges and tragic life events and adjust to new circumstances.

Other children experience extreme feelings of unhappiness that can last for long periods of time. These feelings may or may not be triggered by a particular event. When children experience symptoms of depression or irritability for weeks at a time, they may have a Depressive Disorder.

There are three types of Depressive Disorders. These are based on the severity and duration of depressed feelings.

Adjustment Disorder with Depressed Mood. Adjustment Disorder with Depressed Mood is an exaggerated reaction to a specific event. Such a reaction causes negative effects on a child's behavior at home or in school. An example of this might be a child whose parents have separated. One child might respond to the separation with some sadness or anger and not be diagnosed with Adjustment Disorder with Depressed Mood. Another child might experience major changes in mood or behavior that interferes with schoolwork. This child might qualify for a diagnosis of Adjustment Disorder with Depressed Mood.

Dysthymia. For some children, depression may be long-lasting and not necessarily in reaction to a specific event. Dysthymia is often considered a chronic, low-grade depression that can prevent people from enjoying much of what life has to offer. Low self-esteem, difficulties with concentration, and other symptoms of depression are present over long periods of time. These symptoms are not necessarily severe and so observing them in young people can be difficult. Children with Dysthymia have a 70 percent risk of developing Major Depression.

Major Depression. This refers to depression that can be very serious. Symptoms are usually more severe than those with an Adjustment Disorder or Dysthymia. Children with Major Depression most often experience major changes in the way they feel and behave in school or at home. People may experience Major Depression for various periods of time—ranging from two weeks to several years. Unfortunately, depression has a tendency to recur if it is not treated. Up to 40 percent of children who experience one episode of depression will experience another within two years.

Behaviors and Symptoms to Look For

You will most easily see symptoms of depression when a student shows a sudden change in attitude or behavior. A once enthusiastic and outgoing boy may suddenly seem sullen and begin to withdraw from friends and activities he likes. His change in behavior will alert you that something may be bothering him. In other cases, if you only know a student as soft-spoken, shy, or withdrawn, it may be more difficult to observe depressed feelings.

Symptoms of depression can vary significantly among different ages.

Preschoolers may be more accident prone, subject to excessive and multiple fears, and be self-deprecating.

Children ages six to eight are more likely to exhibit vague physical complaints, exhibit both aggressive and clinging behavior toward parents, and avoid new people and challenges.

Children ages nine to twelve more often have morbid thoughts about death and excessive worry about schoolwork.

Adolescents are more likely to exhibit excessive anger, withdrawal, hypersensitivity to criticism, and suicidal thoughts. They also more commonly abuse drugs and alcohol, have eating disorders, and engage in cutting.

Following are common symptoms of Depressive Disorders:

A generally depressed mood with sadness, anxiety, or irritability. Depressed children often appear sad or worried. They might be very concerned about grades or peer acceptance, and they may be quiet or unproductive in class due to decreased energy.

Social withdrawal. Alienation from peers can be the result of, or partial cause for, depression. Be observant of students who seem isolated from peers.

Academic failure or marked changes in achievement. Children who are depressed may suddenly appear to lose interest in schoolwork, and their grades may drop. This can include students who once performed at a high level.

Loss of interest or pleasure in usual activities. A student's general loss of enthusiasm may indicate depression. Students might continue to participate in activities but not seem to enjoy them.

Frequent absences or tardiness. Depression and lower grades can lead to an increased dislike of school. Students may avoid going to school.

Lethargy or a sudden decrease in energy. Consistent fatigue or a change in a student's energy can suggest a depressed mood. Less energy can lead to poor work production and falling grades.

Fatigue or tiredness. Children with depression often have disrupted sleep patterns. Tardiness can be caused by difficulty getting up in the morning. These students may appear drowsy or even fall asleep in school.

Feelings of worthlessness or guilt. Low self-esteem is a common characteristic of depression and often can be observed in a child's words, demeanor, and behavior. Students may criticize their abilities in the classroom ("I'm no good at math") and other settings ("I shouldn't play, I always strike out"). Feelings of inferiority can lead to withdrawal because students don't feel they are worthy of peers' acceptance ("I'm fat").

Problems concentrating or indecisiveness. Inattention and difficulty making decisions are commonly observed in children with depression. Inattention caused by depression can be confused with Attention Deficit Hyperactivity Disorder (pages 135–146).

Significant weight gain or loss. Students' eating patterns may change in reaction to emotional distress. Some students will eat more and gain weight when depressed. Others will lose their appetite or deliberately limit how much they eat. Eating disorders (pages 167–171) can accompany depression especially among adolescents.

Disruptiveness. Children who are depressed may show oppositional and defiant behavior. A student might be so affected by her feelings that she questions the necessity of a given assignment or rule. ("Why does it matter anyway?") Emotional sensitivity and irritability can fuel these kinds of outbursts.

Recurrent thoughts of death. One sign of severe depression is suicidal thinking. All thoughts or threats of self-harm should be taken seriously and responded to right away. For more information on suicide warning signs and appropriate responses see Self-Injury on pages 173–177.

Classroom Strategies and Interventions

Depressive Disorders, as with all mental health disorders, should only be diagnosed by a qualified mental health professional. If a student has not been diagnosed but you observe symptoms that might represent depression, it's important to inform parents, counselors, and other school staff of any behaviors that concern you.

Following are some suggestions for helping students that you suspect or know are experiencing depression:

Provide students with compassion and empathy. Show students you are genuinely interested in their lives and well-being. Ask about family, friends, interests, and other aspects of their lives. The impact of genuine, sustained interest on the part of an educator cannot be overestimated in the life of a depressed student.

Show flexibility with school policies including absences and tardiness. Students with depression are likely to experience significant sleep disturbances that can affect attendance. A depressed mood may also lead to school refusal. Attending appointments for therapy might also cause some absenteeism. Provide accommodations in your classroom schedule and rules for these students.

Allow for flexibility in workload. Adjust coursework assignments to accommodate a student's mood as well as any extended absences. Large assignments or projects can be broken into smaller steps to avoid overwhelming a student. Consider extended time for exams to help ease a student's difficulties with concentration, decreased energy, and slower processing speed.

Provide for a safe and caring classroom. Bullying may be a partial cause for depression and can make children who are already depressed feel worse. Ensure that your classroom is a place where harassment is not tolerated. Strategies for creating supportive school environments can be found in "Establishing a Safe and Caring Classroom" on pages 35–36.

Offer a place where depressed students can take a break or talk. Students who are overwhelmed by their feelings should be allowed to visit a "safe place" or to speak with a school counselor.

Plan for gradually reintroducing a student to school. It might be necessary for a child to be slowly reintroduced to school after a hospitalization or lengthy home-bound period. Work with counselors and other school staff to establish a plan for a student's return to the classroom.

Carefully observe *all* students. The signs of depression are not always readily apparent and may not emerge in an obvious way in your classroom. It's important to know your students and to note any changes you see in their behavior.

PROFESSIONAL TREATMENTS

Cognitive-behavioral therapy is an effective treatment for Depressive Disorders. This therapy teaches young people how to think differently so they will feel better. Mood tends to improve when a child realizes that a situation is not as bad as she believed. Relaxation training, breathing exercises, and the use of imagery also are used to help decrease negative emotions. Working with a play therapist may be best for young children who cannot yet fully verbalize their thoughts and feelings.

Children with Major Depression may be prescribed medication if symptoms are severe. The most common medications prescribed for depression are *selective serotonin reuptake inhibitors (SSRIs)* and *serotonin-norepinephrine inhibitors (SNRIs)*. Recent evidence shows that increased SSRI prescriptions for youth with mood disorders have lowered the suicide rate among this age group. However, there may be a very small percentage of young people who become more depressed, agitated, and even suicidal in the initial stages of taking this medication. Children must be monitored very closely during the early days and weeks when taking medications. Other possible side effects of medication include drowsiness, insomnia, stomachaches, headaches, nervousness, and weight gain. Any troubling symptoms you observe in a child taking medication should be immediately shared with the school nurse and parents.

MICHAEL

Michael was a bright thirteen-year-old with a lot of heart. He was a popular kid among his classmates and always had a joke for his teachers. But all of this changed after the winter break. Michael seemed to come back to school a different person. He wouldn't speak to others unless he was forced to. His work began to fall off and he didn't seem to care. In the halls, Michael would pull the hood of his sweatshirt over his head as if to become invisible. Teachers knew something was wrong, but Michael wouldn't talk to anyone. No one knew what the problem was.

The school counselor was asked to intervene and brought Michael to her office. They spent a few sessions in silence with Michael avoiding eye contact until he finally revealed that his father left home abruptly over the holidays. The counselor recommended to Michael's mother that she take him to see a psychotherapist. Michael's father and mother remained separated, but with the professional's help, Michael was able to adjust to his new home situation.

Bipolar Disorder

Bipolar Disorder—the current term for what used to be called *manic-depression*—is a brain disorder that causes people to experience extreme and rapid changes in mood and energy. These shifts often result in disruptive (or even destructive) behavior that make it difficult for children to perform at school or have normal relationships with others.

Adults and children experience Bipolar Disorder differently. Adults most often cycle between episodes of depression and intense euphoria or elation. Instead of episodes of depression, younger children are more likely to exhibit anger, explosiveness, or belligerence. These moods cycle with manic periods of increased energy, overly high self-esteem, decreased need for sleep, and thoughts that "race."

Young people also tend to cycle between moods more frequently than adults. Children usually have very rapid mood swings that can occur many times within a single day. A child with Bipolar Disorder could be overly giddy and excited about a project he's working on and the next minute become angry and destroy it. His mood may abruptly change again so that he becomes enthusiastic about repairing the damage. An event may or may not trigger these changes in mood.

Estimates suggest that up to 1% of young people experience Bipolar Disorder. Between 20% and 30% of adolescents who have an initial episode of depression eventually develop Bipolar Disorder.

Distinguishing between symptoms of Bipolar Disorder, Attention Deficit Hyperactivity Disorder (pages 135–146), and Oppositional Defiant Disorder (pages 147–154) can be difficult. Some children can have more than one disorder. Do your best to accurately report behaviors to parents, school staff, and professionals involved in a child's care. As with all mental disorders, a mental health professional needs to make the diagnosis.

Behaviors and Symptoms You Can Look For

Students with Bipolar Disorder often are easier to observe than those with Depressive Disorders. Rapid changes in mood and destructive behavior can signal that a child is having a problem. Younger children often express anger or belligerence, which cycles with manic behavior. Adolescents more often have classical symptoms of Depressive Disorder (see pages 79–84), which cycle with manic thoughts and behavior.

Manic behaviors in children include:

An unrealistically euphoric mood. A student may exhibit an exaggerated mood of elation or giddiness, which may last from a few minutes to a few hours. This euphoric mood does not appear to be justified by real-life events; for example, a child who can't stop laughing and giggling during class for no apparent reason.

Excessive energy and activity. Students may use energy in productive or non-productive ways. A student might suddenly begin completing class work she had previously ignored. Another student may be unable to stop moving or talking, and may cause classroom disruptions.

Need for less sleep. Someone in a manic phase of Bipolar Disorder will sleep much less than usual. The student may not appear tired; he may even be overly active in class.

Fast speech. Students experiencing a manic mood may talk very fast. It can be difficult to understand a student or get in a word of your own.

Have ideas that "fly" or thoughts that "race." A student in a manic episode may have many racing thoughts and not be able to express himself clearly. These ideas may be unrelated to each other and difficult to suppress. Students frequently interrupt class.

Plan or attempt unrealistic and sometimes risky or illegal activities. Students may lack good judgment, which can lead them to endanger themselves (and others). Excessive sexual activity or substance abuse may be common among older students.

Think in grandiose ways. Students may have a very unrealistic self-image. A student may view herself as the smartest student or best athlete when she is actually average in these areas. Grandiosity can be associated with risk-taking tendencies ("I'm much smarter than my teacher so I'm going to tell her how to teach today").

Show irritability, severe rage, and verbal or physical abuse. These students' mood changes can be rapid and extreme. Aggressive, violent behavior can occur with bouts of explosiveness that last for long periods of time.

Think and act in hypersexual ways. Children (even young children) may talk about sexual topics or act out sexually in inappropriate ways.

Classroom Strategies and Interventions

Students can show depressed or manic behaviors at any given time. For suggestions in responding to students with depressed mood, see pages 82–84. To address manic moods, you can use the strategies below. Check with counselors, other school staff, parents, and any mental health professionals involved in the care of a child for insight into a child's behavior and helpful interventions.

Be prepared for extreme mood swings and grandiosity. Students with Bipolar Disorder often experience extreme fluctuations in mood including sadness, giddiness, anxiety, anger, or other emotions. Some students may also express delusional thinking. Accept a student's views as being true rather than risk argument. For example, if a student claims to be smarter than all of her teachers, it's probably best to just say "okay" rather than dispute this opinion with a more realistic statement.

Avoid verbally engaging a student experiencing strong emotions. When a student's emotions are overwhelming him, he won't be able to think or speak logically. Respond to outbursts in a low voice and with a calm demeanor. Anger or criticism can fuel the child's emotions.

Allow students to leave the classroom to talk with someone. Students may experience feelings or behave in ways in the classroom that are very disruptive. Have a school-approved plan in place that allows this student to leave the classroom to talk with a counselor or psychologist.

Allow for flexibility in workload to accommodate energy level. Students with Bipolar Disorder may experience wide variations in their energy levels. Adjust course and homework requirements to accommodate a student's ability to produce work and generally function in the classroom.

Identify any situations that trigger a child's heightened moods. Note events that seem to cause or make worse a student's mood disturbances and take steps to avoid them.

Note: Children with mood disorders often have varying academic difficulties at school. Many strategies and accommodations listed for students with Attention Deficit Hyperactivity Disorder (see pages 135–146) and learning disabilities (see pages 109–133) can also be useful with these students.

GET HELP! If a student is behaviorally explosive, have a prepared plan to call your school's crisis team or personnel designated to respond to such emergencies.

PROFESSIONAL TREATMENTS

Medication is considered essential treatment for children with Bipolar Disorder. *Mood stabilizers*—which steady mood between two extremes—are the most commonly prescribed medications. Some students are prescribed an *antidepressant* or an *atypical antipsychotic medication* in addition to a mood stabilizer. Side effects of medications include excessive thirst and urination, drowsiness, diarrhea, stomachaches, weight gain, and headaches. It's important to allow students on these medications full access to fluids and use of the restroom. Check with parents about any medications being taken and ask them to inform you of any changes. Be observant of side effects, especially during the initial stages of medication use, and report any concerns immediately to a school nurse and parent.

Psychotherapy can also be helpful to teach students how to cope with their mood changes. A child who becomes destructive with rage might be taught healthier ways (like relaxation and breathing exercises) to deal with his intense anger. Family therapy can help families cope with Bipolar Disorder.

Communication Disorders

"Education is all a matter of building bridges."

—Ralph Ellison, author

Children with communication disorders experience difficulties with speech and language. These young people may have challenges forming the sounds of speech, understanding others, or expressing themselves (verbally or through writing).

Language plays an obvious role in learning and socializing. Students who have communication disorders are at risk for falling behind in multiple areas at school. They often have additional learning difficulties, most often a reading disability. Children may also feel self-conscious about language limitations and have difficulty forming friendships. Negative peer reaction (including teasing) to language difficulties can also hurt students' social development.

Approximately 3% of children in early elementary school have a communication disorder. About half of these children outgrow disorders by mid- to late-adolescence.

Communication disorders are one of the most common developmental problems among young students. Fortunately, most children overcome delays and develop full language skills. A small percentage of students continue to have communication difficulties into adolescence and even adulthood.

DISORDERS COVERED IN THIS SECTION

CAUTION! An English language learner should not be diagnosed with communication disorders unless difficulties with comprehension or expression also exist in the student's native language. Nonnative speakers may need to be evaluated by a bilingual speech-language pathologist.

Articulation Disorders

Children with Articulation Disorders have difficulties forming the sounds of speech. Most often these problems occur with the *s, z, l, r, k, g, ch,* and *th* sounds.

Physical problems with the oral motor system are sometimes responsible for a child's difficulties with articulation. *Apraxia,* for example, is a brain disorder that limits mouth and tongue muscle movement and can interfere with speech.

Most children with an Articulation Disorder overcome delays and develop full language abilities before significantly falling behind at school. Those children whose difficulties persist may find it hard to complete some work (such as oral reports) in secondary grades. Difficulties with speech also can lead to problems with socializing and the greater likelihood of being singled out for teasing or harassment.

About 10% of all children under age eight experience an Articulation Disorder. Only between 2% and 3% of these young people have difficulties with articulation past age five.

Behaviors and Symptoms to Look For

Children with Articulation Disorders substitute, omit, or distort sounds of speech. The range of articulation difficulty stretches from a mild problem to one that makes a child nearly impossible to understand.

Following are some examples of articulation difficulties:

Leaving out consonants at the beginning of words. Example: *all* for *ball.*

Leaving out consonants at the end of words. Example: *ca* for *cat.*

Leaving out sounds where they should occur. Example: *tail* for *table.*

Distorting sounds. Examples: *ship* for *sip* or *shursh* for *church.*

Substituting an incorrect sound for a correct one. Examples: *wabbit* for *rabbit, tat* for *cat,* or *dod* for *dog.*

Unintelligible speech. Apraxia is a severe Articulation Disorder that can cause children to speak almost completely unintelligibly. Only those who spend a lot of time with a child are likely to understand him. Example: "My I-her an I ab a dod." ("My sister and I have a dog.")

Classroom Strategies and Interventions

Articulation Disorders can make it difficult for children to participate in class and may have negative effects on how they socialize with others. Some difficulties with articulation may seem to fade over time—others will require intense intervention by you and possibly a speech-language pathologist. Combine your efforts to improve students' speech with those of professionals available to you at your school.

Following are some suggestions for building communication skills and accommodating the needs of students with an Articulation Disorder in your classroom:

Accurately restate the student's inaccurate sound as naturally as possible. Example: If a student has difficulty with the beginning "y" sound and says, "I want the weawo one," repeat the words slowly with greater enunciation and stretch the targeted word: "Oh, you want the YELL-OW crayon. Here you go." This approach is mainly effective with younger children as older students may feel embarrassed or uncomfortable with increased attention on mistakes.

Read a list of words containing the mispronounced sound. Use a list of about ten words. Sit across from the student and encourage her to look at you as you say the words. Show her how you position your mouth, lips, and tongue to make the correct sound.

Encourage students. Talk about any progress a student has made with articulating sounds. Provide specific compliments on sounds he says correctly. Example: "You said the *R* sound correctly in that word!"

Prepare students in advance of classroom requests. Let a student know that you plan to call on her for a particular answer. Ensure she is able to articulate the answer by practicing with her as necessary.

Allow for flexibility in course work. Consider replacing oral reports with written assignments. Keep a child's articulation difficulties in mind when designating roles for group presentations.

Accept inaccurate word pronunciation from the student. Rather than draw attention to or criticize a child's pronunciation in front of others, accept his response as it is given. Students with this disorder often are very sensitive, and increased attention on their errors in speech can make them feel worse.

Eliminate bullying and create safe learning environments. Students who have difficulties with speech are more likely to be bullied or excluded by peers. For ideas you can use to create supportive school environments, see "Establishing a Safe and Caring Classroom" on pages 35–36.

Provide social skills instruction. Children who have difficulties articulating speech may fear embarrassment or mockery by peers. Excessive fear of speaking in public may lead a child to become withdrawn. You can counter this by teaching social skills at a pace comfortable to the student. Some social skills building activities and resources can be found in "Building Social Skills in Students" on pages 37–39.

PROFESSIONAL TREATMENTS

Regardless of how much you are able to help students with Articulation Disorders in the regular classroom, it may also be important for a student to work with a speech-language pathologist. Students should be referred to speech therapy if others find it difficult to understand them, or their speech otherwise significantly varies from that used by peers.

Receptive and Expressive Language Disorders

Students with Receptive Language Disorder have difficulties understanding language used by others. Children with Expressive Language Disorder have difficulty using language to express themselves. The severity of these disorders varies—some students may not have significant noticeable communication problems, while other students' difficulties are apparent and require substantial intervention.

Receptive Language Disorder and Expressive Language Disorder are not caused by hearing difficulties or unfamiliarity with a culture or language. Heredity, differences in how the brain works, and chronic ear infections during the first two years of life are thought to be possible reasons for language delays.

These language disorders create challenges for students in many areas. Due to the difficulty children have understanding or remembering instructions, adults may assume they don't pay attention or behave appropriately. Poor vocabulary recall can lead to writing difficulties and leave students struggling for the right word. Finally, some students' tendencies in speech (such as parroting) seem odd to others and may cause a child to be socially isolated.

Between 3% and 5% of preschool and primary school students experience Receptive and Expressive Language Disorders. About half of these children outgrow disorders during adolescence.

Behaviors and Symptoms to Look For

Receptive Language Disorder and Expressive Language Disorder can create many academic, behavior, and social challenges for students. The pattern of language delays (and the problems they cause) can vary a great deal among students.

Children with Receptive Language Disorder may:

Have poor attention span—especially when listening to others speak. Difficulty understanding someone's speech can cause a student's attention to wander. This behavior can sometimes be misinterpreted as Attention Deficit Hyperactivity Disorder (pages 135–146).

Show difficulty following directions. Students with Receptive Language Disorder often have difficulty understanding and remembering directions and therefore may not *follow* them. Children who appear irresponsible or defiant may simply not know or remember what they are supposed to do. Also watch for students who seem to lean heavily on cues from others to participate in classroom activities or complete assignments.

Show poor ability to process and remember verbal information. Some students may not take a single line of notes during a lecture or class period—even when you have specifically asked them to do so. Children with Receptive Language Disorder often will have difficulties getting down information, because they do not remember it long enough to write it down. Others will be able to repeat isolated facts but miss the main point or perspective you're trying to get across.

Have limited reading comprehension. These students often have difficulties with reading. Those who are able to decode (or sound out) words may have a limited understanding of what a book or passage is about. Poor comprehension is related to very weak vocabulary skills.

Show difficulty understanding words with multiple meanings. In large part due to limited vocabulary, students struggle to understand or remember the multiple meanings of a single word.

Have difficulty with basic "*wh*" questions *(what, where, why, when, who)*. Children may understand parts of a question, but not its entire intention. Examples:

Teacher: Where should your pencils be right now?

Student: I don't need to sharpen them.

Teacher: Why did you like that story?

Student: You read it to us yesterday.

Children with an Expressive Language Disorder may:

Speak in words, phrases, or incomplete sentences. Children may speak in a way that seems to make little sense. Example: *Milk! He bad boy.*

Use gestures and sound effects instead of words to express ideas and feelings. Examples: *Last night my cat* (gestures scratching accompanied by hissing sound). *She wants the* (pointing to object).

Use pronouns, plurals, and possessives incorrectly. Examples: *Me go to bed. Us went there. I have three cat.*

Have difficulty telling a story or describing an event. Students may place events out of sequence, neglecting some and repeating others.

Have limited expressive vocabulary. Example: *I have a new game on the computer—you know, the one with cars and you pick one . . . like the purple one . . . and you go fast, and sometimes they* (makes crashing sound) *and then you have to get them back and go really fast.*

Have difficulty finding the right words to express meaning or referencing objects. Example: *You know, the thing that puts fires out* (instead of saying *fire extinguisher*).

Overuse filler words and imprecise language. Students may rely on *ah, um,* and *you know* when speaking. They may also use *thing, watchamacallit,* or other non-descript terms when they can't think of a word.

Have trouble with written compositions. Students produce work that contains vague ideas in which it is difficult to discover (or follow) a student's point or argument.

Classroom Strategies and Interventions

Students with Receptive Language Disorder and Expressive Language Disorder experience many different challenges. For this reason, a wide variety of strategies may be necessary to address behaviors. Work to match these interventions with the specific needs of a student.

Following are some strategies and accommodations helpful for students who have these disorders:

Repeat and clarify instructions as needed. A child's short attention span and a potentially limited grasp of language may make it necessary for you to repeat instructions. It's important to demonstrate patience and avoid criticizing students. When appropriate, it may help to have students re-state or paraphrase directions.

Deliver information in more than one way. In addition to explaining a concept verbally, provide graphics to help demonstrate it. You might use Venn diagrams, illustrations, or images from magazines or the Internet. Teach students to make simple diagrams to organize information and remind them of important concepts from class.

Simplify daily language use. Example: *Please hand me the pencil* instead of *Please hand me the big black pencil in your hand.*

Help students to compare and contrast objects and ideas. Show how two items are related or different. Example: In comparing a pen and pencil you might say the following: *They're the same because you write with both of them. They're different because a pen has ink and a pencil has graphite. You can usually erase what you write with a pencil, but you usually can't when you write with a pen.* You might also wish to show students how to use a Venn diagram to compare and contrast.

Be specific when giving instructions. Students can be overwhelmed by extensive directions and may be confused about what it is they are supposed to do. Break down assignments into small steps.

Provide written directions. In addition to verbal instructions, write directions on the board. You might also provide a handout on which the student can check off each step as it is completed. A check-off handout can encourage independence and responsibility.

EXAMPLE DIRECTIONS FOR WRITING ASSIGNMENT

1. Get your notebook from the bin.
2. Get a pencil from the cup.
3. Turn to the first blank page.
4. Write today's date on the first line.
5. Think about the writing topics for today.
6. Write about your topic.
7. Done?
8. Read what you wrote.
9. Does it make sense?
10. Are words missing?
11. Read it again.
12. Return your notebook to the basket and your pencil to the cup.

Provide a preview of a class or lesson. Preview a lesson or an assignment with an overview of what students will be expected to learn. Ask students to think about a few key questions or concepts when reading or working on a project.

Show a sample of the finished product you're assigning. Students may have a hard time picturing what is expected of them solely based on verbal instructions. A sample or another visual representation can help them to understand what you'd like them to do.

Teach students how to draw conclusions. To model drawing inferences, you might use a picture and talk about what is happening in it. Example: *Oh, I see a man carrying a can of paint and a paintbrush. Hmmm, there's a ladder leaning against the house. The man is walking away from the house with the paint and brush. I guess he just finished painting the house.*

Pre-teach vocabulary. Explain vocabulary words to be used in a discussion or lesson before presenting the lesson. You might also provide a list of these words on a handout and ask students to fill in their meanings as the terms come up in the class discussion.

Teach pre-writing skills. Students with language disorders often have difficulty organizing and fluently expressing their thoughts. Counter this by teaching pre-writing strategies such as mapping (or webbing).

EXAMPLE OF MAPPING

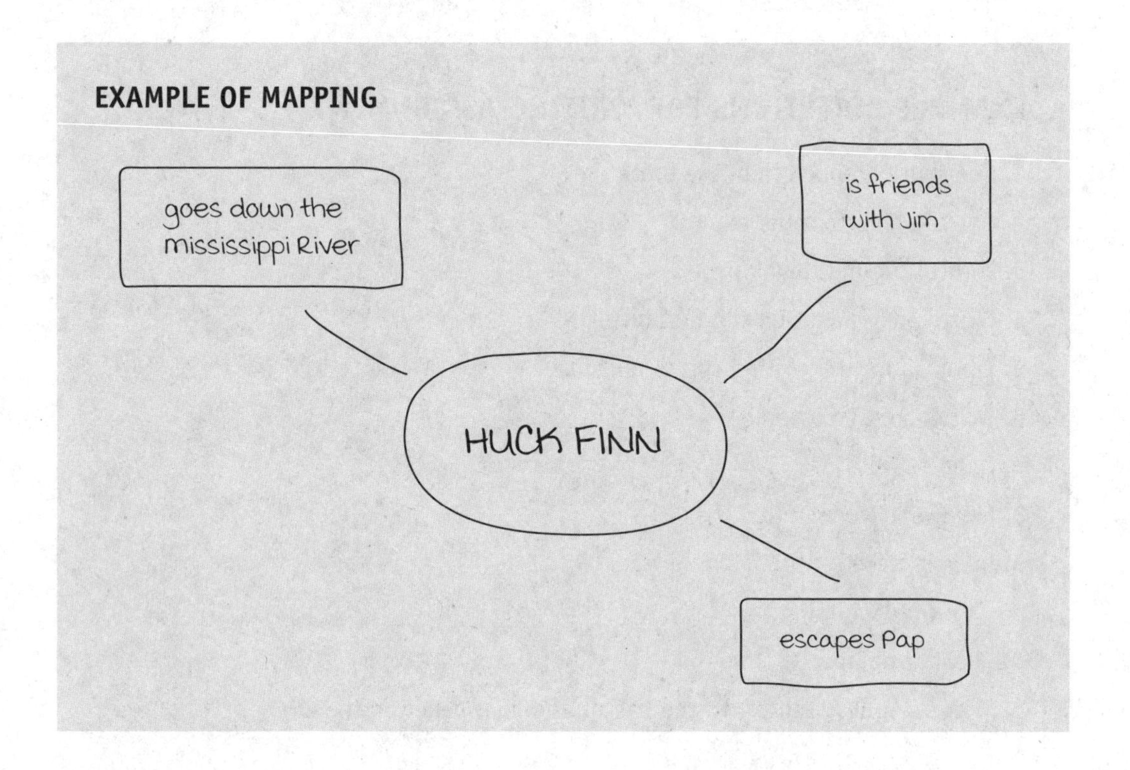

Allow for flexibility in course work. Adjust the work you assign based on a student's respective strengths and weaknesses. Replace tasks that are especially difficult for students with others that still allow them to show their knowledge in content areas.

Eliminate bullying and create safe learning environments. Students who have difficulties with communication may be susceptible to teasing and bullying by peers. Ensure that students are not harassed or excluded. For ideas toward creating supportive school environments, see "Establishing a Safe and Caring Classroom" on pages 35–36.

Provide social skills instruction. Children who have language disorders may fear teasing by peers. Excessive fear of making mistakes in speech may cause children to become withdrawn. You may counter this by teaching social skills at a pace comfortable to the student. Some social skills building activities and resources can be found in "Building Social Skills in Students" on pages 37–39.

PROFESSIONAL TREATMENTS

It's important to make use of the speech-language pathologist at your school. Report students' communication difficulties that concern you to this specialist so children can be evaluated and helpful strategies found.

JASON

Fourteen-year-old Jason seemed to know a lot about history. He often raised his hand in class to answer Mr. Locke's questions. That's why Mr. Locke was surprised to read Jason's essay on the three branches of government. Jason had included some of the relevant details, but they were poorly organized; the paper was difficult to follow.

Mr. Locke decided to meet with Jason to discuss the essay. He learned that Jason has always had problems writing papers. "I'm a whiz at remembering stuff," Jason said. "I just have a hard time getting it down on paper. I can't seem to get the words right."

Mr. Locke referred Jason for a language evaluation, which revealed he had mild Expressive Language Disorder. Jason was relieved to know why he struggled with writing. "No wonder I have troubles with papers!" Mr. Locke replaced written papers and essay tests with projects and multiple-choice tests. These accommodations were kept in place until Jason learned strategies he could use to improve his writing ability.

Stuttering

Children who stutter repeat sounds or words, hesitate, or have broken speech. It is a myth that stuttering is caused by nervousness, stress, or other psychological problems. Instead, it is caused by differences in the way the areas of the brain responsible for speech process information.

About 1% of young people experience periods of stuttering at some point during childhood. Most of these children outgrow the disorder by age six or seven.

Academic problems for children who stutter are generally limited to difficulties participating in class. These students often are extremely self-conscious about their speech and may be particularly reluctant to talk in front of groups—including classmates. They also are more likely to be teased or bullied by other students. Sometimes a fear of stuttering will cause them to be severely isolated socially.

Behaviors and Symptoms to Look For

The most obvious difficulty in school for children who stutter is participating in class. Following are some behaviors you may observe at school:

Students repeat sounds, words, and phrases. Examples:

- Sounds (*c-c-candy*).
- One-syllable words (*I-I want more*).
- Multi-syllable words (*Swimming-swimming is fun*).
- Phrases (*I want-I want to see that*).

Sound prolongations and drawn-out words. Example: *The water looks bluuuuue.*

Substitution of simple words to avoid difficult ones. Example: *tin foil* instead of *aluminum foil.*

Audible or silent blocking. Filled or unfilled (silent) pauses in speech. Example: Filled pauses include breaks in speech with filler words like *um, uh,* and *er.*

Abrupt changes of words or thoughts. Example: *I went to. . . . Where did you get that?*

Physical expressions of tension. Children may grimace, blink, or contort their face in expressions of discomfort.

Social isolation. Students who have difficulties with speech are more likely to be mocked or teased by peers. Students with these disorders may choose to isolate themselves, avoiding games and other group activities.

Classroom Strategies and Interventions

Stuttering can create many difficulties for children at school. Work with speech-language pathologists and other school staff to help children succeed academically. In addition, try to address any social problems students may be experiencing.

Following are some suggestions for helping students who stutter adjust in the classroom:

Show patience. Always wait for a student to finish speaking. Students often are sensitive about their difficulties with speech. Showing impatience or irritation is likely to make students feel worse about these challenges.

Reduce your rate of speech while speaking to a student. Students who stutter frequently feel pressure to quickly finish what they are trying to say. If you model a slower rate of speech, students may emulate your speed. Speaking at a slower rate may improve their fluency of speech.

Try to maintain eye contact with a student while he is stuttering, even if he resists looking at you. Some people tend to look away when another person is stuttering because they feel uncomfortable for him. The person who is stuttering may interpret this avoidance as a discomfort with him. He may think you're impatient and tired of listening to him stutter. By maintaining eye contact, you're letting the student know you're interested in what he has to say.

Make it clear to others that you're waiting for a student to finish. Don't acknowledge other students who may be getting impatient and interrupting or answering the question. You might maintain an expectant gaze toward the student while at the same time holding up your index finger to discourage other children from talking.

Ask a student questions that she can answer simply. You might call on children who stutter when only brief responses are required. This might include single-word short answers or solutions to multiple-choice questions. You might wish to check in with a student before calling on her so that she feels confident in her reply.

Minimize students' oral reading requirements and oral reports. Consider assigning written work or projects to replace oral reports and avoid asking students who stutter to read long passages. Modify curriculum in any other appropriate ways. For additional accommodations you might make for students, see "Effective Teaching Strategies for Meeting Diverse Student Needs" on pages 31–33. **Note:** Some children who stutter can read fluently when reading in unison with another child.

Create a special time outside of class when a student may speak with you. The regular class period may not be an appropriate time for a student who stutters to share concerns. Let students know they can speak with you outside of class when something is bothering them. You might set up a daily or weekly appointment with a student.

Take immediate action if any student mimics, laughs at, or teases a child who stutters. Students who stutter often are taunted or bullied by peers. Put an immediate end to any teasing you observe. For ideas toward establishing supportive school environments, see "Establishing a Safe and Caring Classroom" on pages 35–36.

Provide social skills instruction. Children who stutter are more likely to be teased by other students. Intense fear of embarrassment may lead to a child becoming withdrawn. Try to diminish this by teaching a student social and conflict resolution skills. Some social skills building activities and resources can be found in "Building Social Skills in Students" on pages 37–39.

If student and family approve, educate the class about a child's stuttering. Classmates are less likely to tease (and more likely to help) a student when they understand why she stutters. In taking this step, ensure written student and parent permission and involve a guidance counselor or school psychologist if possible.

Avoid finishing a student's statements for him. Students who stutter may be extremely sensitive. It's important that you're an ally to students who stutter. This means being someone who understands a child's difficulties, empathizes with him, and shows respect. You also want to value his contributions to the class. Finally, reiterate to other students in your class the importance of allowing others to speak.

Avoid telling a student to slow down or think about what she wants to say. A seemingly commonsense reaction to a child who is stuttering might be to ask her to slow down, take her time, and think about what she wants to say. Unfortunately, the reason a child stutters is much more complicated than trying to talk too fast. She's probably been told to "slow down" many times before. Suggesting a child slow down does not work and the student may feel worse because she feels she's failed again.

PROFESSIONAL TREATMENTS

A speech pathologist can help a student form his initial speech sounds more easily. The therapist might model a more breathy quality to his initial sounds to reduce the severity and frequency of his "blocked" speech. Speech is blocked when lips or throat tighten or the tongue doesn't move smoothly to the palate. The result is that not enough air comes out to produce sound and a child stutters.

SEAN

Mrs. Perez had the following discussion with her fourth-grade class:

"You know we've all heard Sean repeat sounds when he speaks. His speech is a little bumpy. Sean is working on making his speech smoother without the bumps. How can you be a friend to Sean when he speaks?"

Mrs. Perez waited for responses but no one offered any. She went on:

"You could wait for Sean to finish what he wants to say before you start talking. You could also look at Sean when he's speaking. You might think about what Sean is saying instead of how he's saying it. For example, we've all heard Sean say teeeeeecher and we know he's talking about me."

Mrs. Perez concluded: "Thanks to each of you. You're a great class, and I know you'll help Sean to do his best."

Pragmatic Language Disorder

Students who experience Pragmatic Language Disorder have difficulties communicating socially. Also called *social communication disorder*, this condition limits a child's ability to say the right things at the right times in the right ways.

Communication is a very complex system of spoken words, body language, and facial expressions. For most students, each of these aspects of communication comes fairly naturally as they develop socially. Children with Pragmatic Language Disorder have great difficulties with small talk and other social functions of language. They may not understand the nuances of another's speech or nonverbal cues (like a facial expression), and they misinterpret meaning. They may not understand that communication is meant to be reciprocal or a shared experience—instead of paying attention to what others are saying they pursue their own agenda with a conversation.

There have not been enough studies to determine the numbers of children who have Pragmatic Language Disorder. The majority of students with the disorder also have autistic spectrum disorders (pages 155–162) and Nonverbal Learning Disability (pages 129–133).

Because of these difficulties, conversations may seem disconnected or awkward. Students may be perceived as self-centered or rude. It's common for children with Pragmatic Language Disorder to be considered odd (or worse) by peers and to be socially isolated.

Behaviors and Symptoms to Look For

Pragmatic Language Disorder has wide-ranging effects in the classroom. Children affected may have difficulty working with others and experience challenges forming and maintaining friendships. A student who talks incessantly, invades others' personal space, or shows other social miscues can create classroom disruptions and might be alienated from peers.

Pragmatic Language Disorder can also have a negative impact on students' academic performance. In the same way students communicate with others without regard for another person's interest, they may write an essay or a report that doesn't address the most important aspects of an assignment. Instead their focus may be on information relevant to a narrow area of their own interest.

Students with Pragmatic Language Disorder show a variety of behaviors that can make social communication difficult or cause them to break classroom rules. These may include:

Dominating a conversation. Students may talk incessantly with little regard for what others say or feel. These children steer conversations onto narrow topics that interest them but have no relevance to the other person. These students do not seem to share or seek information from others or share enjoyment speaking with others. Instead it can seem as if a student is talking for his own benefit.

Little grasp of conversation turn-taking. Students may say very little or be completely silent when others initiate conversation. These children may not know what to say or even realize another person expects them to respond. Those who are able to converse may speak in a way that is difficult to follow. They may also not realize you expect them to speak or provide an answer when called on in class.

Poor grasp of body language and facial expressions. Students with Pragmatic Language Disorder not only struggle with speech, but also with the more subtle aspects of social communication. They may have little appreciation for facial expressions or body language. They may have difficulties understanding the concept of boundaries and consistently invade others' personal space.

Tactlessness. Children may have little notion of social graces or politeness. They make remarks they believe are factual and do not understand why someone is upset at what they have said. *(If you eat all that food you'll get even fatter.)* Students may also speak to everyone in the same manner—regardless of age or social status.

Literal interpretation of language. Students with Pragmatic Language Disorder may have difficulty understanding abstractions and misinterpret idioms or figurative language. (Teacher: *How are you finding the work in seventh grade?* Surprised student: *What do you mean? I never lost it.*) Literal interpretation of language can lead to academic difficulties in language arts courses.

Unusual speech. Students may speak with peculiar intonation or inflection. They may speak much too loudly or too quietly for a given situation.

Poor reading comprehension. Children often have difficulties drawing conclusions based on what they have read. Difficulties understanding event sequence and a character's thoughts and feelings may add to reading comprehension problems.

Classroom Strategies and Interventions

Pragmatic Language Disorder creates a variety of social and academic challenges. Following are some strategies that can be helpful when working with these students.

Use precise and literal language. Clear, specific directions are important to address a student's literal interpretation of language. (Instead of saying *Use your time wisely*—an abstract expression a student may not understand—say, *Keep working on your assignment without taking any breaks or doing anything else until you're done.*)

Be thoughtful about classroom activities. Students with Pragmatic Language Disorder may struggle a great deal with group work because of their difficulties with social communication. Pair up these students with others who are kind and understanding and who model positive behavior.

Provide explanations for academic work. Students may understand the world primarily from their own perspective and may resist doing classroom work they don't believe is meaningful to them. It may be important to explain to them why students have to learn some content.

Encourage a student to focus on his behavior, not that of others. In addition to a tendency to interpret language literally, children may also interpret rules literally (and rigidly). Unfortunately, they may also insist others do the same and assume the role of rule enforcer in the classroom. Ask students to pay attention to only their own behavior and suggest it is your job to enforce classroom rules.

Teach students how to draw inferences. Students may not understand how events relate to one another. It is important for you to show them how to reach understanding. *Example:* You ask your class to settle down after lunch, but many of the students continue talking. You start but immediately stop your lesson and look around at the students who continue to talk. Your facial expression shows impatience and you say that everyone will miss tomorrow's lunch recess. A student with Pragmatic Language Disorder may think you are angry at him—even if he wasn't talking. When students with Pragmatic Language Disorder misinterpret communication, it is necessary for you to explain how an initial event led, step-by-step, to a conclusion. (**Note:** These students may also need to be told step-by-step how to problem solve.)

Work to improve reading comprehension. Asking a student to reread material more carefully likely won't improve his understanding. Instead, you may need to structure an assignment so the student answers Who, What, Where, When, and

Why questions about a reading. Visual organization of information (such as Venn diagrams and mapping) can help students differentiate important concepts and outline plot.

Eliminate bullying and create safe learning environments. Students with Pragmatic Language Disorder are at high risk for teasing and bullying. Ensure that your classroom is a place where all students feel accepted and respected. For ideas toward creating supportive school environments, see "Establishing a Safe and Caring Classroom" on pages 35–36.

Provide social skills instruction. Use examples of real-life scenarios to teach students appropriate social interaction. These scenarios can be read in story form or role-played in the classroom. Some social skills building activities and resources can be found in "Building Social Skills in Students" on pages 37–39.

Note: Many of the strategies for helping students with Asperger's Syndrome (pages 155–162) and Nonverbal Learning Disability (pages 129–133) may also be helpful with students who have Pragmatic Language Disorder.

Learning Disabilities

"Teaching should be such that what is offered is perceived as a valuable gift and not as a hard duty."

—Albert Einstein, physicist

Children who experience learning disabilities have neurobiological disorders that affect their ability to process information. These students generally have average to above average intelligence but differences in the way the brain functions can cause them to perform poorly at school. They may have difficulties understanding or using language (spoken or written), listening, and reasoning due to these brain differences.

Ever since special education legislation was first adopted more than thirty years ago defining learning disabilities has been an issue of debate. The methods used to identify students for special services have changed a great deal. These aspects of special education continue to evolve with each reauthorization of the Individuals with Disabilities Education Act (IDEA). The type of special education services students receive also is in flux. Special education teachers used to address most of the needs of students with learning

School districts consider only about 5% of students to have learning disabilities, but it is believed that learning disabilities are under-diagnosed and that up to 15% of the population may be affected. Young people with learning disabilities are at a higher risk for Attention Deficit Hyperactivity Disorder (pages 135–146), which some people believe overlaps with these disorders.

disabilities (in pull-out classes or other special settings), but today many regular classroom teachers are responsible for helping these students.

This section provides information you can use to better understand and help students who have learning disabilities in the regular classroom. These strategies can help you raise academic achievement and foster positive self-esteem in these children.

SPECIAL EDUCATION TODAY

Identification of students with learning disabilities for special education services used to be based on the discrepancy between a child's IQ and academic achievement. The latest model focuses less on labeling students and more on providing additional instruction and interventions to improve academic performance before the term "learning disabled" is applied.

In this new model, students will be labeled "learning disabled" only after it's been shown a student is generally proficient with the English language, has received adequate instruction in reading and math, and does not respond to interventions that assessments indicate will improve performance. For more information on IDEA law, special education trends, and related issues see "The Role of Schools in Addressing Mental Health and Learning Disorders" on pages 7–39.

DISORDERS COVERED IN THIS SECTION

Reading Disability

(Including Dyslexia)

Students with a reading disability have difficulties sounding out new words, identifying words automatically, reading fluently (with adequate speed), and comprehending text. Children might experience one or more of these difficulties.

Dyslexia involves difficulties with phonetic decoding (or the "sounding out" of words), automatic word recognition, and spelling. The brain of a person with Dyslexia processes these tasks in a different (and very inefficient) way.

Some students with dyslexia may still read somewhat well. More often these students read with reduced speed and comprehension because difficulty reading words hinders fluency and understanding. Receptive and Expressive Language Disorders (pages 94–99) and Attention Deficit Hyperactivity Disorder (pages 135–146) may also create fluency and comprehension problems independent of difficulties with word recognition.

Because reading is essential in all school subjects, poor readers struggle in multiple content areas. A student's writing ability also is affected, making it difficult for students to demonstrate what they know in various subject areas.

The type and severity of a reading disability can vary among children. Some students are strong in one area of reading and very poor in others. Others may benefit from additional help in all areas of reading. This section is designed to identify and address different aspects of reading disabilities.

Between 10% and 15% of all students have a reading disability. These students account for more than 80% of students identified as learning disabled.

Behaviors and Symptoms to Look For

Difficulties with reading occur in three major areas:

DYSLEXIA (decoding and automatic word recognition)

Children with Dyslexia may:

- Have difficulty decoding "nonsense" or unfamiliar words.

- Have difficulty reading single words accurately and fluently.
- Have poor spelling skills.
- Read aloud inaccurately or in a choppy way.
- Have poor ability to hear the sounds that make up words (such as the difference in sound between *cat* and *cut*).
- Guess at words that appear visually similar to those they recognize (reads *between* instead of *because*).
- Have difficulty naming letters and numbers rapidly.
- Read silently at a very slow pace.
- Have weakness in reading comprehension, vocabulary, and written composition skills in middle and high school.
- Transpose words or letters (such as *b* for *d,* or *bog* for *dog*).
- Struggle with other academic subjects.

FLUENCY

Students with fluency difficulties:

- Read only with a lot of effort.
- Read with little expression (monotone).
- Read with inconsistent (and generally slow) speed and inappropriate pauses.
- Read words in isolation but not in text.

COMPREHENSION

Children with comprehension difficulties:

- Have difficulty understanding or identifying main themes or conclusions of text (even though they may recall specific facts).
- May have a limited vocabulary.
- Have difficulty using strategies to understand what they are reading (such as thinking and asking questions about what they're reading, looking ahead or back in the text for facts, and understanding a piece of text before going on in reading).

Classroom Strategies and Interventions

Kindergarten students with weak phonological skills (for example, difficulty naming letters, distinguishing different sounds of letters, and blending sounds) may continue having difficulties in the first and second grades with skills such as matching sounds with printed letters, rapidly identifying words, and sounding out unknown words. These challenges may in turn lead to difficulties with reading speed, comprehension, and vocabulary in later grades. Early intervention therefore is important. Children who have difficulty *learning to read* in the early years will have trouble *reading to learn* in later years.

The exact form of your literacy efforts will depend on your school's reading program and the areas in which your students are struggling—whether with Dyslexia, fluency, comprehension, or a combination of these.

Despite your best efforts to build reading skills, some children will continue to experience difficulties and will require accommodations in the classroom. As with teaching strategies, these classroom accommodations should not be thought of as "one size fits all." Instead match interventions with students' respective needs. In the material below, strategies and accommodations are followed (in parentheses) by the reading difficulty they may most benefit, though suggestions may prove effective with any given student.

Provide reading and vocabulary instruction accompanied by images. Pictures from books, magazines, or other media can give children a concrete image with which to associate words. Ask students to visualize a given word as you provide a visual representation. (Dyslexia)

Encourage children to use kinesthetic learning methods. Ask students to say new words while also tracing them with their fingers on their arms or desk. Incorporating multiple senses can aid memorization. (Dyslexia)

Use already acquired word knowledge. When children struggle phonetically with particular words, bring to their attention similar words they are able to pronounce. This can help them recognize how a given letter or letter pattern sounds and should be spoken. For example, a student who is able to say the *o* sound in *rock* can apply it to the word *clock*. (Dyslexia)

Provide visual cues and tools to reinforce language instruction. Consider posting new or difficult words in a prominent place within the classroom. You might do this by using markers on a whiteboard or creating a bulletin board display specifically for vocabulary. (You might also use this technique to display common words that are often misidentified or misunderstood by weak readers.) Encourage students to create flashcards for use outside of class. (Dyslexia)

Use music and rhythm in language instruction. Most children enjoy music and rhyme. Songs, raps, and rhymes can be effective toward reinforcing word sounds and meanings. (Dyslexia)

Teach specific skills for finding the main idea, finding facts, and drawing conclusions. When discussing a reading assignment, ask, "Who, what, when, where, and why" questions. ("Who was the main character? What was the big problem she had to solve? When did the story take place? Where did the character live? Why did the character have this problem?"). Teach students to summarize the facts of a story in a logical sequence so they can verbalize or write a summary. In class discussions, call on students who have comprehension difficulties only if you're reasonably certain they might provide the right answer. (comprehension)

Ask students to make predictions. Provide consistent breaks in reading to ensure that everyone understands themes from a story or book. At important points, ask students to make predictions of what will occur next in a story. ("Okay, so we know that George has just found out where the dragon lives. What do you think will happen next?") Predictions can help prepare weaker readers for upcoming content in reading assignments. (Dyslexia, comprehension)

Model fluent reading. Read out loud frequently to students. Teach students how to read smoothly and with expression. ("Did you hear how I said, 'up on the roof'? These words go together. That's how we know where the cat went. Then, when I read that the boy was asking how the cat got up on the roof, I raised my voice at the end because he was asking a question and there is a question mark (pointing to it) after 'How did he get up there?'") Also encourage students to practice reading out loud with an adult at home. (Dyslexia, fluency, comprehension)

Provide repeated practice in oral reading. Having a student repeat the same text multiple times will increase his fluency especially if he is given feedback. The text should contain words the student knows so that word recognition problems are not interfering and the text should be relatively short. (Dyslexia, fluency)

Practice repetitive, unison reading. Ask students to read as a class or in groups. This strategy allows students to work on reading aloud without exposing an individual student's reading weaknesses. (Dyslexia, fluency)

Teach reading comprehension strategies. Provide students with tools they can use to focus on particular elements of a story and visually organize information. For example, a Venn diagram might be used for comparing and contrasting two concepts from a nonfiction text. Semantic and graphic organizers may also be helpful. You may suggest a student create a story map as he reads. Older students can be taught to use the SQ3R method (survey, question, read, recite, review) to organize and reinforce ideas from a given text. (comprehension)

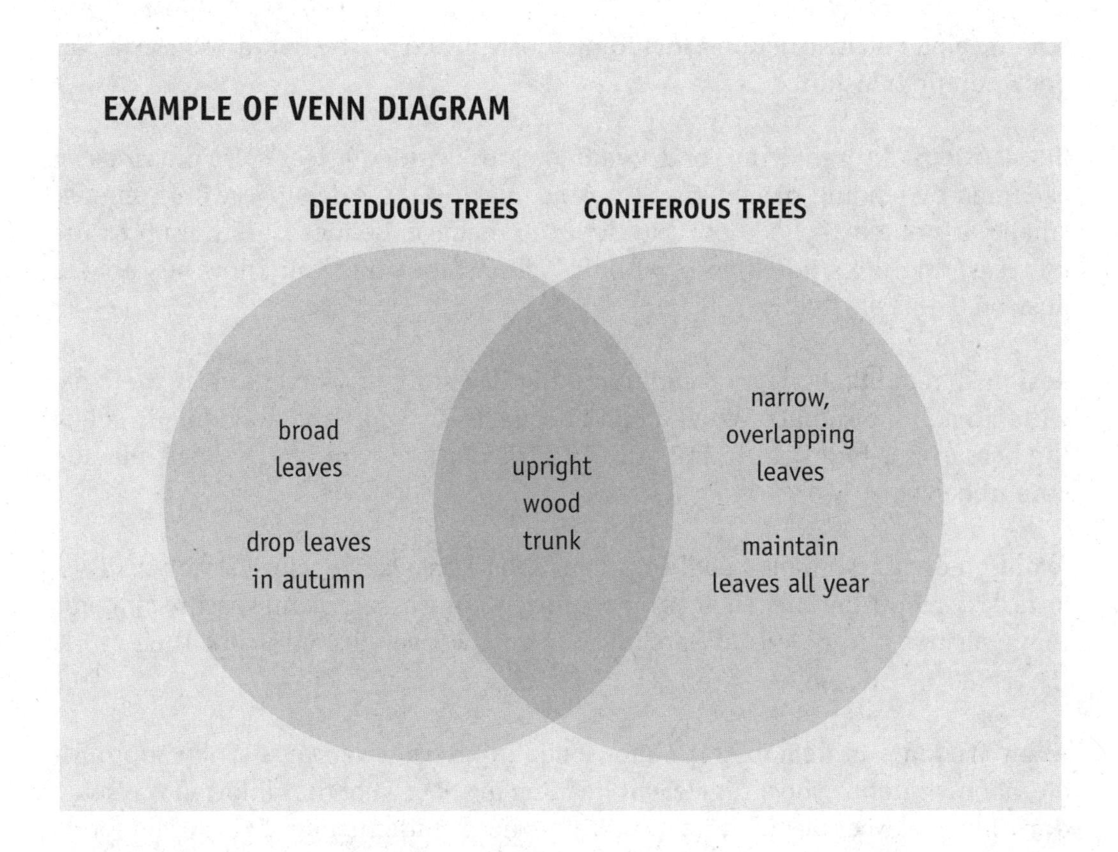

Use audiotape or CD-assisted reading. Ask students to read along in their books as they listen to another reader on a tape or CD. This can help a student read more smoothly and with expression. (Dyslexia, fluency, comprehension)

Emphasize vocabulary instruction. Reading is a primary contributor to vocabulary development, but students with reading difficulties tend to avoid reading. Consequently, their vocabulary may be limited. This cycle further hinders their reading fluency and comprehension. Vocabulary development using computer-based instruction has shown impressive results. You also can preview a text by explaining certain vocabulary words. Show students the same word in multiple contexts and show them how to use a dictionary to look up meanings. (fluency, comprehension)

Shorten reading assignments. Children may be very slow readers. As appropriate, reduce the amount of reading you assign to students to accommodate this pace and emphasize comprehension of the material they are able to complete. Encourage students and provide genuine praise on their progress. (Dyslexia, fluency, comprehension)

Read written instructions. Students often make mistakes on assignments and tests because they don't fully comprehend written instructions. Help avoid this by reading aloud all instructions, including those posted on the board. (Dyslexia, fluency, comprehension)

Be cautious in requiring oral reading. Most students feel self-conscious or ashamed of reading disabilities. To avoid making these feelings worse, choose small parts of a text you know a student can manage. Reduce classroom pressure by reassuring the student you will only call on him when you know he's able to answer. (Dyslexia, fluency)

Assign a reading buddy. A reading buddy is a student who sits near the child with a reading disability. When a child begins to struggle, she may quietly solicit the help of this buddy to sound out words or clarify meaning. (Dyslexia, fluency, comprehension)

Avoid grading a student's spelling. Poor spelling skills typically accompany Dyslexia. When appropriate (such as on creative writing assignments) assure students they will not be graded on spelling but on the overall content of their work. (Dyslexia)

Allow students to demonstrate knowledge in alternative ways. When appropriate, allow students who struggle with reading to show what they know in ways that don't involve excessive reading or writing. These students might give oral reports or create art projects in place of reading lengthy books or writing reports. Consider administering tests orally to students who have reading or writing difficulties. (Dyslexia, fluency, comprehension)

Allow extra time for assignments and tests involving reading. Students with weak literacy skills may need more time to show they understand and can answer questions based on reading material. Relax deadlines and time constraints on assignments and tests. (Dyslexia, fluency, comprehension)

Monitor student progress on assignments. Verify that a student is on schedule with a reading assignment. Ask him if he has any questions and encourage the progress he has made. (Dyslexia, fluency, comprehension)

Provide background information on assignments and tests. When assigning stories or books for students to read, give weaker readers copies of notes, story summarizations, outlines, lists of key vocabulary words, and other tools that can help prepare them for what they will read. (Dyslexia, fluency, comprehension)

Consider using multimedia formats in the classroom. Recorded texts are available through Recording for the Blind and Dyslexic (www.rfbd.org). These can help students understand a text that may be too difficult or lengthy for them to read. Following along in a book while listening to a recording also can help students recognize words and improve reading speed. Encourage the use of other technology such as highlighter-type word scanners or computer-based reading software that scans textbooks and audibly reads material back to the student. Big Books—large, illustrated editions of texts—and CDs of texts also are available from many publishers. (Dyslexia, fluency, comprehension)

Make accommodations or exemptions for learning a foreign language. Students with Dyslexia will likely have difficulty learning a foreign language. Accommodations or exemptions from a foreign language requirement should be considered. (Dyslexia, fluency, comprehension)

Increase student interest and engagement. Poor readers often don't like to read. These students experience reading as boring or too difficult and they tune out or give up. Counteract this disengagement by including in your classroom (and within curricula) reading materials from a wide range of ability levels and interests. If you know a particular student likes animals, for example, suggest she read a book about them in place of a text she's found too boring or difficult. (Dyslexia, fluency, comprehension)

Promote an attitude of enthusiasm for reading. Talk about all of the great things about reading and how it can be a lot of fun. You may want to talk about some of the books that have excited you. Ask students to talk about books they're interested in and why. Avoid making judgments on reading preferences. For example, if a student loves reading comic books or a particular Web site, reinforce the act of reading itself without offering any opinion about the content. (Dyslexia, fluency, comprehension)

Build students' self-esteem as you teach reading skills. Children who have difficulty reading often think of themselves as "stupid" and may choose to give up on reading efforts because they feel they'll "never learn." Emphasize that reading difficulties are not an indication of low intelligence. Rather, some students merely have not found the right reading strategies to succeed. Talk about how you are teaching them tools they can use to read better. (Dyslexia, fluency, comprehension)

Eliminate mistreatment and bullying. Many children who struggle with reading may be singled out for teasing. Immediately stop any harassment you observe. For ideas toward creating supportive school environments, see "Establishing a Safe and Caring Classroom" on pages 35–36. (Dyslexia, fluency, comprehension)

Coordinate literacy efforts with other teachers, special education services, and parents. Work with other school staff to improve reading ability in multiple settings and across content areas. This may involve making others aware of student accommodations you have found helpful or setting up a cross-disciplinary project. Also engage adults at home to encourage and support students as they work to improve their reading abilities. (Dyslexia, fluency, comprehension)

PROFESSIONAL TREATMENTS

Some students may require more individual reading instruction or remediation than is available in school. They may require the help of reading specialists who are well-trained in research-based reading instruction methods.

ELEMENTS OF CLASSROOM READING INSTRUCTION

Reading instruction may vary a great deal between schools. Following are some key elements that should be included in all reading programs.

- Instruction must be *explicit*. Learning fundamental reading skills of letter-sound relationships cannot be left to chance. It cannot be assumed that a student knows that "t" makes a certain sound, or that "a" can make multiple sounds or that "au" sounds different from "ae." These "connections" must be taught, repeated, and practiced.
- Instruction must be *systematic*. Phonics instruction should be taught in a logical sequence. For example, teaching and mastering all single letters before teaching letter combinations.
- Instruction must be *intensive*. Students identified as weak readers should be provided with considerably more reading instruction as early as first grade.
- Instruction must be delivered *sequentially and gradually*. Students should learn, practice, and master one skill before moving on to tackle another skill.
- Phonics instruction should not be taught in isolation but in the *context of academic content*. Fluency and comprehension also should be emphasized.
- Students with any type of learning difficulty require more *positive emotional support and reinforcement*. Teachers should be "cheerleaders" for these students.

For more information on specific reading strategies and programs, see "Resources" on page 187.

Math Disability

Children with a math disability (sometimes called *dyscalculia*) often struggle in many different areas of mathematics. These challenges may range from an inability to recognize numbers to difficulties problem solving and understanding patterns or relationships between shapes.

A math disability may be caused by a number of possible cognitive difficulties, such as with memory, attention, and visual-spatial ability. Much like reading, math relies on a language of signs and symbols. Children with a math disability struggle to decode symbols and to memorize the equations or processes important to solving problems. Children with a reading disability are likely to have difficulties with math—especially with word problems.

About 6% of students have a math disability.

It's difficult to anticipate exactly what difficulties a student will have; most often it is a specific pattern of strengths and weaknesses. For this reason, it's important to observe specific skills that students need to develop and match strategies accordingly.

Behaviors and Symptoms to Look For

Students have difficulties performing math due to a number of possible skill deficits. These may include:

Memory. Some students have trouble memorizing basic facts of math. Addition, subtraction, and multiplication facts need to be learned and stored in memory or they won't be available for subsequent recall. Other students can learn and store facts initially, but they have difficulty retrieving the facts quickly from memory. Still other students have difficulty remembering sequences for solving calculation problems. This type of difficulty involves *working memory*, which is the ability to hold certain information in memory while performing some other task. For example, solving a long division or algebra problem requires recalling a number of steps in the correct order while simultaneously working on one step in the sequence. Any or all of these memory difficulties can interfere with a student's ability to solve math problems successfully.

Comprehension/problem solving. Some students have difficulty understanding various aspects of math problems. For example, young children just beginning to learn math may have difficulty understanding math symbols. Some students have difficulty mastering concepts of counting or place value. Language processing or reading problems can interfere with a student's ability to understand and solve word problems. The ability to systematically solve a math problem can present difficulties for other students. These students may also have little understanding of patterns and relationships between objects or numbers' real-world significance or application. In lower grades, they may have difficulties telling time or counting money.

Organization. Organizational difficulties can interfere with a student's ability to solve a problem on paper in a way that he and his teacher can understand. Some students' written solutions to math calculations "travel" around the page so much that the student confuses himself. This disorganization can lead children to lose track of what step they're completing and make reviewing work difficult.

Attention/impulse control. Problems paying careful attention or an impulsive, hurried response style can lead to excessive errors in math. These students' preference for solving problems in their heads instead of writing down numbers also contributes to careless errors.

Slow speed. Students may exhibit very slow speed in retrieval of facts or procedures from memory. Their problem is with cognitive fluency (speed of retrieval of information from memory) rather than absence of information or understanding. Problems with cognitive fluency also make it difficult for students to turn in work or tests on time.

Anxiety. Math seems to evoke more anxiety than any other academic subject. Students who worry about math typically have some weaknesses in math and their anxiety compounds their difficulties.

Classroom Interventions and Strategies

Strategies for helping students in the classroom should be chosen based on the specific math skills that need to be developed. Instructional strategies for building math ability follow; the area of weakness a strategy best addresses is included in parentheses. Keep in mind, however, that any strategy may be relevant at any given time for a particular student.

Even with consistent efforts to build students' math skills, some children may require curriculum accommodations. As with strategies, match appropriate accommodations with the needs of individual students.

Model step-by-step problem solving methods for students. When solving problems in front of the class, clearly state the steps you are performing. Also have students restate the steps as they solve their own problems. (memory, comprehension/problem solving)

Have students estimate answers or evaluate potential solutions before they begin computing. This checks for a basic understanding of the problem and the mathematical procedure. It may prevent students from arriving at answers that make no logical sense. (comprehension/problem solving)

Use real-world problems to demonstrate math concepts. This strategy is particularly relevant when teaching word problems, but it also can be used with number problems (percentages). Real-world applications illustrate math's relevance and are great opportunities to add interest to a subject many students feel is boring. (attention/impulse control)

Ask students to explain or teach a solution to the class. Talking about math procedures helps integrate them into a student's memory. Check with a student to ensure he can complete a given problem in advance. ("Do you think you might be able do number ten in front of the class tomorrow?") (memory, comprehension/problem solving)

Monitor students' progress on class assignments. Check in frequently with students to ensure they're on task. Offer guidance and encouragement as a student works on respective tasks. (attention/impulse control)

Consider small group work. Students with a math disability often will benefit more from group brainstorming than working alone. (comprehension/problem solving)

Introduce new skills using concrete examples. It is important students understand math in the context of real objects and shapes. When possible, ground concepts in the physical world by utilizing concrete manipulatives. Hands-on learning is very effective in teaching concepts to kinesthetic learners. (attention/impulse control, comprehension/problem solving, memory)

Allow students to quietly self-verbalize at their desks. Quietly repeating to themselves problem-solving steps and mathematical procedures can help students execute math equations. (attention/impulse control, comprehension/problem solving)

Allow time for questions. Conclude each teaching period with time for students to ask about anything they may have missed or not fully understood. (anxiety, attention/impulse control, comprehension/problem solving, memory)

Allow the use of calculators. When appropriate, allow students to solve problems or check their answers with a calculator. (anxiety, memory, speed)

Adjust time pressures and workload as necessary. Give a student who is struggling the time he needs to complete an assignment or a test, or reduce the number of problems due in class or for homework that are required to demonstrate skill mastery. (anxiety, attention/impulse control, memory, speed)

Practice high frequency/low intensity repetition. For example, give two ten-minute practice assignments each day instead of one twenty-minute assignment. (attention/impulse control, memory)

Encourage students to check answers. Students who have difficulty sitting still or paying attention may rush through a test or an assignment, making many careless errors along the way. Address this problem by telling a student you will not accept his test or work until at least half of the class has finished. (attention/impulse control)

Slow down presentation of lesson. Summarize concepts at key points to reinforce them and check in with students frequently for understanding. (anxiety, attention/impulse control, comprehension/problem solving, memory)

Observe the importance of verbal explanation. Some students have visual-spatial deficits that make it difficult for them to understand concepts by looking at pictures or diagrams alone. Your verbal explanation will be important to these children. (organization)

Have students use graph paper. Children who have difficulty organizing math problems on the page may find it easier to line up numbers and equations with vertical lines on graph paper. An alternative is to turn lined paper sideways. (organization)

Be cautious when calling on struggling students. Difficulties with math can harm a child's self-esteem. Refrain from calling on students unless you are sure they have a reasonable probability of answering a question correctly. To encourage participation, prepare a student by letting her know in advance you'd like to call on her for a particular answer. (anxiety, comprehension/problem solving, memory, speed)

Allow students to review corrected assignments and tests. This allows children to see what they are doing incorrectly and to learn from their mistakes. For a student who struggles with a particular type of problem, you might provide in the margins key information toward solving that problem. (anxiety, attention/impulse control, comprehension/problem solving, memory, organization)

Allow students to arrive at answers using alternate methods. Short cuts and alternative problem-solving techniques often are not allowed during math instruction. Allow students with math disabilities to solve problems in whatever way they can if they show their work and the method they use. (comprehension/problem solving, organization)

Break up the curriculum into small parts. Provide frequent, shorter quizzes on single concepts rather than long tests that incorporate multiple math procedures. With less material to remember, students are likely to perform better. Frequent quizzes also allow you to monitor a child's progress and provide appropriate interventions. (attention/impulse control, comprehension/problem solving, memory)

Emphasize the importance of sequence. Students may not understand (or remember) that multiple-step problems need to be completed in a specific sequence. Reaffirm this idea and provide helpful reference materials as necessary while the student completes an assignment or a test. (comprehension/problem solving, memory, organization)

Allow procedure sheets or students' notes to be used during tests. Students with weaknesses in math often forget important procedural steps or formulas they'll need to do well on exams. To counter this and ease anxiety, allow students to reference sheets with equations and other information that will help them succeed. (anxiety, attention/impulse control, comprehension/problem solving, memory, organization)

Allow use of multiplication table. Students who struggle with multiplication may use valuable test time figuring out basic problems. Allow them to reference a multiplication table if it means they'll be able to focus on the actual concept being tested. (speed, memory)

Build students' self-esteem. Children who have difficulties with math may worry that they'll never "get it." Talk about the progress a student has shown and express optimism in the belief that she can improve even more. (anxiety)

Work with other teachers, special education services, and parents to improve math skills. Work with other teachers and parents to build up student skills in targeted areas. Designate a student for a specific role in a cross-disciplinary project or encourage parents to practice skills with students at home.

Writing Disability

Children with a writing disability may have difficulties in several areas of writing. These can include writing legibly, spelling accurately, or expressing ideas clearly.

A helpful distinction to keep in mind is that writers perform two functions—those of "author" and "secretary." The author thinks about the message, the organization of ideas, and the language in which to express the message. The secretary, on the other hand, focuses on mechanical concerns like spelling, punctuation, capitalization, spacing, and handwriting. Students with problems in more than one area may become overwhelmed by the multiple demands of writing. Concentrating on the tasks of the author may sacrifice secretarial skills and vice versa.

At least 10% of students have a writing disability. It is the most common learning disability among young people with ADHD (pages 135–146). Many young people with severe reading disabilities (pages 111–118) also have a writing disability.

Behaviors and Symptoms to Look For

Writing disabilities range from the inability to properly form letters, words, and punctuation markings to difficulties formulating or organizing thoughts. The two main kinds of writing disability are:

Developmental Coordination Disorder. Also called *dysgraphia,* these are difficulties involving the legibility of handwriting. Children may:

- Have illegible or very poor writing.
- Have an awkward pencil grip or wrist position.
- Poorly space letters and words.
- Form letters and punctuation very slowly and with great effort.
- Experience "hand fatigue" while writing.

Disorder of Written Expression. Children with this disorder have difficulty expressing their ideas. Children may:

- Have poor grammar, use punctuation incorrectly, and have problems spelling.
- Omit letters from words or words from sentences.
- Write run-on or incomplete sentences.
- Have difficulty organizing thoughts, constructing paragraphs, and writing compositions.

Students with a writing disability can have a combination of these problems, and most of these children dislike writing. The effects of a writing disability are far-reaching because they compromise skills important in essentially every academic area. Students, for example, who struggle with writing may not elaborate on content when writing an essay because they need to concentrate so heavily on the mechanics of writing.

Classroom Strategies and Interventions

A student's writing ability depends on writing legibly, using proper spelling, grammar and punctuation, and expressing thoughts in an organized way. All of these aspects are essential and should be addressed by writing instruction programs. Even with intense efforts to build writing skills, however, some children will continue to experience challenges. While consistent efforts to build skills are important, accommodations may also be needed to allow students to show their knowledge in content areas.

Following are some strategies for building skills and accommodating students with writing difficulties. Children often have a unique pattern of writing strengths and weaknesses that you'll want to match with interventions.

Model and reinforce proper pencil grip and paper position with young writers. Particularly with students in kindergarten and first grade it's important to watch for the correct basic mechanics for writing. An incorrect method can be a difficult habit to reverse.

Use multi-sensory techniques to teach letters and numbers. Letter and number formation may be easier for some students when multiple senses are used during instruction. For example, a struggling student might benefit from your placing your hand over hers as she forms letters. You might ask a student to say a letter as he stands and traces its shape in the air with an index finger. When students practice writing on their own, encourage them to whisper letters and numbers quietly as they form them.

Allow students to show what they know in the ways they work best. Let certain students demonstrate content area knowledge in ways that do not require extensive writing. Consider replacing written reports with oral presentations. In place of essay tests use short answer or multiple choice formats.

Avoid criticizing any aspect of written language. Remove neatness, spelling, and punctuation from grading criteria so poor writing does not undermine a student's grades. Emphasize the importance of understanding key concepts and evaluate writing mechanics outside of content areas.

Be cautious about asking students to write on the board. Many students with poor writing skills are self-conscious about their abilities. To encourage participation, select small portions of text you feel a student can handle writing on the board. Prepare her in advance so she can practice and feels confident in the task.

Reduce copying assignments from the board. The mere task of copying an assignment or problem can be very time consuming and difficult for students. Counter this by providing information on handouts. For example, a sheet of math problems could be provided on paper rather than copying them from the board.

Allow print or cursive. Some students struggle with printing, others with cursive. Encourage students to use whichever form of writing works best for them.

Encourage the use of pencil grips. Comfortable pencil grips can make handwriting easier and less painful on a student's hand and fingers.

Use multiple kinds of paper. Match a student's writing ability and preference to wide or narrow ruled paper. Encourage the use of graph paper in mathematics. Vertical lines allow students to more easily line up problems and keep track of place values.

Provide class notes for students with writing difficulties. Students may have difficulty not only creating legible notes, but also focusing on main concepts from a given class period. Give these students your lecture notes (or those of an assigned note taker) so they may have material to reference as you progress through the unit. You might also consider providing handouts that require students to write in a single word or short phrase while listening in class. Another strategy is to record lectures and have a student transcribe them on a computer at a later time.

Encourage the use of technology. Technology offers many possible benefits for students who struggle with writing. For example, typing may be easier than writing. Word processing programs can check for correct spelling and grammar. Voice recognition software can be useful for completing written assignments at home.

Stress one or two aspects of writing at a time. For earlier drafts of a report, tell students not to worry about spelling, punctuation, or legibility but to make organization and expressing ideas the priority. Prior to a final draft, the language and mechanics can be reviewed and improved.

Modify curriculum and relax classroom deadlines. When appropriate, consider reducing the length and number of written assignments. Allow additional time for all written tasks including note taking, copying, and test taking.

Teach composition strategies. Make students familiar with the different stages of writing a report or another assignment: outline the paper, organize its ideas, write a draft, edit the draft, and revise to produce a final paper.

Teach pre-writing strategies. The goal of pre-writing is to help students come up with and evaluate ideas for specific writing assignments. Popular pre-writing strategies include clustering, diagramming, and drawing.

Teach and encourage the use of diagrams and other visual tools to organize information. Visual outlining tools can be effective for helping students plan writing projects, carry out research, and organize research into clear writing. Clustering is a diagrammatic activity that can help students generate ideas and see patterns in their thoughts. Story mapping can help students plot how they'd like a story to go. Venn diagrams can help compare and contrast two items in preparation for an analytical essay.

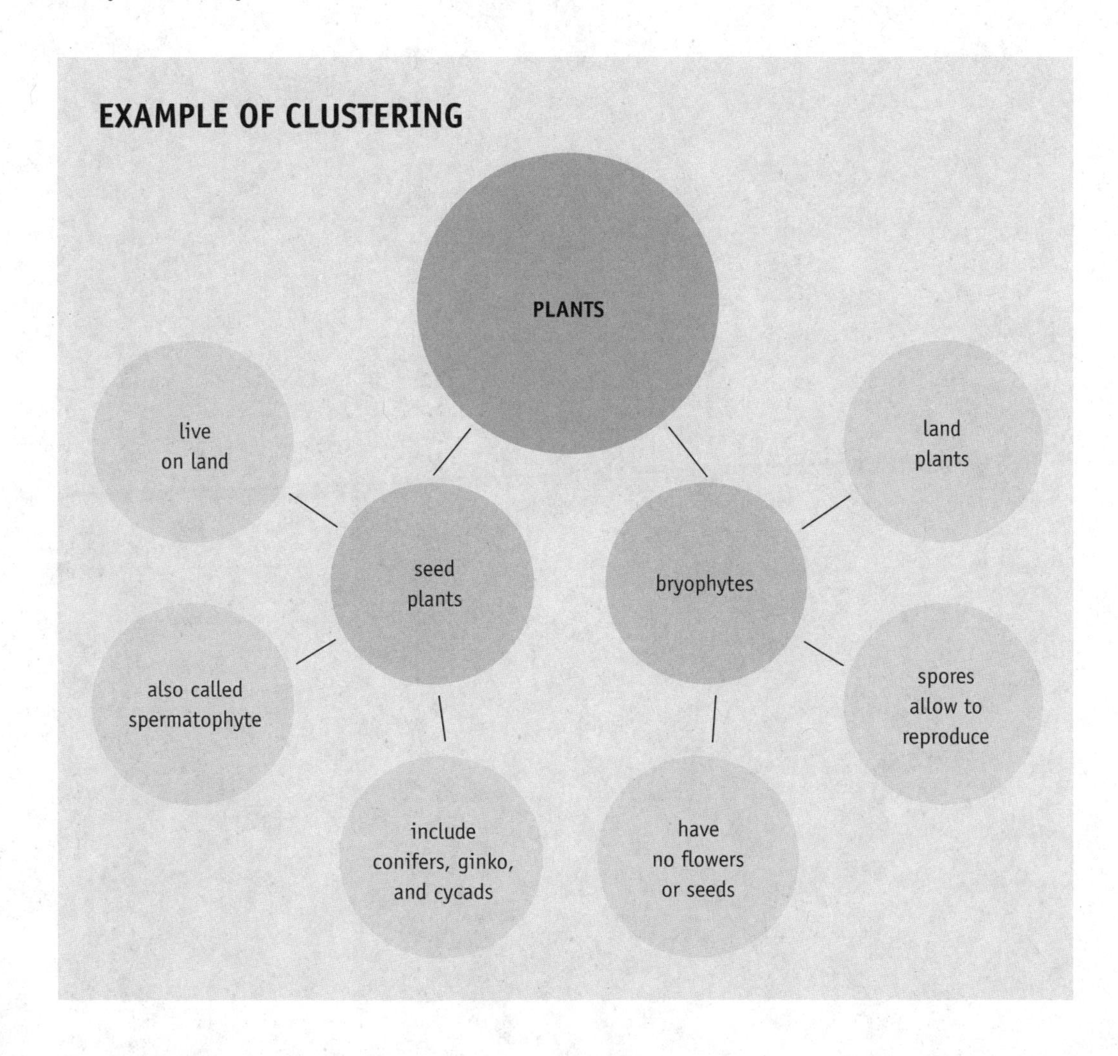

Ensure student interest. Poor writers often think of writing with displeasure. They may believe it is too difficult. Counteract a dislike of writing by ensuring assignments incorporate high interest topics. If you know a particular student likes sports, for example, suggest she write a script for a sports report. As much as possible, allow students to select their own writing topics. Also include journal writing as an option.

Teach and encourage use of computer writing programs. Computer writing programs have multiple benefits. They allow students to type information (as opposed to physically writing it), help to come up with and organize ideas, and add interest to what many think of as a "boring" activity.

PROFESSIONAL TREATMENTS

Some children with a Developmental Coordination Disorder may need to work with a professional outside of the classroom to improve fine motor skills. For students with poor handwriting, recommend an evaluation by a children's occupational therapist.

Nonverbal Learning Disability (NVLD)

Nonverbal Learning Disability is a neurobiological disorder caused by abnormalities in the right hemisphere of the brain. The disorder is very different from other learning disabilities in that it is not language based. NVLD often is overlooked because students who experience it have some learning strengths (including rote memory) that temporarily allow them to perform well at school—especially in younger grades.

The effects of NVLD on students often grow more severe over the course of time. Elementary students with the disorder often are good readers and have excellent memorization and vocabulary skills. As students get older, reading ability drops. Children in middle and high school must learn to read for comprehension; the rote memory that allows students with NVLD to perform well in younger grades is no longer sufficient to help them maintain grade-level abilities. Other difficulties with visual-spatial-organizational and motor skills and social communication also surface.

Less than 1% of the population has Nonverbal Learning Disability. Children with NVLD are frequently misidentified as having other conditions including Attention Deficit Hyperactivity Disorder (pages 135–136), Asperger's Syndrome (pages 155–162), and other behavioral disorders because of similar symptoms.

Visual-spatial-organizational skills. Children with NVLD may have limited skill for visualizing imaginary objects, poor memory for things they have seen, faulty spatial perception, and difficulty with spatial relationships.

Motor skills. Students may have poor coordination, problems with balance, and difficulties with handwriting.

Social skills. Students often have difficulty picking up on nonverbal cues, show poor social judgment, and have troubles forming and maintaining relationships. Difficulty with transitions and new situations also is common. Reasoning skills are much weaker than verbal skills.

NVLD can be a frustrating disorder because often it is not identified and children struggle at school without understanding why. With no firm idea that NVLD is affecting children, teachers may also feel at a loss as to how to effectively address their learning weaknesses. Students are most commonly diagnosed with NVLD in middle school, by which time they may already be behind in many academic areas and feel frustrated at school. Peers often alienate them by this time due to their social and motor difficulties. Early identification is therefore very important for reducing the severity of this disorder's effects.

ACADEMIC STRENGTHS AND WEAKNESSES OF CHILDREN WITH NVLD

Strengths:

- Word decoding and identification
- Spelling
- Rote memory
- Auditory verbal learning

Weaknesses:

- Reading comprehension
- Mechanical computation and reasoning
- Handwriting
- Organization

Behaviors and Symptoms to Look For

In addition to a specific pattern of academic strengths and weaknesses, students with NVLD often experience behavioral and social aspects of the disability. Clumsiness, a tendency to become lost or disoriented, and marked social skills deficits can lead these children to be labeled "odd" (or worse). For this reason, students' behavior and social skills require as much, if not more, attention as their areas of academic difficulty.

Children with Nonverbal Learning Disability may:

Be easily disoriented or lost. Visual-spatial-organizational deficits cause children to have difficulty becoming familiar with new physical locations. Even after children have attended a school for days or weeks they may have trouble finding their way around.

Have difficulty coping with changes in routines. These students are comfortable with routines and can become upset when a physical environment or set of procedures is modified.

Have difficulty generalizing previously learned information. Students with NVLD may be able to recall very specific details about a story or a topic of class discussion. Summarizing the material in a general way, however, often is difficult.

Have difficulty following multiple-step directions. If you provide this student with a direction or procedure involving several steps, he may forget one or more steps or confuse the order of the sequence.

Make very literal interpretations of speech. These students are very "concrete" and may have difficulty detecting sarcasm or understanding idioms. A student may offer her hand, for example, when a teacher asks her to "give a hand" with some task.

Have problems understanding nonverbal communication. Social ability often is hampered in children with NVLD by an inability to read facial expressions, body language, and other social cues. Poor social skills often result in these children being isolated or bullied.

Ask excessive questions. Due to the tendency to be confused by both verbal and nonverbal communication, these students sometimes "don't get it." They may ask lots of questions to clarify something that is obvious to others.

Become easily overwhelmed and anxious. If these students don't understand what or why something is happening around them, they can become upset.

Note: Students with NVLD also exhibit many similar behaviors to students with Asperger's Syndrome (pages 155–162).

Classroom Strategies and Interventions

Nonverbal Learning Disability affects students in a variety of academic and social areas. These students may perform well in some areas and very poorly in others. You can match the following instructional strategies with a given student's particular difficulties.

Provide background information for lectures, assignments, and tests. Prepare students as much as possible for upcoming material and expectations. Outlines of lectures can help students follow along in class and process content. Study guides handed out prior to tests can help students focus on the key areas in which they will be evaluated.

Teach students strategies for organizing their ideas. Students with Nonverbal Learning Disability often struggle with summarizing information. Work to build these skills by teaching outlining and other strategies for organizing information.

Break curriculum and assignments into small parts. Long units can overwhelm students with NVLD because they have challenges processing large amounts of information at a time. Long assignments also can present difficulties because of problems they experience with handwriting.

Monitor students' progress. Check in often with students to ensure they are on track with assignments, projects, and tests. A student with NVLD may seem to have understood directions but really have little idea what's expected of her.

Be precise in communication. Use specific and concrete language with these students. State directions and classroom expectations simply and clearly. Check in with students to ensure they heard and processed what you said.

Adjust reading instruction and pacing. Allow a student to proceed at his advanced pace in the early grades. With older students, be prepared to provide additional assistance for reading comprehension tasks.

Allow for math accommodations. Explain math procedures verbally with a step-by-step approach—minimizing the use of drawings, diagrams, and other visual displays. Provide graph paper for students to better organize and line up equations. Simplify word problems by omitting extraneous information. When appropriate, allow students to solve problems or check answers with a calculator. **Note:** You may wish to consider exempting these students from geometry due to a heavy focus on visual-spatial skills.

Avoid grading written language. Remove neatness from grading criteria so that poor handwriting does not sabotage a student's grades. Emphasize the importance of understanding the material and evaluate the mechanics of writing outside of content areas.

Modify curriculum and relax classroom deadlines. When appropriate, consider reducing the length and number of assignments in areas with which a student struggles. Allow additional time for tasks that may be difficult for the student.

Assign the student a buddy. A buddy should be compassionate and helpful. He may sit next to the student with NVLD to help her stay organized or understand what she is supposed to be doing. A buddy may also help an easily disoriented or lost student navigate the school.

Monitor peer interactions, particularly during unstructured time. Children may act "oddly" or lack social judgment among peers. Observe students with NVLD closely when interacting with other children and ensure they are not experiencing teasing or bullying. "Establishing a Safe and Caring Classroom" (pages 35–36) provides some ways in which you can address inappropriate student behaviors.

Teach students strategies for staying organized. Familiarize students with organizational strategies such as color-coding to coordinate materials. Encourage the use of binders, organizers (including electronic), and assignment notebooks.

Reduce visual stimuli. These students' strength is their ability to process rote verbal information rather than visual directions and spatial concepts. Reduce your reliance on visual instructions and translate visual instructions into verbal directions. For example, instead of showing a student directions on a school map for getting to another classroom, have the student remember to "take 2 rights, 1 left, and 1 right."

Teach and model social skills. Students with Nonverbal Learning Disability often need to be taught basic or obvious social behaviors. Emphasize turn-taking, social cues, nonverbal behavior, and rules of conversation. Some social skills activities and resources can be found in "Building Social Skills in Students" on pages 37–39.

Note: Some students with NVLD also have Pragmatic Language Disorder (pages 104–107). The strategies and interventions in that section may be useful in helping these students.

PROFESSIONAL TREATMENTS

Students with NLVD benefit from working with speech-language therapists on voice tone and social skills. These professionals may use techniques such as Social Stories™ and Comic Strip Conversations that are helpful with students who have Asperger's Syndrome (pages 155–162). Students with NVLD may also work with occupational therapists to strengthen visual-motor and spatial skills.

Attention Deficit Hyperactivity Disorder (ADHD)

"Tell me and I'll forget; show me and I may remember; involve me and I'll understand."

—Proverb

Students with ADHD experience difficulties with attention and impulse control. They may struggle to concentrate on lessons and complete schoolwork. These problems often lead to poor academic performance. Children with ADHD are more likely to get into trouble for inappropriate behavior. They often have difficulties forming friendships with others.

In most cases, ADHD is caused by differences in how several parts of the brain function. These differences make it difficult to perform certain tasks—especially those that require attention and controlling behavior. Because students with ADHD have chemical differences in the brain, medication is used to help people with ADHD. Behavior management strategies at home and accommodations in school also are important to help students succeed.

■ About 8% of young people experience Attention Deficit Hyperactivity Disorder (ADHD). Boys are diagnosed with the disorder more than twice as often as girls. ADHD places young people at higher risk for a variety of other mental health and learning disorders.

Many educators believe that helping children with ADHD is one the biggest challenges facing today's schools. It is important to remember that ADHD is a neurobiological condition—children are not willfully defiant or disinterested in schoolwork. Working with school counselors, other staff, parents, and any involved mental health professionals, you can address students' performance and behavior difficulties and help them be more successful. The strategies in this section can help you do this.

Behaviors and Symptoms to Look For

Children who have ADHD show different symptoms. Some struggle primarily with schoolwork. They are not generally disruptive and may at first glance appear to be doing well at school. Other students have difficulties with hyperactivity and impulse control that can lead to behavior problems. It may seem that the majority of your time is spent reminding these students to remain seated, silent, and on task. Often children have a mixture of symptoms, all of which make them more at risk for disciplinary action and academic underachievement.

These symptoms are reflected in three different types of ADHD. Only a qualified mental health professional can make a diagnosis, but information on the types of ADHD are included here to help you match students' needs with potentially helpful classroom ideas in the "Classroom Strategies and Interventions" section.

Attention Deficit Hyperactivity Disorder, Predominantly Hyperactive-Impulsive Type. This form of ADHD is diagnosed when children are overactive and misbehave because they don't think about the consequences of their behavior. Students may fidget, stray from their desks, or otherwise move around. This type of ADHD is usually diagnosed in preschool or kindergarten children who do not necessarily have difficulty with attention, though challenges in this area may be seen as they grow older and are required to focus and stay on task for longer periods of time.

A child is diagnosed with ADHD, Predominantly Hyperactive-Impulsive Type when she frequently shows six or more of the following behaviors that cause significant problems in at least two settings:

- Fidgets with hands or feet or squirms in seat.
- Leaves seat in classroom or other situations where remaining seated is expected.
- Runs or climbs excessively in situations where it's inappropriate.
- Has difficulty playing quietly.
- "On the go" or acts as if "driven by a motor."
- Talks excessively.
- Blurts out answers before questions have been completed (or before raising hand in school).

- Has difficulty waiting turn.
- Interrupts or intrudes on others.

Attention Deficit Hyperactivity Disorder, Predominantly Inattentive Type. This form of the disorder is sometimes referred to as "ADD"—with the "H" referring to hyperactivity omitted. Young people with this diagnosis have very little or no impulsivity or hyperactivity and primarily experience difficulties with attention, alertness, organization, memory, and planning. These children may be described as slow moving, "spacey," or lethargic. They often are misinterpreted as lazy, unmotivated, or irresponsible because they have difficulty initiating, remembering, and following through on tasks.

Many people believe that ADHD, Predominantly Inattentive Type is underdiagnosed because highly visible, disruptive behavior is not a symptom. As a result, many children who struggle with concentration may be in need of academic support but are not getting it. It's likely more girls than boys are diagnosed with this type of the disorder.

A child is diagnosed with ADHD, Predominantly Inattentive Type when he frequently shows six or more of the following behaviors that significantly interfere with his functioning in at least two settings (at home and in school, for example):

- Doesn't pay close attention to details; makes careless errors.
- Has difficulty sustaining attention in tasks.
- Doesn't seem to listen when spoken to directly.
- Does not follow through on instructions and fails to finish schoolwork or chores.
- Has difficulty with organization.
- Avoids, dislikes, or is reluctant to engage in tasks that require sustained mental effort.
- Loses things necessary for tasks and activities.
- Easily distracted by extraneous stimuli.
- Forgetful in daily activities.

Attention Deficit Hyperactivity Disorder, Combined Type. Children with this form of ADHD have difficulties with impulsivity, hyperactivity, and inattention. They often get the most attention because they experience a wide variety of challenges in the classroom related to both behavior and academic performance.

Children are diagnosed with ADHD, Combined Type when they frequently show a combination of six or more behaviors from both the Predominantly Inattentive and Predominantly Hyperactive-Impulsive types of ADHD. These behaviors must create significant problems for the child in at least two areas of life.

Despite its name, this type of ADHD is not primarily a disorder of attention. It's an impulse control disorder that makes it difficult for children to resist behaving in ways that feel good or they would enjoy at the moment. They may show no signs of having ADHD when watching television or playing video games, but have considerable difficulties paying attention or remaining still when doing things they have to do but do not necessarily enjoy. During class time it's hard for them to keep from doing things they'd enjoy more—like moving around, talking with others, or "having fun." For the same reason, it's difficult for them to resist playing until after their homework is done.

Besides difficulties with concentration and impulse control, young people with all types of ADHD have weaknesses with *executive functions*—"high level" functions of the brain that allow students to start tasks, plan, organize information, and remember what they learn.

SOMETHING TO THINK ABOUT . . .

Ruth E. Harris has created a "Bill of Rights" for students who have ADHD.

"Help me to focus." Please teach me through my sense of touch. I need hands-on and body movement.

"I need to know what comes next." Please give me a structured environment where there is a dependable routine. Give me an advanced warning if there will be changes.

"Wait for me, I'm still thinking." Please allow me to go at my own pace. If I rush, I get confused and upset.

"I'm stuck, I can't do it!" Please offer me options for problem-solving. I need to know the detours when the road is blocked.

"Is it right? I need to know NOW!" Please give me rich and immediate feedback on how I'm doing.

"I didn't forget, I didn't 'hear' it in the first place." Please give me directions one step at a time and ask me to say back what I think you said.

"I didn't know I WASN'T in my seat!" Please remind me to stop, think, and act.

"Am I almost done now?" Please give me short work periods with short-term goals.

"What?" Please don't say, "I already told you that." Tell me again in different words. Give me a signal. Draw me a symbol.

"I know, it's ALL wrong, isn't it?" Please give me praise for partial success. Reward me for self-improvement, not just for perfection.

"But why do I always get yelled at?" Please catch me doing something right and praise me for my specific positive behavior. Remind me (and yourself) about my good points when I'm having a bad day.

"Reward me for my effort." Please remember to say, "Thanks for trying so hard." It takes extra effort to stay on task.

Classroom Strategies and Interventions

Because students with different types of ADHD have diverse challenges, there is no one-size-fits-all approach for helping children. A student who benefits from your interventions to help her organize her work and plan ahead won't necessarily need reminders to show appropriate classroom behavior. For this reason the following strategies and accommodations are organized by areas of difficulty. Many of the suggestions will be helpful for students with multiple areas of difficulty.

When you see a student struggling, match your approach with specific needs you observe. Teach, model, and encourage the continued use of the strategies that benefit specific children. Often, students are able to gradually wean themselves from teacher support and require fewer classroom accommodations as they get older.

INATTENTION

Be thoughtful about where you seat a student. As much as possible, seat students away from distractions (such as the door or a window). Seat children near other students who are good role models and pay attention. It can also be helpful to seat a student near you at the front of the room.

Develop a system of signals with a student. In private with the student, tell him that you will give signals when you'd like him to do something. This might be an index finger to the mouth or a tug on your left ear as a reminder to remain quiet or stay on task.

Make direct eye contact with a student. Frequent eye contact can help keep a student engaged in classroom discussion. If a student is distracted, say her name and ask her to look at you as you teach.

Write instructions on the board. If a student misses a verbal instruction because he wasn't been paying attention, instructions written on the board can direct him. You might also provide a handout that has detailed instructions.

Provide students with copies of notes. Even with your best efforts to engage distractible students, it's common they will miss important information they're supposed to be recording. As necessary, provide children with class notes so that they have the information they need to take tests or do coursework.

Encourage students to check their work. Students with ADHD often make careless mistakes on schoolwork. Ask them to look over assignments or tests before they hand them in. You may also wish to provide a checklist of frequent mistakes students can use to check their work.

Minimize writing on tests and assignments. Use the rule of "more white than black" on any handout. The fewer words on a page, the easier it will be for visually overwhelmed students to maintain focus.

Prepare the class in advance for transitions. Students with ADHD have difficulty with change. Ensure all of your students know when transition times will occur.

Use computerized instruction. Most students enjoy working with computers. Learning software may be more engaging for children who are visual or tactile learners. Use these programs to promote interest in content and reinforce your lessons.

Modify instruction for diverse learning styles. Teaching students through different learning styles can be a powerful way to engage them. Consider curriculum that incorporates a student's learning styles and interests. For more information on strategies for motivating learners, see "Effective Teaching Strategies for Meeting Diverse Student Needs" on pages 31–33.

SLOW OR INEFFICIENT WORK PRODUCTION

Allow students extra time to complete work. Students with ADHD often struggle to complete work and tests. Receiving poor grades because an assignment is late can discourage these students from giving full effort. As necessary, relax deadlines and give some credit for work that is turned in late. Place emphasis on the importance of learning the skills that assignments are meant to develop.

Reduce quantity of assigned class and homework. Problems with attention and focus can make it very difficult for students with ADHD to complete as much work as peers. They may feel that meeting the workload is impossible and choose not to try. When appropriate, reduce the amount of work a student is given.

Use a timer for student's work. Having a time limit for a task motivates a student by transforming schoolwork into a game of "beat the clock." This "fun" incentive can help a student stay focused.

Break longer assignments into shorter parts. Ask students to check in with you after completing portions of an assignment or test. Frequent breaks allow students with ADHD to regain their focus when starting again on work. Having them check in also allows you to monitor their progress and ensure they are on the right track.

Recommend students do the easiest tasks first. Some students with ADHD may get stuck on work that is difficult for them. Suggest students do as much of an assignment or test as they can and return later to problems that are giving them trouble.

EXCESSIVE PHYSICAL ACTIVITY AND IMPULSIVITY

Allow students to move in ways that do not distract others. Let students stretch quietly or play with an object (like a stress ball) when they feel the urge to move. You might also suggest children twirl their thumbs, tap a leg, or otherwise expend energy in quiet ways.

Provide opportunities for physical activity. It can be very difficult for children to stay still over the course of an entire class period. When possible, incorporate physical activity into your lessons. This may be as simple as asking students to walk to the front of the class to respond to questions or write answers on the board.

Prevent students from turning in work or tests too quickly. Children with ADHD may impulsively rush through assignments and tests and make many careless mistakes. Tell students you will not accept work they haven't put their full effort into.

Allow students to run errands for you. Let children who struggle with staying seated to periodically run errands (like bringing something to the school office). If you notice that a student needs to move, create "errands." Arrange for a student to occasionally drop off or pick up mail at the office and return to class.

Closely monitor behavior during transitions and unstructured activities. Children with ADHD may struggle to behave appropriately during lunch, recess, and other unstructured times. Reiterate rules for these periods and closely supervise them when activities are underway.

Address misbehavior with a minimum of attention. Some children enjoy negative attention. If you become upset their misbehavior may increase. As much as possible, address inappropriate behavior without drawing a lot of attention to it. Keep verbal comments to a minimum and try to give feedback through eye contact, a light touch on the shoulder, walking by a student's desk, or pointing at her work as a reminder to stay on task.

Involve students in monitoring their own behavior. Provide a student with a self-monitoring checklist on which he can make marks when he shows an inappropriate behavior. If a student tends to call out without raising his hand, have him place a check on his form each time this occurs. Self-monitoring helps increase awareness and improve the ability to control behavior. You may tie self-monitoring performance into goals for behavior contacts. For an example of a self-monitoring checklist, see page 23.

Set up behavior contracts. Focusing on one or two behaviors at a time, work with students to diminish inappropriate classroom actions. Create a behavior contract (see page 27) that specifically spells out what a student agrees to do as well as the reward. For a sample of a filled out behavior contract, see page 22.

Provide positive reinforcement for appropriate behavior. Even when students with ADHD are not behaving "perfectly," encourage and reinforce progress children have made. Be specific in your praise. ("It's great the way you lined up this morning without touching anyone else.")

Use classroom management techniques that specifically address ADHD. Russell Barkley, a leading authority on ADHD, emphasizes several essential points regarding behavior management strategies for students with ADHD. More information on classroom management strategies can be found in "Effective Classroom Policies and Procedures" on pages 19–25.

1. Classroom rules and instructions must be delivered *clearly, briefly, and frequently.*
2. Positive consequences must be implemented prior to punishments. It's unlikely punishment will work in an environment with little positive reinforcement.
3. Consequences must be delivered more *frequently* and *swiftly* and be *more powerful* compared to students without ADHD.
4. Consequences need to be changed or rotated more frequently for children with ADHD.
5. Behavioral interventions may need to remain in place indefinitely and be modified periodically to maintain effectiveness.

DISORGANIZATION AND POOR MEMORY

Establish routines and clarify expectations. Students with ADHD benefit from organization and order. Consider posting a daily schedule and behavior guidelines so students know schedules and rules. For more information on establishing consistent classroom routines and expectations, see "Effective Classroom Policies and Procedures" on pages 19–25.

Encourage the use of an assignment notebook. All students can benefit from using an assignment notebook or a planner. Ensure that those with ADHD have a single place where they keep track of assignments and check off items as they complete them. Each day, ask to see a student's assignment notebook to be sure assignments have been written accurately. You can ask parents to check completion of homework and ensure it is brought to school the following day.

Encourage students to use a three-ring binder. Binders should be separated by subject with dividers and include loose-leaf paper and a small pouch that contains pens, pencils, erasers, highlighters, and other common supplies students need. There should be separate folders or compartments for items students need to take home, items that return to school, and completed work.

Make clear where items are found in the classroom. Share with students where containers of supplies can be found and set up specific places where work can be turned in. Keep the placement of these items consistent.

Help students organize their desks or lockers. Give extra assistance to students who struggle with organization and encourage them to clean out desks or lockers regularly. Help students decide what can be recycled, brought home, or left at school.

Encourage parents to provide an extra set of books at home. Many students with ADHD are forgetful and don't bring home the right books to complete homework. An extra set of books at home can address this problem.

Provide checklists for students and encourage their use. Checklists can be helpful toward guiding children through routines. For example, if first thing each morning you want students to turn in homework and take out their math book, math notebooks, rulers, and pencils, you might write down each of these steps under "First Thing."

Color code and coordinate objects to be remembered and organized. Using a different color folder and notebook for each subject makes it easier for students to group together and organize class information than using folders with written labels.

Develop a balance between accommodating students' forgetfulness and disorganization and holding them accountable. After the implementation of accommodations, students need to be accountable for not turning in an assignment. Consequences for late work should be included in a student's IEP or 504 plan.

THE IDEAL TEACHER (AND PARENT) FOR AN ADHD CHILD*

- Thoroughly knowledgeable about ADHD and accepts the legitimacy of the disorder.
- Tough as nails about rules but always calm and positive.
- Ingenious about modifying teaching strategies and materials in order to match the child's learning style.
- Tailors academic material to suit child's abilities and skills.
- Creates assignments that require as much activity on the child's part as possible—hates dittos and endless seatwork.
- Mixes high and low interest tasks in tune with child's predilections.
- Isn't into homework in a major way.
- Knows to back off when student's level of frustration begins to peak.
- Knows to back off when teacher's level of frustration begins to peak.
- Speaks clearly in brief, understandable sentences.
- Looks the child straight in the eye when communicating.
- Runs an absolutely predictable and organized classroom.
- Controls the classroom without being controlling.
- Provides immediate and consistent feedback (consequences) regarding behavior.
- Develops a private signal system with child to gently notify him when he's off task or acting inappropriately.
- Maintains close physical proximity without being intrusive.
- Ignores minor disruptions—knows how to choose battles.
- Has no problem acting as an "Auxiliary Organizer" when appropriate and necessary.
- Makes sure the child is organized for homework and parents are notified about school events.
- Maintains interest in the child as a person with interests, fears, and joys—even after a trying day.
- More than willing to call or meet with parents frequently to keep in step with other efforts.
- Has a sense of humor you wouldn't believe.

*From *ADHD/Hyperactivity: A Consumer's Guide* by Michael Gordon. Used with permission.

PROFESSIONAL TREATMENTS

Symptoms of ADHD may be decreased through a number of different approaches including medication, behavior modification, and counseling. Medication has been shown to be the most effective of these treatments. It helps those parts of the brain affected by ADHD to function more normally. Some children may take more than one medication due to another mental health disorder. Possible side effects of medication are headaches, stomachaches, fatigue, irritability, tics, nervousness, and sadness. Any troubling symptoms you observe in a child taking medication should immediately be shared with the school nurse and parents.

Behavior modification at home and in school can help children with ADHD be more aware of their behavior and improve it. A uniform behavior management plan is most effective as these students benefit from predictability and structure. Such a plan provides for very clear rules with a consistent system of consequences. Mental health professionals frequently consult with parents of children with ADHD to help them develop these strategies. Learning strategists or educational coaches are also sometimes used to teach children effective organization and time management skills. Traditional counseling or psychotherapy may be useful when a child with ADHD has another mental health disorder (such as anxiety or depression).

Students with ADHD frequently have difficulties surrounding sleep (including snoring and sleep apnea). These and other medical concerns should be evaluated by a physician.

WHAT IT'S LIKE . . .

CHRIS—ADHD, Predominantly Hyperactive-Impulsive Type

A preschool teacher writes:

"Chris is having trouble following our rules. He doesn't sit on the circle with other children and he doesn't want to listen to stories—he seems to want to do 'only what Chris wants to do.' When we use crayons, Chris scribbles and doesn't seem to try to stay inside the lines. On the playground, he pushes, kicks, and takes toys from other children. When we're lined up for snack or for lunch, he can't stay in the line and he wants to run instead of walk. Chris doesn't listen well and isn't learning his letters and numbers as well as other children. I'm concerned Chris might not be ready for kindergarten next fall."

KIM—ADHD, Predominantly Inattentive Type

An eighth-grade teacher writes:

"Kim is the sweetest girl. She's never a behavior problem. I do see her doodling in her notebook more often than other students. And while she appears to be listening to me most of the time, when I call on her she sometimes hasn't heard a question. She also seems to easily get confused about where we are in our books—that is if she remembers to bring hers to class. I've spoken with other teachers and they've seen similar behavior from Kim. Her grade in my class is suffering because of incomplete homework. She often forgets to write assignments down or bring her book home to complete work. At other times, she's completed her homework (according to Kim and her parents) and somehow it doesn't make it to class!"

ANTHONY—ADHD, Combined Type

A third-grade teacher writes:

"Anthony is easily distracted by sounds. Another thing is that he doesn't actually sit at his desk—he either stands or sits on one leg. His work is careless with answers that are very brief and lack detail. Anthony has trouble calming down after recess. He also has difficulty working in a group without getting loud and physical. He's impulsive and blurts out answers, too. In P.E., Anthony's too rough and quick to complain about 'injustices.' His behavior makes him the last one chosen on teams. Anthony's grades are bad mostly because he doesn't give school enough attention. When he decides to do his best, the quality of his work is good. I have to be very conscientious about engaging him and helping him to develop social skills."

Disruptive Behavior Disorders

(Including Oppositional Defiant Disorder and Conduct Disorder)

"A master can tell you what he expects of you.
A teacher, though, awakens your own expectations."

—Patricia Neal, actress

Disruptive behavior disorders include Oppositional Defiant Disorder (ODD) and Conduct Disorder (CD). Children with ODD are excessively argumentative, defiant, and angry. They may break home and school rules and blame others for their behavior. Students with CD have more serious patterns of behavior that may include hurting others (and animals), destroying others' property, lying, theft, and other serious violations of rules or laws.

About 10% of children and adolescents have disruptive behavior disorders. Half of these young people have Attention Deficit Hyperactivity Disorder (pages 135–146). Mood disorders (pages 77–88) also are common in these students.

Identifying a disruptive behavior disorder can be difficult because all children are angry or defiant at times. It's also natural for young people to test (or protest) parent limits and teacher directions. Some questioning of authority—especially during adolescence—can be a healthy sign of developing independence and assertiveness. A severe pattern of negative behavior that causes problems at school or home may suggest a disorder.

Reasons behind a child's poor behavior may vary. It may be the result of limited parental expectations or discipline. These children don't have a mental disorder but simply haven't been taught how to behave appropriately. Other children's behavior can be linked to mental disorders. Students with ADHD commonly are diagnosed with behavior disorders. Poor self-control leads them to be defiant and disruptive. These young people may not intentionally misbehave, but difficulties controlling impulses or hyperactivity can lead to behavior difficulties.

GET HELP! Students with disruptive behavior disorders are among the most behaviorally explosive children at school. It's important to alert other personnel at the first sign of out-of-control behavior.

Behaviors and Symptoms to Look For

Children with disruptive behavior disorders are likely the most visible in your classroom. These students argue, break rules, disrupt class, and take your attention away from teaching. They're probably the students who try your patience and require the most discipline.

Disruptive behavior disorders can be thought of as existing on a continuum—the more severe a child's problem, the more serious the defiant behaviors and rules' violations are. Children whose more severe oppositional behavior is not addressed are at greater risk to develop Conduct Disorder.

A child with Oppositional Defiant Disorder may frequently:

- Lose her temper.
- Argue with adults.
- Defy or refuse to comply with adults' requests or rules.
- Deliberately annoy others.
- Blame others for her mistakes or misbehavior.
- Be easily annoyed by others.
- Be angry and resentful.
- Be spiteful or vindictive.

Nearly every child at some point shows some of these behaviors. A student will be diagnosed with ODD if he engages in multiple behaviors (four or more) in a way that causes major problems in school, at home, or in relationships. Classifying behaviors (and their severity) should be left to the judgment of a mental health professional.

Conduct Disorder is more severe than ODD. Defiant or angry behavior leads to serious violations of rules or the law. Children with CD may:

- **Show aggression toward people or animals.** These behaviors may include threatening or fighting others, using weapons, torturing animals, or stealing from others while physically threatening them.
- **Destroy property.** This may include arson and other destructive behaviors.
- **Deceive or steal.** Behaviors may include breaking and entering, "conning" people, or shoplifting.
- **Break the law and serious rules at school or home.** Behaviors include running away from home or skipping school.

Not all students who violate these rules or laws have Conduct Disorder. It's possible a child will break a serious rule once, realize her mistake, and amend her behavior. Those with CD show a pattern of serious misbehavior. Only a mental health professional can diagnose the condition.

Classroom Strategies and Interventions

The strategies and accommodations you choose to use with children will depend in large part upon the severity of behavior problems. Check school and district policies to be certain your interventions fall within guidelines. Interventions should not embarrass or humiliate a student but serve to keep her from continuing problem behaviors.

It's important to address students' behavior with the help of administrators, counselors, and other school staff. Parents and any mental health professionals involved in the care of children can also be good resources. In severe cases—especially with older students—it's possible that you'll be working with community agencies and law enforcement to effectively manage students' behavior.

Following are some ways to address difficulties with behavior in your classroom:

Build strong relationships with students. Students often resent teachers and other authority figures. These children may think you're only looking to punish them. Your best antidote to resentment is to gain the trust of students. Greet children by name as they enter class. Show genuine interest in them and talk about the ways in which you'd like to help improve their behavior. Reaching out to challenging students can be very effective because they may not expect such a gesture; your willingness to give them a chance to prove they can behave at school may help them do just that.

Clearly establish rules and behavior expectations. It's essential for students to know classroom rules if they are to follow them. Rules should be clear, consistent, and posted prominently in the classroom. Many schools and teachers involve students in the creation of rules to promote buy-in with children. For more information on establishing consistent classroom routines and expectations, see "Effective Classroom Policies and Procedures" on pages 19–25.

Provide positive reinforcement. Children with behavior problems often receive more critical feedback than positive reinforcement. The result is that they know how not to act but may not know what behaviors are appropriate. As much as possible reinforce positive behaviors. Help students see that you do not view them as "trouble makers" but as important individuals who can have a positive impact at school. You might reward positive behaviors by creating a "Certificate of Respectful Behavior" (or some other form of recognition students can bring home) for a child who shows desirable behavior. When positive actions are acknowledged, children are less likely to seek attention by being disruptive. A sample form can be found on page 26.

Teach anger management and conflict resolution skills. Show children positive ways to deal with strong feelings and disagreements. Help build social skills and reinforce the benefits of resolving differences with others peacefully. Some activities and resources for helping students get along well with others can be found in "Building Social Skills in Students" on pages 37–39. You might include some brief calming or conflict resolution suggestions on a "tip sheet" that a student can keep in her pocket to reference throughout the day.

EXAMPLE OF A TIP SHEET

FIVE QUICK COOL-DOWNS

1. Take deep breaths. Count to five as you take in and let out each breath.

2. Count by fives. When you reach 100, count down by fives.

3. Think of positive words like "happy" and "calm."

4. Close your eyes and imagine yourself at a place you like.

5. Smile.

Facilitate kind acts. Pair disruptive students with other children they can help in some way. For example, a child who struggles with behavior but excels in math may become so caught up in helping another student learn that his difficult behaviors diminish. Helping others can help students see the value of kind, positive actions and create in them a sense of belonging and importance in the classroom. You might acknowledge kind acts with a note home to parents or "documentation" similar to the "Certificate of Respectful Behavior."

Use a behavior contract to address misbehavior. Ask students to agree to appropriate behavior in writing and tie positive behavior to rewards. Parents should be aware of and involved in your efforts to improve behavior. Also check in with other staff for behavior modification strategies being used with a student. A sample of a behavior contract can be found on page 22.

Establish provisions for students to cool off. Work out a plan with students for times when they feel frustrated and about to act out. Allow them to go to a quiet place in the classroom or visit with a counselor to calm down. This may include a system of silent signals in which you indicate it's okay for them to leave. The "Student Coping Plan" on page 30 can be used to create these classroom accommodations.

Remain calm. Many students with behavior problems enjoy seeing teachers and other adults become upset. Regardless of how frustrated you may feel, do not allow these feelings to show. Instead, administer disciplinary action in a firm, detached way.

Use a timer to encourage positive behavior. Tell a student privately that you will give her a sign when she is behaving inappropriately. She will have a certain amount of time to correct her behavior before she receives a punishment. The next time the student misbehaves, walk to the timer as you continue to teach and set it. The student will know that she has to amend her behavior or face the punishment you privately discussed. An hourglass works well because the impact on other students is minimal.

Teach children to self-monitor their behavior. In private, provide a student with a behavior tracking form. Ask him to focus on decreasing one negative behavior (such as talking back to you). Develop a silent signal you can use during class to let him know when he has committed the behavior so that he can mark it on his form. Set weekly goals with the student (perhaps in conjunction with a behavior contract) and tie progress to rewards. As a student becomes more aware of his behavior, he may no longer need a signal to tip him off to it. Eventually his self-monitoring can make a behavior cease altogether. A sample behavior tracking form can be found on page 28.

Closely monitor behavior during transitions and unstructured activities. Children with behavior disorders may have difficulties controlling themselves during lunch, recess, and other unstructured times. Reiterate rules for these periods and closely supervise students when activities are underway. Quickly step in to end any teasing, fighting, or bullying behaviors.

Consider asking parents to sit in on class. Many students will be embarrassed about behaving in a certain way if a parent or caregiver is present. Asking a parent to join your class for part of the day may help address difficult behavior in a student.

Make students aware of why their negative behaviors aren't appropriate. Children often fail to see the reasons for rules—and may complain when they get into trouble. When children are aware of why rules are in place, they're more likely to follow them. Use a behavior modification plan (see page 29) to help students understand rules and come up with constructive strategies for when they are frustrated or need to solve a problem.

Provide a warm and encouraging environment. Show all students genuine concern and support—including those who can be a challenge. Do not tolerate bullying or teasing and work to promote kindness and respect in students. Strategies for creating supportive school environments can be found in "Establishing a Safe and Caring Classroom" on pages 35–36.

Set up an Academy. Some students will *repeatedly* defy, protest, and refuse to change their behavior despite numerous interventions. Behavioral experts Ray Levy and Bill O'Hanlon describe an approach for these students called "The Academy." There are four steps in an Academy:

1. Privately explain to a child that repeated rule infractions are telling you he needs more help to behave appropriately.
2. Ask a student to practice the behavior you want him to perform at a time that is inconvenient for him (such as after school).
3. Ask the child to practice the appropriate behavior over and over again.
4. When a student is successful showing appropriate behavior, praise him and tell him that you hope you don't have to go through additional Academies.

Example: A student refuses to clean up after a science lab. Instead of helping, he complains and says that others should put away the equipment. Schedule an Academy with the student after school. Have him get out items that he typically uses during the lab. Ask him to please dispose of these items properly and put them back in their appropriate place. Thank him and have him take out other materials and repeat the procedure. Repeat this procedure several times until he's successful. This gives you the opportunity to praise him for behaving appropriately. If the exercise is effective, he'll realize it's a lot easier to comply with your requests the first time than it is to participate in Academies.

Refer for alternative placement. Some students, especially those with Conduct Disorder, may not be able to function in the regular classroom. In cases of severe behavior problems, work with a school specialist to determine if outside placement (whether a special class or another school) is appropriate.

Note: Many strategies and accommodations listed for students with Attention Deficit Hyperactivity Disorder (see pages 135–146) can also be useful with students who have disruptive behavior disorders.

TIPS FOR AVOIDING POWER STRUGGLES

Many young people with disruptive behavior disorders thrive on confrontation. Behavioral experts Ray Levy and Bill O'Hanlon describe five communication strategies that can help end power struggles. These strategies often are effective because they don't provide students with the satisfaction they may get from upsetting adults.

Use Brain-Dead Phrases. These are responses that let a child know that you're not going to be manipulated by arguing and that you refuse to take responsibility for her behavior. These phrases follow a child's demand, protest, or misbehavior. Example:

Student: "I didn't do it!"

Brain-dead responses might include: "I understand" (said with sadness), "I'm sorry you feel that way," "It really doesn't matter," "Good try" (with a little smile).

Cool It. Anger from an adult can fuel an angry child. Don't feed the anger; instead douse it with sadness. As you administer a consequence, respond as though you'd rather the situation weren't happening. (You may not actually feel sad, but you need to react as if you do.) Example: Instead of (angrily) "Jessica, you will not go on our field trip," say, "Jessica, I'm sorry you'll not be able to join us on tomorrow's field trip. I hope your behavior improves so you can come along next time."

Give More Choices. Since control is what many defiant children want, give it to them by offering more than one choice. As much as possible offer positive choices that teach (instead of simply punish). Examples: "I can give you a detention or we can talk about why what you did was wrong. Which would you like to do?" "I listen to disagreements at lunch and after school. When would you like to share your side of the story?"

Zip It! If a penalty or consequence must be administered, name it and don't say another word about what's happened. Lecturing is not only a waste of time, it empowers a child by giving him the opportunity to debate or argue.

Don't Tell Children What They Just Learned. Never say, "I told you so." It's counterproductive to rub a lesson into a child's face. He's figured it out for himself although he may not give you the satisfaction of telling you.

PROFESSIONAL TREATMENTS

Teaching parents well-established principles and strategies of child behavior management is the most effective therapeutic intervention for this type of student. A mental health professional typically teaches parents over a period of months how to modify different aspects of their parenting technique. These modifications include how to establish and communicate rules, how to pay more attention to positive behavior, how to establish appropriate penalties, how and when to impose positive and negative consequences, and how to respond to protests and noncompliance.

These students can cause serious problems in a classroom and there are no simple answers for teachers. The literature on the treatment of CD includes terms such as "intractable," "highly resistant to treatment," and "notoriously hard to treat." Group treatment has advantages and disadvantages. Residential programs and "boot camps" have demonstrated some positive short-term outcomes but worsening outcomes in the long run.

Asperger's Syndrome

"A good teacher is like a candle—it consumes itself to light the way for others."

—Proverb

Asperger's Syndrome is a neurobiological disorder that can have wide-ranging effects on children. Difficulties include poor social ability and repetitive or ritualistic behaviors that make students stand out as "odd." Differences in the way these children process sensory information create additional challenges at school.

Asperger's Syndrome occurs in about .05% of children. It is much more common in boys. Up to 40% of children with Asperger's Syndrome may have other mental disorders—most often Attention Deficit Hyperactivity Disorder in children and depression and anxiety in adolescents.

Asperger's Syndrome is considered an *autistic spectrum disorder* and is sometimes referred to as *high-functioning autism.* While it features similar symptoms to more severe disorders on this spectrum, it is much less debilitating. A child with full-blown *autism* may be nonverbal; engage in isolated, repetitive play; and seem oblivious to the activity or people around him. Children with Asperger's Syndrome have some autistic tendencies, but often are highly verbal and have more social awareness. Strong rote memory allows them to excel in science, math, and other subjects that require concrete thinking.

Socializing is often the most severe difficulty for young people with Asperger's Syndrome. These students may not know what to say in social situations. They struggle taking turns in conversation and frequently interrupt others or talk exclusively about themselves or their own interests. Students also have difficulty understanding facial expressions, body language, and other nonverbal communication. They often show obsessive patterns of behavior and interests that further alienate them from peers.

Asperger's Syndrome and other autism spectrum disorders are on the rise, because people on the higher functioning end of the spectrum—those often not diagnosed in the past—are now being identified. While the cause of Asperger's Syndrome is still under study, many researchers believe there are strong genetic factors. Environmental toxins have also been cited to play a role in the disorder's development.

Behaviors and Symptoms to Watch For

As a result of limited social ability, students with Asperger's Syndrome have difficulties relating to people and forming friendships. Most often these children want friends but they have underdeveloped social skills. While alienation from peers may be the most obvious of these students' difficulties, many academic challenges also are seen.

Children with Asperger's Syndrome may:

Use formal language. Students frequently use words such as "frankly," "typically," "in fact," or "ordinarily." They may begin most of their sentences with "Well." Children with Asperger's Syndrome often seem "book smart" but lacking in common sense. Their speech may also have an unusual tone or inflection.

Have a very literal interpretation of language. Literal interpretation can make it difficult for students to understand jokes, sarcasm, idioms, or nuances of speech. As a result they may respond strangely to questions. (Example: "Will you give me a hand with these books?" Student, looking confused, extends hand.)

Have poor ability to understand abstract concepts. While students may have a strong concrete understanding of language and factual information, their ability to think abstractly is limited. This leads to difficulties in language arts and other subjects that require abstract thinking. Their view tends to be in "black or white" terms; behavior is viewed rigidly as right or wrong. Students may frequently tattle on other students for rules violations.

Be preoccupied or obsessed with one or two areas of interest. Interests often include video or computer games, works of art, fictional books (frequently science fiction), or TV programs. Strong rote memory can make these children seem like "walking encyclopedias."

Show poor conversational ability. Students may not know when to speak or may say things that are irrelevant to a situation. They begin, end, and interrupt conversations inappropriately. Children with Asperger's Syndrome most often have little regard for another person's reactions, feelings, or interests. They go on at length, not realizing when others are bored with a topic of conversation. Poor social skills can result in these children being isolated or bullied.

Have problems understanding nonverbal communication. Social ability is further hampered in children with Asperger's Syndrome by an inability to read facial expressions, body language, and other social cues. They misinterpret others' expressions and react with inappropriate behavior. For example, a student may not realize that someone's expression indicates anger or irritation and continue showing the problematic behavior as though nothing were wrong.

Be tactless. Students have little knowledge or understanding of social etiquette. They may be extremely rude without realizing it. (Example: "It's obvious you have a weight problem. I wouldn't lean on that if I were you.") Children also have difficulties judging personal space and may ask invasive personal questions that violate another's privacy.

Show differences in sensory reactions. Students may be especially sensitive to sound, movement, light, temperature, and other classroom conditions. Their senses of touch, taste, and smell may also be strong.

Have difficulty understanding and discussing feelings. While these children are highly verbal, they have a limited ability to discuss how they are feeling. As a result they become very upset (or even explosive) with little indication as to what is bothering them. This can make it especially challenging to address a student's difficulty. In addition, students have little ability to empathize with or attribute feelings to others.

Have difficulty coping with changes in routines. These students often feel the need to engage in repetitive routines. Students may become upset or defiant when routines are changed.

Have difficulties with attention and organization. Students may appear to be listening but instead be thinking about something else—often one of their favorite interests. Staying on top of work at school can be difficult for these students because of poor organizational skills.

Have poor motor skills. Students may walk or move in peculiar ways that draw attention (or ridicule) from others. Children may perform poorly in physical education classes, sports, and other activities. Because extracurricular activities are a way for students to socialize, motor difficulties can further separate children from peers. Weak fine motor skills can create handwriting challenges for these students.

CAUTION! At times, a student with Asperger's Syndrome may have a "meltdown." Children will scream, cry, run out of the room, or become aggressive. If a situation gets out of control, immediately get help from someone else on staff.

Classroom Strategies and Interventions

Students with Asperger's Syndrome show a variety of behaviors that call for multiple interventions. Depending on a student's particular needs, social development often needs to be as much of a priority as academic achievement.

The following strategies and accommodations can be helpful.

Work together with the school staff, parents, and any outside professionals. Though students with Asperger's Syndrome usually are able to participate in general education settings, many may also qualify for special services. It's important to align your efforts with those of classroom aides, counselors, and other school staff. Asperger's Syndrome also affects children at home. Parents and mental health professionals can provide valuable insight into classroom coping strategies.

Use precise and literal language. Clear, specific directions are important to address a student's literal interpretation of language. Students with Asperger's Syndrome might miss or misinterpret a nonverbal signal or facial expression that would seem obvious to other students.

Teach rules in a step-by-step manner. Students may need to be taught rules and social behavior in specific detail. A written "tip sheet" can be helpful.

EXAMPLES OF TIP SHEETS

Answering a Question in Class

1. Raise your hand if you want to ask or answer a question.
2. Wait until a teacher calls on you before you speak.
3. Put your hand down if the teacher asks another student to answer a question.

Hallway Behavior

1. Walk the same speed as other students are walking.
2. Walk on the same side of the hallway as the students going in the same direction as you.
3. Try not to touch or bump into other students.
4. Speak in a voice that's only loud enough to be heard by a person next to you.

Establish a structured environment and minimize surprises. Students with Asperger's Syndrome thrive on predictability, structure, and routine. They may become anxious when they don't know what to expect or when plans change suddenly. Prepare these students in advance for any anticipated changes in routine. This might take the form of frequent explanations of contingency plans. (Example: "This afternoon we're going to watch a DVD about the solar system. But if for some reason the DVD isn't available, we'll be doing our regular science work.") Visual schedules also are useful so students can refer to them throughout the day to know what's coming next. For more information on establishing consistent classroom routines and expectations, see "Effective Classroom Policies and Procedures" on pages 19–25.

Explain classroom rules. Students may acknowledge a rule but not understand why it exists. Without this basis of understanding, they may fail to comprehend situations in which it may be broken. (Example: "You must raise your hand and be called on if you want to answer a question. If you answer out loud when you haven't been asked, you might be interrupting the teacher and not letting other students have the chance to answer a question.") Be cautious, though, as students may wish to engage in extended debates about rules.

Modify instruction to match student strengths. Students with Asperger's Syndrome have difficulties with abstract and critical thinking. As you work to develop these skills in students, match up content work to their strengths. Rather than compositions or essay tests, for example, these students will benefit from assignments and tests that require short, factual answers. They're more comfortable with topics that are fact-based and involve data. Also consider curriculum that incorporates a student's learning styles and interests. For more teaching methods, see "Effective Teaching Strategies for Meeting Diverse Student Needs" on pages 31–33.

Monitor sensory hypersensitivity. Students with Asperger's Syndrome may be particularly sensitive to sound, light, touch, taste, and smells. Noisy, crowded environments (such as the cafeteria or playground) can overstimulate and be upsetting for students. Work to minimize exposure to a student's particular sensory sensitivity. Their sensory needs may require that you get the help of an occupational therapist to eliminate environmental stressors (such as bright, glaring light) in your classroom.

Establish provisions for times when students are emotionally upset. Make sure there's a private place where students can go and a person (such as a school counselor or psychologist) they can see when they are having emotional difficulties. The "Student Coping Plan" on page 30 can help you set up provisions.

Teach and model social skills. Students with Asperger's Syndrome often need to be taught basic or obvious social skills. Emphasize turn-taking, tact, manners, nonverbal behavior, and rules of conversation. Some social skills activities and resources can be found in "Building Social Skills in Students" on pages 37–39.

Closely monitor children at unstructured times. Students' lack of social skills can be apparent especially during unstructured periods like recess or lunch. Observe students closely during these times to ensure they are not being teased or bullied. "Establishing a Safe and Caring Classroom" (pages 35–36) provides other ways to create school environments supportive of all children.

Assign a student buddy. Choose an empathetic student who naturally helps others to provide a child who has Asperger's Syndrome with quiet classroom guidance and aid in social situations.

Gently discourage inappropriate classroom commentary. Students with Asperger's Syndrome may talk endlessly about something that is off-topic or of interest only to themselves. Not only can this create classroom disruptions, but it may also alienate other students. Tell the student that he can talk with you further about a topic after class.

Appreciate a student's difficulties. Realize that students aren't acting or speaking this way to deliberately upset you or other children. A student's behavior is often the result of a lack of social understanding. Don't take inappropriate comments personally.

If the student and family approve, educate your whole class about Asperger's Syndrome. Classmates are less likely to tease (and more likely to befriend or help) a student when they understand why she acts the way she does. In taking this step, ensure you have written student and parent permission and involve a guidance counselor or school psychologist if possible.

Note: Some of the strategies and interventions for helping students with Attention Deficit Hyperactivity Disorder (pages 135–146), Nonverbal Learning Disability (pages 129–133), and Pragmatic Language Disorder (pages 104–107) may also be helpful with students who have Asperger's Syndrome.

WHAT IT'S LIKE . . .

From a thirteen-year-old who has Asperger's Syndrome:

"Apparently I am very pedantic and speak slowly and monotonously. I am also told that I have a problem with communication because I do not know when I am boring someone. I like to talk about computers and don't usually realize that others don't want to. Well actually I do, but when I am thinking about computers I am not thinking about anyone else. Sometimes, well most of the time, my mind is so full of computers that I don't stop to think about myself or other people at all. It is very difficult for me to recognize that I may go on too intensely about my special subject as I am me and cannot imagine myself as any different.

"For any kid, whether they enjoy it or not, school is a whole minefield of challenges and new experiences. For kids on the autistic spectrum it seems as if we spend all of our time stepping on these mines (don't worry kids reading this, there are no mines really—I am just using metaphors) and the whole school experience becomes a very difficult one. School is one place where children are expected to be sociable and have friends. It is very difficult for kids with Asperger's Syndrome to have these expectations pushed on them as well as having all the hassles of school to contend with.

"Asperger's people have a great difficulty with social stuff. There seem to be lots of hidden rules and subtle ways of speaking and behaving that are just impossible to fathom. Most Asperger's kids don't usually even bother. Difficulties with facial expressions, the use of language, and body language all make us targets for ridicule."

PROFESSIONAL TREATMENTS

Treatment for children with Asperger's Syndrome will vary a great deal depending upon the pattern and severity of behaviors. Most children benefit from social skills development in individual or group counseling settings. Many will work with someone to develop study and organizational skills. Others may be helped by an occupational therapist who can address sensory problems and difficulty with motor skills.

Some students with Asperger's Syndrome also experience anxiety, depression, or attention deficits and take medication to address these problems. Children should be very closely monitored when taking medications—especially early on. Possible side effects of medications include increased feelings of depression, drowsiness, insomnia, stomachaches, headaches, nervousness, and weight gain or loss. Any troubling symptoms you observe in a child taking medication should be immediately shared with the school nurse and parents.

Tic Disorders

"Teachers who inspire realize there will always be rocks in the road ahead of us. They will be stumbling blocks or stepping stones; it all depends on how we use them."

—Anonymous

Children with tic disorders experience repeated, sudden, and involuntary movements. Tics can occur with varying frequency, in combinations, and over different periods of time.

Some tics resemble "normal" actions that are not commonly thought of as tics. As a result they may be overlooked. A child who is sniffing or clearing her throat may be thought to have a cold or allergies. If she does not have respiratory problems and the behavior continues over a long period of time, these behaviors could be tics.

The frequency and severity of tics determine the degree to which a student is affected. Tics may become more frequent or pronounced when a student feels stressed or fatigued. Tics that go unnoticed by most people are not likely to cause a child any significant problems. (Students may also attempt—with varying success—to suppress tics). Tics that are obvious and frequent put children at greater risk for teasing.

Between 1% and 2% of people experience chronic tic disorders—many others develop tics that fade. Boys are more likely to be affected by tic disorders. The majority of young people with a tic disorder also have Attention Deficit Hyperactivity Disorder (see pages 135–146).

Tic disorders often overlap with Attention Deficit Hyperactivity Disorder (pages 135–146) and Obsessive-Compulsive Disorder (pages 50–56).

Behaviors and Symptoms to Watch For

Tics are considered *transient* when they last for no longer than one year. They are considered *chronic* when they occur nearly every day for at least a year. There are two different kinds of tics:

Motor tics. Simple motor tics include repetitive muscle movements such as eye blinking, facial twitching, tooth clicking, neck jerking, shoulder shrugging, nose twitching, head turning, lip licking, mouth twisting, jaw snapping, finger movements, or any other jerking part of the body.

Complex motor tics seem more purposeful and longer lasting. They can include sustained "looks," licking, jerking one's shoulder, clapping, tapping, tensing certain muscles, or any other body movements.

Vocal tics. Simple vocal tics include sounds made with the nose, mouth, or throat. These include throat clearing, coughing, spitting, grunting, gurgling, whistling, hissing, sucking, snorting, and sniffing.

Complex vocal tics may include spoken words or phrases. Most often these words seem random or out of context. (Example: In the middle of class, a student says—and keeps repeating—"I want the blue bike.")

TOURETTE SYNDROME (TS)

Tourette Syndrome is a tic disorder diagnosed in children who experience two or more motor tics and at least one vocal tic many times a day. These tics may occur at the same time or independent of one another over the course of at least a year. Tics may wax and wane but are never absent for more than three months at a time.

Classroom Strategies and Interventions

Tic disorders can cause significant difficulties with learning as well as negative effects on a child's social development and emotional health. Following are some strategies you can use to address tic disorders in the classroom:

Avoid commenting on tics. Students often are very self-conscious about tics—especially those that are severe and draw negative attention from peers. Avoid commenting on a student's tic—or worse—asking her to stop. Tics are involuntary and these comments can make self-conscious students feel even worse.

If a student and family approve, educate your whole class about tic disorders. Classmates are less likely to tease (and more likely to befriend) a student when they understand why he acts the way he does. In taking this step, ensure written student and parent permission and involve a guidance counselor or school psychologist if possible.

Provide accommodations for testing. Stress can make tics more pronounced. Students may feel pressure to suppress tics during a test, taking away from their ability to focus on their exam. As appropriate, provide a separate room where she can take the test. This also keeps a child's tic from distracting other students.

Provide accommodations for writing difficulties. Children with tics often struggle with writing. As necessary, reduce written work and allow students to show knowledge in content areas in other ways. Additional accommodations can be found in "Writing Disability" (pages 124–128).

Allow students extra time to complete work. Tics can interrupt a student's workflow, so students with tic disorders may be slow in completing work and tests. As necessary, relax deadlines, shorten assignments, and provide for other accommodations to address this slow place.

Repeat instructions and give reminders as necessary. Tics can interrupt a child's thoughts so she may miss something you say. Write instructions on the board or hand out a sheet of paper that includes them. Students occasionally get "stuck" on tasks. Give a student a gentle reminder to move on.

Create a special time outside of class when a student may speak with you. Students with tics may be reluctant to ask questions or participate in class discussions. Invite a student to meet with you outside of class time to address any concerns she might have. Set up a daily or weekly appointment (such as during recess or lunch).

Build students' social skills. Students with tics may have low-self esteem and be reluctant to join play or activities with others. Help diminish a student's fears by providing socials skills instruction. Some social skills building activities and resources can be found in "Building Social Skills in Students" on pages 37–39.

Eliminate bullying and create safe learning environments. Children with tics are more likely to be teased or excluded by peers. It's important to prevent bullying throughout the school (including in classrooms, hallways, gymnasiums, lunchrooms, and locker rooms, and on playgrounds and buses) so students feel safe. Find suggestions for creating a supportive school environment in "Establishing a Safe and Caring Classroom" on pages 35–36.

Note: Many of the strategies for helping students with Attention Deficit Hyperactivity Disorder (pages 135–146) and Obsessive-Compulsive Disorder (pages 50–56) may also be helpful with students who have tic disorders.

PROFESSIONAL TREATMENTS

Many parents take children to a physician for tic behaviors to rule out other medical problems. A physician may refer a child to a psychologist for behavior therapy treatment if tics are causing a significant problem in the child's life. Habit reversal training with a psychologist can be effective in helping to control tics. Medication is used to suppress more serious tics. Medication can cause side effects and teachers should inform the school nurse and parents about any concerning behaviors they observe after a child begins taking medication.

WHAT IT'S LIKE . . .

From a father about his son:

My son Scott has Tourette Syndrome, a strange, little known, and less understood neurological disorder. He suffers every day because his body does things he doesn't want it to do—shake his head, blink his eyes, make faces, twitch and jerk his arms or legs, hop when he tries to walk, squeak, cough, or shout. They call these symptoms "tics." He can't stop them.

When he was four years old we noticed him making strange sounds—little squeaking noises. Continual, annoying, squeaking noises. We asked him to stop—he said he couldn't. We said, "Sure you can—just don't make those noises!" He said he couldn't stop. We sent him to his room. This was before we knew about Tourette Syndrome. Sure enough, after a few months of pressuring him, he stopped making the squeaking noises. We said, "See, we knew you could stop those annoying noises! But why are you shaking your head like that all the time?" Thinking his hair must be in his eyes, we took him for a haircut. He still shook his head all the time. We didn't know why. He said he couldn't stop it.

When we thought we had him "cured" of the head shaking, we noticed he was blinking his eyes. Not a regular eye blink like we all do; he was squashing his eyelids down, and sometimes squinting. We took him to an eye doctor—nothing wrong with his eyes. He kept blinking. We took him to more eye doctors. "His eyes are fine," they'd say. "Must be a nervous habit he picked up. He'll grow out of it." When we asked Scott, he would say, "I can't stop it." By the age of six, Scott had seen several different eye doctors. Finally, one suggested a neurological specialist. The neurologist diagnosed Scott's problems as Tourette Syndrome.

Eating Disorders

"Teachers teach because they care. Teaching young people is what they do best. It requires long hours, patience, and care."

—Horace Mann, education reformer

Millions of young people have anorexia, bulimia, binge-eating disorder, or a combination of these disorders. Many other students not diagnosed with an eating disorder obsessively exercise, severely restrict their diets, or have other unhealthy attitudes toward weight and food.

While it's common for people to be concerned about food and weight, those with eating disorders have extreme attitudes and behaviors that extend beyond healthy dieting. Underlying issues in eating disorders often are psychological—about 90 percent of those affected have an additional diagnosable mental disorder. Adolescents may have low self-esteem, anxiety, depression, perfectionism, or post-traumatic stress. Feelings of guilt, fear, shame, anger, or helplessness can lead a student to "solve" a problem through eating. This may include eating excessively for comfort or limiting food intake in an attempt to have some sense of control.

While exact figures are not known, up to 4% of the population may have anorexia or bulimia and another 5% may have binge-eating disorder. While these percentages reflect the total population, young people are most affected. One-third of people with eating disorders report their disorder began between the ages of 11 and 15. About 90% of people with eating disorders are women.

Unhealthy attitudes toward weight and food may also begin with a wish to fit some model of thinness students see in the mass media. Children who are teased about their weight may take extreme measures to become thinner. Wrestlers, gymnasts, dancers, and other athletes might try to reduce their weight in unhealthy ways. A tendency toward eating disorders can be hereditary or influenced by family or cultural attitudes toward food.

Students with eating disorders often don't realize their habits are self-destructive. They may even pride themselves on how much more disciplined they are than others. In truth, eating disorders are potentially life-threatening illnesses that can cause heart conditions, strokes, kidney failure, and other medical complications that result in almost half a million deaths a year.

Behaviors and Symptoms to Look For

Adolescence is the age most affected by eating disorders, though younger and younger children are now showing unhealthy attitudes toward food and diet. Students often are secretive about their eating habits. They may deny or try to cover up symptoms so they can continue their behavior. In addition to problems with food and weight, these students may engage in cutting or other self-harming behaviors (see pages 173–177).

The three main types of eating disorders are:

Anorexia. Students with anorexia severely limit how much they eat and often obsessively exercise in an attempt to control their weight. Body image is distorted in these young people; they may perceive themselves to be "fat" regardless of how they look or much weight they lose. Often young people with anorexia are perfectionistic and overachieving. Their very regimented attitudes toward food and exercise can lead to extreme weight loss and potentially are deadly. Symptoms of anorexia may include:

- Rapid weight loss
- Paleness, dark circles under eyes, and gaunt features
- Dizziness and fainting spells
- Complaints of being cold
- Intense, dramatic mood swings
- Hair loss
- Abuse of laxatives, diuretics, and diet pills
- Cessation of menstruation
- Frequent excuses for not eating
- Preoccupation with food, calories, and cooking
- Frequent self-weighing or measuring

- Excessive and compulsive exercise
- Wearing loose, baggy clothes

Bulimia. People who have bulimia may eat normal or excessive amounts of food. In order to prevent weight gain, they make themselves vomit or use laxatives or diuretics shortly after meals. Students with bulimia can be particularly difficult to observe because they often maintain a normal weight. Like anorexia, bulimia can lead to medical illness and death. Symptoms of bulimia may include:

- Binging and purging
- Visits to the bathroom after meals
- Secretive eating
- Average weight with some minor fluctuation
- Swollen glands in neck and puffiness in cheeks
- Complaints of sore throat
- Broken blood vessels in eyes
- Tooth decay and erosion of enamel
- Abuse of laxatives, diet pills, ipecac, and diuretics
- Excessive and compulsive exercise

Binge-Eating Disorder. Young people with this disorder may eat much more quickly than normal and not stop until they're uncomfortably full. They may eat large amounts of food even when they don't feel hungry, or they eat alone because they are embarrassed about how much they eat. Those who engage in these behaviors often feel disgusted, depressed, or guilty after overeating. While binge-eating disorder hasn't been recognized as a formal disorder by the American Psychiatric Association, it is thought to be more common than either anorexia or bulimia. Symptoms of binge-eating disorder include:

- Frequently eating abnormally large amounts of food until uncomfortably full
- Inability to control eating
- Secretive eating
- Negative feelings after binging

People do not always fall neatly into one category of eating disorders. Some have more than one disorder or a combination of symptoms. For example, an adolescent with anorexia may periodically binge and purge in addition to limiting what they eat.

Beyond watching for unhealthy eating patterns and changes in physical appearance, it's important to notice signs of emotional distress that may underlie eating disorders.

CHILDHOOD OBESITY

Another eating disorder that's rapidly gaining visibility is *childhood obesity*. These children may be at higher risk for other eating disorders. Especially if criticized or teased, they may develop unhealthy eating habits (such as restricting diet to lose weight or eating excessive amounts to comfort themselves).

Classroom Strategies and Interventions

Eating disorders should only be diagnosed by a qualified health professional. If a student has not been diagnosed but you observe symptoms, it's important to report any concerning behaviors to parents, counselors, the school nurse, and other school staff.

Following are some suggestions for helping students with eating disorders:

Build strong relationships with students. Students often are secretive about unhealthy attitudes about food and body image. Your best antidote to secrecy is to gain the confidence of your students. Showing empathy and genuine interest in a student can help you establish trust. If a student does share information about an eating disorder, work with her, her parents, and other school staff to provide support.

Avoid insensitive comments. Eating disorders are serious and potentially deadly. Off the cuff remarks ("You look like a skeleton, you should eat something." "You could use some exercise.") can have a strong negative effect upon students. Instead say something that shows you care about a student ("I'm really concerned about how much weight you seem to have lost.").

Talk about unhealthy body image and model healthy eating habits. Whether or not you teach a health course, take opportunities to address the media's unrealistic notions of the "perfect" body. Shift students' thinking from looking a certain "perfect" way to being healthy. Talk about healthy attitudes you have about body image, nutrition, and exercise.

Provide students with consistent reassurance. Compliment students on talents, accomplishments, creativity, and values. Teach students that they're much more than what they look like—that people are valued based on "what's on the inside."

Address perfectionism in your classroom. Many students with eating disorders are perfectionistic. Their pursuit of a "perfect" body may coincide with being perfect in other areas—including schoolwork. Impress upon students that perfection is an impossible (and debilitating) goal.

Discontinue use of calipers. If calipers to measure body fat are being used by a health, physical education, or personal fitness instructor, this practice should be stopped. For whatever benefit this procedure is presumed to have, it's thought to be one of the most powerful triggers for eating disorders.

Eliminate teasing. Children with eating disorders may get criticized about their weight. Establish a zero tolerance policy on teasing, taunting, ridiculing, and other negative statements from students. "Establishing a Safe and Caring Classroom" (pages 35–36) provides ways you can address teasing and other bullying behaviors.

Allow for flexibility in a student's workload. Eating disorders and the physical problems they cause can make it difficult for students to focus on schoolwork. As appropriate, reduce classroom pressures.

Be available when a student needs to talk. As an educator, you play an important role in the lives of students. Closely monitor those who seem troubled; initiate conversation with these children and be aware of times in which it seems they might want to talk with you. These students might appear anxious and come to class early, hang around after a period, or start a conversation with you but seem to talk around a problem. If students do open up to you, make time to listen, avoid judgment, and share information as appropriate with parents and other school staff.

PROFESSIONAL TREATMENTS

Eating disorders are most effectively addressed by a multi-disciplinary team that includes psychiatrists, psychologists, physicians, nutritionists, and other medical professionals. Sometimes, these disorders can be treated on an outpatient basis, but more serious cases require hospitalization or treatment in an inpatient facility. A student may continue to struggle with an eating disorder after beginning treatment. Full recovery can be a long process.

GET HELP! If a student discloses an eating disorder or unhealthy attitudes toward food and eating, it's your obligation to share this information. Speak with a counselor or another person on staff to determine the best way to proceed and whether a parent should be contacted. Never volunteer to keep a student's secret safe if it might jeopardize her health.

Self-Injury

(Including Cutting and Suicide)

"Teachers don't just teach; they can be vital personalities who help young people to mature, to understand the world, and to understand themselves."

—Charles Platt, author

When people self-injure, they deliberately cut, mark, burn, bite, bruise, or otherwise mutilate themselves. They may pick skin or scabs so injuries aren't allowed to heal. *Cutting*—carving or scratching the skin—is rapidly increasing as one of the most common self-injurious behaviors among adolescents. In fact, it is perceived by some as trendy; even students without psychological difficulties are engaging in it because of increased publicity and peer pressure.

Estimates suggest that between 1% and 2% of the U.S. population may engage in some kind of self-injury. Specific statistics for young people aren't available, but the behavior is more common in adolescents. Females and people with eating disorders, Bipolar Disorder, a history of childhood abuse, or personality disorders may be more likely to self-injure.

Acts of cutting and self-injury serve many purposes. They are a response to overwhelming negative emotions (like fear, anger, grief, and helplessness) a child is feeling. As contradictory as it sounds, hurting themselves makes these students feel better. Negative emotions that are not expressed can build up over time and cause a student to feel pressured; the act of physically hurting themselves provides students relief from this pressure. In effect, emotional pain is exchanged for physical pain. Self-injury may be a visible "cry for help"—

especially for those students who are not able to share strong negative feelings they are having.

Cutting and other self-injurious behaviors may serve as evidence of one's psychological suffering. Emotional pain is invisible and may be doubted by the person who is feeling it. Making the pain "physical" confirms its existence. Another motivation for self-injury may be to create a reason to nurture herself—an attempt to heal from some psychic wound or trauma. Through bandages and ointments or through the natural healing process, an individual can engage in self-care.

Probably the most obvious reason for self-injury is self-hate. Victims of child abuse may be candidates for self-injury due to self-hate—they may blame themselves for the abuse and feel they deserve punishment.

Self-injury can be addictive. Endorphins are released in the brain when a person experiences pain. Endorphins are the body's natural painkillers and create temporary positive sensations. This feeling may mask much of the pain mutilation causes. Self-injurers may become addicted to the positive feeling of endorphins. Recent research suggests that certain abnormalities in brain chemistry may make some people more likely to engage in self-injury.

Behaviors and Symptoms to Look For

It is unlikely you'll observe students in acts of self-harm. They often are secretive about the behavior. More likely you'll notice suspicious looking scratches, scars, or burns—especially on a student's wrists or arms. Students may be quick to make excuses for these markings. They also might attempt to hide the markings by wearing long sleeves or pants—even in very warm weather.

Note: Alteration of the body for the purpose of decoration (such as piercing or tattooing) is not considered self-injury. Family adults, of course, should be involved in a young person's decision to have these procedures done. Many states require this parental permission.

Classroom Strategies and Interventions

Students who self-injure are in need of help from qualified health professionals. In addition to any physical wounds that require treatment, these children may be experiencing a mental disorder that needs to be addressed. If you suspect a child of self-injury, it's important to inform a counselor, school nurse, and other relevant school staff right away.

Following are some suggestions for supporting students who self-injure:

Provide students with compassion and empathy. Show students you are genuinely interested in their lives and well-being. Ask about family, friends, interests, and other aspects of their lives. Genuine, sustained interest in a student can have a positive impact. Students are more likely to share their feelings when they regard you as someone who sincerely cares about them.

Respond to students calmly. Observing cuts, carvings, or scars on a student's skin can be shocking. Try your best to respond calmly to a child if you observe suspicious marks. Ask about any wounds you observe in a concerned, nonjudgmental way to try and determine what has caused them. If a student admits to injuring himself, tell him that his sharing information is an important first step toward getting help.

Show sensitivity. Avoid responding to self-injury with shock or disgust—which can be perceived by a student as negative judgment. Also avoid invasive questions. ("Why would you want to do that to yourself?") Offer your support and talk about how you will need to involve a counselor in getting help.

Educate yourself about self-injury. Cutting and other self-injurious behaviors are on the rise. Do your best to stay up-to-date with this trend. The resources at the end of this section are good places to begin your efforts.

Talk openly with students about self-injury. Acknowledge you are aware that cutting and other forms of self-injury are thought by some to be trendy or cool. Talk about the addictive and destructive nature of self-injury and encourage students to reject any peer pressure they might feel to engage in these behaviors.

PROFESSIONAL TREATMENTS

Students who self-injure need treatment from a mental health professional. Self-harm is often considered a symptom of some deeper problem that becomes the focus of therapy. Issues leading to the feelings that trigger self-injury are discussed with the goal of resolving these problems. Therapists also teach people alternative ways to deal with the strong feelings that precede self-injury.

GET HELP! Distinguishing whether a student's scratches, burns, or scars are a result of self-injury or simply the effects of a recent accident can be difficult. It's always best to be proactive. If any marks on a student's body make you suspicious, get the help of a school nurse or counselor and make preparations to inform parents. If you have reason to believe marks are the result of parental abuse, a student's injuries should be reported to the appropriate state agency. Visit www.smith-lawfirm.com/mandatory_reporting.htm for information on reporting child abuse in your state.

Suicide

Suicide is the most severe and irreversible form of self-injury. It is the third-leading cause of death for people ages 10–25. Depression is the most common reason for attempted suicide. Warning signs of suicide include:

Talking or recurrent thoughts about suicide. Students who talk about suicide ("I wish I were dead" "Things would be better if I wasn't here") are not just "looking for attention." They're making a cry for help and need immediate professional help.

Feelings of helplessness or hopelessness. Young people may feel overwhelmed and talk about how there is no possible way for them to overcome problems. ("There's no point in anything without my girlfriend," "I'll never heal from abuse." "Life sucks.")

Feelings of worthlessness or guilt. Students may express these feelings generally or in regard to a specific event. ("I can't do anything right," "My parents would still be together if it weren't for me.")

A generally depressed or irritable mood. Students may appear deeply upset or sad. These feelings may persist, regardless of what happens throughout the course of a student's day—even fortunate events may be met with apathy or pessimism. These moods may be especially obvious in children who were once generally happy and positive.

Loss of interest or pleasure in usual activities. Hobbies or extracurricular activities students once enjoyed may no longer seem important. Students may drop out of these activities or simply "go through the motions" so as not to alarm parents and other adults about depressed feelings.

Changes in relationships. Young people may become detached or isolated so that friendships suffer. When asked what is wrong, these students may refuse to open up and further internalize problems.

Significant weight gain or loss. Large fluctuations in weight may suggest a child is experiencing emotional disturbances.

Disturbances in sleep. Students may have difficulty sleeping due to anxiety or depression. Too much sleep may suggest attempts to escape from problems.

Fatigue or loss of energy. Students may be lethargic due to disturbances in sleep or depression.

Risky behaviors. Students may seem to have little regard for their own safety. They may drive recklessly or otherwise act in ways that suggest they don't care about their own lives.

Recent loss or life-changing event. Students are at greater risk for depression and suicide attempts in reaction to loss, serious health concerns, or another significant life event (such as separation or divorce of parents).

Problems concentrating or indecisiveness. Students may have difficulties in the classroom as a result of constant emotional tension. Children who were once good students may lose interest in school.

Saying good-bye or giving things away. Students may indirectly say good-bye or give away prized possessions to friends. ("If I don't see you again, have a good life." "You can have my mp3 player—I won't need it anymore.")

Note: Students who attempted suicide in the past are at greater risk to do so again.

RESPONDING TO SIGNS OF SUICIDE

Take all threats of suicide seriously. Don't dismiss suicidal talk or suspicious actions as attention-seeking behaviors.

Listen to what students have to say. Be supportive and nonjudgmental in your response to students. Avoid cliché responses that may not sound sincere to students. Instead, genuinely empathize with and listen to students. Affirm that sharing depressed or suicidal feelings is the first step toward getting help.

Don't agree to keep a student's secret. It is your responsibility to inform others at school about a student's suicidal thoughts or wishes. Show appreciation for a student's trust in you and offer your full support. Also let her know that the responsibility you feel to help her necessitates involving a counselor (or another specialist on staff).

Get immediate help. Don't take responsibility for a student's life. As soon as possible get the assistance of a counselor or school psychologist. If you feel a student is an imminent danger to herself, do not to leave her alone.

A Final Word

"I have come to a frightening conclusion.
I am the decisive element in the classroom.
It is my personal approach that creates the climate.
It is my daily mood that makes the weather.
As a teacher I possess tremendous power to make a child's life miserable or joyous.
I can be a tool of torture or an instrument of inspiration.
I can humiliate or humor, hurt or heal.
In all situations, it is my response that decides whether a crisis
will be escalated or de-escalated, and a child humanized or de-humanized."

—Haim Ginott, educator and author

The writing and editing of this book is done, so now the task begins to make something positive happen. This is where you come in. You have the dedication and the tools to bring a new understanding, empathy, and responsiveness to your students with mental health and learning disorders. With this resource guide and your commitment to being compassionate and responsive to children with special needs, you can make it happen. If your students are to actualize their full potential, they need you. Thank you for being committed to the education of all the children.

Resources

Anxiety Disorders

GENERALIZED ANXIETY DISORDER (GAD)

Anxiety Disorders Association of America. 8730 Georgia Avenue, Suite 600, Silver Spring, MD 20910; 240-485-1001; www.adaa.org. A national, nonprofit organization dedicated to improving the research, education, and treatment of anxiety disorders. The Web site links to numerous articles, a therapist locator, and outside resources.

Anxiety Disorders Association of Canada. P.O. Box 117, Station Cote-St-Luc, Montréal, Québec H4V 2Y3; 1-888-223-2252; www.anxietycanada.ca. A nonprofit organization that works with government and research institutions in Canada to improve the quality of services for people suffering from anxiety disorders.

Chansky, Tamar E. *Freeing Your Child from Anxiety: Powerful, Practical Solutions to Overcome Your Child's Fears, Worries, and Phobias.* New York: Broadway Books, 2004. Examines the many manifestations of childhood fear and provides strategies to improve children's social and emotional health.

Childhood Anxiety Network. www.childhoodanxiety.net. A Web site dedicated to providing professionals and adults with current, practical information about anxiety in children.

Crist, James J. *What to Do When You're Scared & Worried.* Minneapolis: Free Spirit Publishing, 2005. Reassuring advice and practical strategies for kids ages 9–13 about how to deal with worries, large and small. Includes information about when and where to go for help for hard-to-handle fears.

Dacey, John S., and Lisa Fiore. *Your Anxious Child: How Parents and Teachers Can Relieve Anxiety in Children.* New York: Jossey-Bass, 2000. A step-by-step program for teachers and parents to help children manage a variety of anxiety problems.

Foa, Ena B., and Linda Wasmer Andrews. *If Your Child Has an Anxiety Disorder: An Essential Resource for Parents.* New York: Oxford University Press, 2006. Discusses the various kinds of anxiety disorders as well as the treatment methods, diagnosis procedures, and contributing factors for each.

Foxman, Paul. *The Worried Child: Recognizing Anxiety in Children and Helping Them Heal.* Alameda, CA: Hunter House, 2004. Discusses childhood anxiety in the context of contemporary social issues and stressors. Includes advice about how to identify anxiety disorders in children and when it is necessary to seek professional help.

Freedom from Fear. www.freedomfromfear.com. A national nonprofit organization for mental health advocacy, this Web site links to fact sheets and resources about various anxiety problems.

Last, Cynthia G. *Help for Worried Kids: How Your Child Can Conquer Anxiety and Fear.* New York: Guilford Press, 2006. Presents case histories and clinical research to help parents make a distinction between common childhood fears and clinical anxiety.

Lite, Lori. *A Boy and a Bear: A Child's Relaxation Book.* Plantation, FL: Specialty Press, 1996. A fictional story that teaches kids how to relax and de-stress. For kids ages 3–10.

Lite, Lori. *The Goodnight Caterpillar: The Ultimate Bedtime Story.* Marietta, GA: LiteBooks, 2004. Teaches kids ages 3–10 how to slow down, relax, and reflect.

Manassis, Katharina. *Keys to Parenting Your Anxious Child.* Hauppauge, NY: Barron's Educational Series, 1996. Discusses how to recognize anxiety problems in children and how to help them deal with anxiety in specific situations at home and at school.

Meiners, Cheri J. *When I Feel Afraid.* Minneapolis: Free Spirit Publishing, 2003. Helps children ages 4–8 understand their fears. Encourages kids to talk with trusted adults about their worries.

Rapee, Ronald M., Sue Spence, Vanessa Cobham, and Ann Wignall. *Helping Your Anxious Child: A Step-by-Step Guide for Parents.* Oakland, CA: New Harbinger, 2000. Explains the causes of childhood anxiety and offers practical strategies for parents to help children cope.

Schab, Lisa M. *The Anxiety Workbook for Teens.* Norwalk, CT: Instant Help Publications, 2005. A workbook for teens to help them develop skills to control their anxiety.

Sisemore, Timothy A. *I Bet . . . I Won't Fret: A Workbook That Helps Kids Beat the Worries.* Norwalk, CT: Instant Help Publications, 2004. A workbook filled with activities to help kids manage worrying.

Sisemore, Timothy A. *Tools & Techniques for Helping Children with General Anxiety Disorder.* Norwalk, CT: Instant Help Publications, 2005. Gives background information about worrying and provides many reproducible forms for teachers, parents, and clinicians to use with kids. Includes a CD-ROM.

Spencer, Elizabeth DuPont, Robert L. Dupont, and Caroline M. DuPont. *The Anxiety Cure for Kids: A Guide for Parents.* Hoboken, NJ: John Wiley & Sons, 2003. Helps parents learn how to recognize anxiety in children, how to talk about anxiety with children, and how to be a supportive parent. This book also offers advice for teachers, therapists, and other school staff.

Wagner, Aureen Pinto. *Worried No More: Help and Hope for Anxious Children.* Rochester, NY: Lighthouse Press, 2002. Helps adults to understand anxiety in children and gives them ways to help kids manage their worries. Covers Generalized Anxiety Disorder and Obsessive-Compulsive Disorder.

OBSESSIVE-COMPULSIVE DISORDER (OCD)

Chansky, Tamar E. *Freeing Your Child from Obsessive-Compulsive Disorder: A Powerful, Practical Program for Parents of Children and Adolescents.* New York: Three Rivers Press, 2000. Shows parents how to help children understand and overcome OCD and gives specific strategies for helping kids manage the common symptoms of OCD. Includes a substantive list of outside resources.

Fitzgibbons, Lee, and Cherry Pedrick. *Helping Your Child with OCD: A Workbook for Parents of Children with Obsessive-Compulsive Disorder.* Oakland, CA: New Harbinger, 2003. Explains the causes and symptoms of OCD in children and discusses treatment methods. Contains assessment guides and progress charts for parents.

Landsman, Karen J., Kathleen M. Rupertus, and Cherry Pedrick. *Loving Someone with OCD: Help for You and Your Family.* Oakland, CA: New Harbinger, 2005. Examines how OCD affects family and friends. Offers advice for strengthening relationships and how family members can respond to someone with OCD.

March, John S. *Talking Back to OCD: The Program That Helps Kids and Teens Say "No Way"—and Parents Say "Way to Go."* New York: Guilford Press, 2007. The first half of this book teaches kids and adolescents how to manage their OCD. The second half shows parents and other adults how to be supportive and encouraging of their child's efforts to manage the disorder.

Niner, Holly L., and Greg Swearingen. *Mr. Worry: A Story About OCD.* Marion Grove, IL: Albert Whitman, 2004. Kids ages 4–8 learn about overcoming fears associated with OCD through the story of Kevin and Mr. Worry.

Obsessive Compulsive Foundation. 676 State Street, New Haven, CT 06511; 203-401-2070; www.ocfoundation.org. An international nonprofit organization for people with OCD, their families, and their friends. The Web site contains fact sheets about OCD, weekly newsletters, and resources for educators.

The Obsessive-Compulsive Information Center. Madison Institute of Medicine, 7617 Mineral Point Road, Suite 300, Madison, WI 53717; 608-827-2470; www.miminc.org/aboutocic.html. The Information Center has a comprehensive database of OCD articles and resources you can request. The Web site gives detailed information about the OCD packets and services they offer.

Organized Chaos. www.ocfoundation.org/organizedchaos. A Web site written by teens with OCD for teens with OCD. Contains a regularly updated news section and features personal stories by teens living with OCD.

Penzel, Fred. *The Hair-Pulling Problem: A Complete Guide to Trichotillomania.* New York: Oxford University Press, 2003. This is a comprehensive guide with authoritative information on compulsive hair pulling for both patients and professionals.

Talley, Leslie. *A Thought Is Just a Thought: A Story of Living with OCD.* New York: Lantern, 2004. Kids ages 4–8 learn about living with OCD through the reassuring story of Jenny.

Wagner, Aureen Pinto. *Up and Down the Worry Hill: A Children's Book About Obsessive-Compulsive Disorder and Its Treatment.* Rochester, NY: Lighthouse Press, 2000. Explains OCD and treatment methods to kids ages 4–8.

Wagner, Aureen Pinto. *What to Do When Your Child Has Obsessive-Compulsive Disorder: Strategies and Solutions.* Rochester, NY: Lighthouse Press, 2002. A step-by-step guide to helping kids with OCD.

Waltz, Mitzi. *Obsessive Compulsive Disorder: Help for Children and Adolescents.* Cambridge, MA: O'Reilly Media, 2001.

Discusses the symptoms of and treatment methods for OCD. Helps parents navigate through health insurance plans and the special education system.

SOCIAL ANXIETY DISORDER (SAD)

Antony, Martin M., and Richard P. Swinson. *The Shyness and Social Anxiety Workbook: Proven Techniques for Overcoming Your Fears.* Oakland, CA: New Harbinger, 2000. A step-by-step self-help guide for teens with social anxiety. Includes tools for self-assessment and self-reflection.

Cain, Barbara S. *I Don't Know Why . . . I Guess I'm Shy: A Story About Taming Imaginary Fears.* Washington, DC: Magination, 1999. Shows kids ages 4–8 that shyness doesn't have to get in the way of making friends and having fun.

Carducci, Bernardo, and Lisa Kaiser. *The Shyness Breakthrough.* New York: Rodale, 2003. Provides methods for how to develop functional shyness in socially timid or anxious children. Includes advice and information about shyness in tweens and teens.

Frank, Tip, and Kim Frank. *The Handbook for Helping Kids with Anxiety and Stress.* Chapin, SC: Youthlight, 2003. Teaches parents how to help kids overcome a variety of fears and anxieties including school phobias and separation anxiety. For parents of kids ages baby–preschool.

Markway, Barbara, and Greg Markway. *Nurturing the Shy Child: Practical Help for Raising Confident and Socially Skilled Kids and Teens.* New York: St. Martin's Griffin, 2006. Helps parents distinguish between functional shyness and debilitating social anxiety. Explains the most current research about social anxiety and suggests ways parents can help and support their child.

Moore-Mallinos, Jennifer, and Nuria Roca. *Are You Shy?* Hauppauge, NY: Barron's Educational Service, 2006. Helps kids ages 4–8 cope with shyness and encourages them to explore their feelings.

SelectiveMutism.org. www.selectivemutism.org. Selective mutism is an extreme form of social anxiety. This Web site provides information on the disorder and advice for helping those who have it.

ShyKids.com. www.shykids.com. A Web site for shy kids and teens that helps them deal with their social worries and fears. Contains a section for parents and teachers on social anxiety and provides links to outside resources.

Social Phobia/Social Anxiety Association. www.socialphobia.org. A nonprofit organization founded in 1997 to meet the needs of people with social anxiety. The Web site contains articles, essays, and links to resources about social anxiety.

POST-TRAUMATIC STRESS DISORDER (PTSD)

Brohl, Kathryn, and Joyce Case Potter. *When Your Child Has Been Molested: A Parent's Guide to Healing and Recovery.* New York: Jossey-Bass, 2004. Explains current research about the affects of molestation on children, discusses various treatment methods, and gives advice about how to help children heal.

Brooks, Barbara, and Paula Siegel. *The Scared Child: Helping Kids Overcome Traumatic Events.* New York: Wiley, 1996. Describes and explains the various traumatic events that can cause kids and teens to become afraid. Covers traumas related to abuse, divorce, natural disasters, world events, and more.

Holmes, Margaret M. *A Terrible Thing Happened: A Story for Children Who Have Witnessed Trauma or Violence.* Washington, DC: Magination Press, 2000. A gently told, comforting story for kids ages 4–8 who have witnessed violence.

Mather, Cynthia L., and Kristina Debye. *How Long Does It Hurt? A Guide to Recovering from Incest and Sexual Abuse for Teenagers, Their Friends, and Their Families.* New York: Jossey-Bass, 2004. Written by an incest survivor, this step-by-step guide for teens helps them work through their feelings in healthy ways. Includes powerful first-person testimonials from other teens recovering from sexual abuse.

PTSD Alliance. www.ptsdalliance.org. A group of professional and advocacy organizations that provide educational resources to people with PTSD and their loved ones.

Schiraldi, Glenn R. *Post-Traumatic Stress Disorder Sourcebook: A Guide to Healing, Recovery, and Growth.* Los Angeles: Lowell House, 2000. Even though this book addresses adult PTSD, it provides parents with a great deal of insight about the causes, symptoms, and treatment methods for the illness.

Sidran Institute for Traumatic Stress Education & Advocacy. 200 E. Joppa Road, Suite 207, Towson, MD 21286; 410-825-8888; www.sidran.org. A national nonprofit organization and a leader in traumatic stress education and advocacy. The Web site contains fact sheets, articles, and resource links about traumatic stress in children.

PANIC DISORDER

Berman, Carol W. *100 Questions & Answers About Panic Disorders.* Sudbury, MA: Jones and Bartlett Publishers, 2005. Facts about panic disorder in an easy-to-undertand Q&A format.

Mattis, Sarah G., and Thomas H. Ollendick. *Panic Disorder and Anxiety in Adolescence.* Oxford: BPS Blackwell, 2002. Information about identification and treatment of panic disorder in teens.

SCHOOL REFUSAL

Crary, Elizabeth. *Mommy, Don't Go.* Seattle: Parenting Press, 1993. Gives children ages 4–8 with a history of separation anxiety new ways to approach separation and personal safety.

Csóti, Mariána. *School Phobia, Panic Attacks, and Anxiety in Children.* Philadelphia: Jessica Kingsley, 2003. A positive, practical book for parents with kids who experience school phobia. Includes information about treatment methods, social anxiety, and school bullying.

Eisen, Andrew R., and Linda B. Engler. *Helping Your Child Overcome Separation Anxiety & School Refusal: A Step-by-Step Guide for Parents.* Oakland, CA: New Harbinger, 2006. Helps parents empower their children with coping skills to ease separation anxiety. Provides methods to monitor children's progress and a list of helpful resources.

Fabian, Hilary. *Children Starting School: A Guide to Transitions and Transfers for Teachers and Assistants.* London: David Fulton Publishers, 2003. Advice for schools and teachers about how help young children adjust to school and separation from their parents.

Heyne, David, and Stephanie Rollings. *School Refusal.* Lake Oswego, OR: Blackwell Publishers, 2002. Helps parents, educators, and counselors identify and understand school refusal. Contains assessment forms, checklists, and a reproducible "hints for parents" section.

Kearney, Chris. *Getting Children to Say "Yes" to School: A Guide for Parents of Youth with School Refusal Behavior.* New York: Oxford University Press, 2007. Step-by-step instructions and worksheets make this book a practical resource for families with children who refuse school.

McEwan, Elaine K. *When Kids Say No to School.* Colorado Springs, CO: Shaw, 2000. Examines why some kids and teens develop anxieties about school. Includes strategies for parents on how to prevent school stress from becoming school failure.

Pando, Nancy. *I Don't Want to Go to School: Helping Children Cope with Separation Anxiety.* Far Hills, NJ: New Horizons, 2005. An illustrated story that shows young kids that they can miss their parents and still enjoy school. Includes coping tips for kids and parents.

Mood Disorders

DEPRESSIVE DISORDER

Barnard, Martha Underwood. *Helping Your Depressed Child: A Step-by-Step Program for Parents.* Oakland, CA: New Harbinger Publications, 2003. Helps parents analyze and understand the symptoms of childhood depression. Gives advice about how to create a wellness plan and where to go for help.

Berlinger, Norman T. *Rescuing Your Teenager from Depression.* New York: HarperResource, 2005. Shares 10 Parental Partnering Strategies to help parents work with mental health professionals and other adults to support depressed teens. Includes numerous interviews with parents, teens, and mental health professionals.

Carlson, Trudy. *The Suicide of My Son: A Story of Childhood Depression.* Duluth, MN: Benline Publishers, 1996. The author shares her personal story of loss to help parents recognize the warning signs of teen depression and teen suicide.

Cobain, Bev. *When Nothing Matters Anymore: A Survival Guide for Depressed Teens.* Minneapolis: Free Spirit Publishing, 2007. In teen-friendly language, this book defines depression and describes its symptoms. It includes personal stories from teens and provides current information on medication, nutrition, and health.

Crist, James J. *What to Do When You're Sad & Lonely.* Minneapolis: Free Spirit Publishing, 2006. Gives kids ages 9–13 strategies and tips to beat the blues and get a handle on their feelings. Covers both short-term feelings of sadness and more serious problems like depression and Bipolar Disorder.

Cytryn, Leon, and Donald H. McKnew. *Growing Up Sad: Childhood Depression and Its Treatment.* New York: Norton, 1996. Discusses the interplay between genetics and the environment as it relates to childhood depression. Explains research and theories about the diagnosis, treatment, and causes of depression in kids.

Depression and Bipolar Support Alliance. 730 North Franklin Street, Suite 501, Chicago, IL 60610-7224; 1-800-826-3632; www.ndmda.org. A nonprofit organization that provides up-to-date, scientific information about Depressive and Bipolar disorders. The Web site includes information about treatment plans and directs readers to support centers all over the United States.

Depression and Related Affective Disorders Association. 2331 West Joppa Road, Suite 100, Lutherville, MD 21093; 410-583-2919; www.drada.org. This organization is dedicated to assisting self-help groups, providing education and information, and lending support to research programs. The Web site includes information on childhood and adolescent depression and provides a list of resources on the topic.

Empfield, Maureen, and Nicholas Bakalar. *Understanding Teenage Depression: A Guide to Diagnosis, Treatment, and Management.* New York: H. Holt, 2001. Summarizes the causes, contributing factors, and treatment methods of depression in teens.

Fassler, David, and Lynne S. Dumas. *Help Me, I'm Sad: Recognizing, Treating, & Preventing Childhood and Adolescent Depression.* New York: Penguin, 1998. Explains how depression develops and how it may be accompanied or compounded by other social-emotional problems. Covers teen suicide and depression's affect on the family.

Fristad, Mary A., and Jill S. Goldberg Arnold. *Raising a Moody Child: How to Cope with Depression and Bipolar Disorder.* New York: Guilford Press, 2004. Provides information on how to help depressed or bipolar kids develop coping skills, how to find the right professional help, and how to handle stress and find support when raising a bipolar or depressed child.

Garland, E. Jane. *Depression Is the Pits, But I'm Getting Better: A Guide for Adolescents.* Washington, DC: Magination, 1997. Helps teens understand their depression and develop coping skills. Advises teens on when and where to go for professional help.

Ingersoll, Barbara D., and Sam Goldstein. *Lonely, Sad, & Angry: How to Help Your Unhappy Child.* Plantation, FL: Specialty Press, 2001. Helps parents recognize signs of depression and anger in children, find professional help, and select the best treatment options.

International Foundation for Research and Education on Depression. P.O. Box 2257, New York, NY 10116; 1-800-239-1265; www.ifred.org. An organization that offers support to people dealing with depression and combats the stigma associated with the disease. The Web site contains articles and fact sheets about depression and links to many outside resources.

Irwin, Cait. *Conquering the Beast Within: How I Fought Depression and Won . . . and How You Can, Too.* New York: Three Rivers Press, 1999. Written by the author when she was a teenager, this book for young people recounts her struggle with depression.

Manassis, Katharina, and Anne Marie Levac. *Helping Your Teenager Beat Depression: A Problem-Solving Approach for Families.* Bethesda, MD: Woodbine House, 2004. A program to help parents identify, empathize with, and change depressive attitudes in teens.

McCoy, Kathy. *Understanding Your Teenager's Depression: Issues, Insights, and Practical Guidance for Parents.* New York: Berkley Publishing Group, 2005. Analyzes the manifestations of depression in teens. Covers eating disorders, truancy, suicide, anger, and rebellion, and discusses the effects of gender and cultural factors on today's teens.

Miller, Jeffrey A. *The Childhood Depression Sourcebook.* Los Angeles: Lowell House, 1998. Discusses how to identify the signs of depression in kids at different developmental stages and how to choose the right treatment plan.

Mondimore, Francis Mark. *Adolescent Depression. A Guide for Parents.* Baltimore: Johns Hopkins University Press, 2002. Discusses Depressive Disorders, Bipolar Disorder, and their differences. Includes sections on eating disorders, attention disorders, alcohol and drug abuse, and cutting.

Oster, Gerald D., and Sarah S. Montgomery. *Helping Your Depressed Teenager: A Guide for Parents and Caregivers.* New York: Wiley, 1995. Provides information on how to prevent depression in teens, how to tell the difference between moodiness and clinical depression, how to recognize the warning signs, and where to go for help.

Spelman, Cornelia Maude. *When I Feel Sad.* Morton Grove, IL: Albert Whitman, 2002. Helps kids ages 4–7 understand and manage feelings of sadness.

BIPOLAR DISORDER

Anglada, Tracy. *Brandon and the Bipolar Bear.* Victoria, British Columbia: Trafford Publishing, 2004. Helps kids ages 9–12 understand Bipolar Disorder and its treatment.

Birmaher, Boris. *New Hope for Children and Teens with Bipolar Disorder.* New York: Three Rivers Press, 2004. Explains the causes of Bipolar Disorder in kids and teens and helps parents help their children deal with the daily social and academic problems they may encounter.

Carlson, Trudy. *The Life of a Bipolar Child: What Every Parent and Professional Needs to Know.* Duluth, MN: Benline Press, 2000. Outlines the symptoms of Bipolar Disorder and its diagnosis, explains different medication types and therapies, and provides insight into the experience of raising a child with Bipolar Disorder.

Child and Adolescent Bipolar Foundation. 1000 Skokie Boulevard, Suite 570, Wilmette, IL 60091; 847-256-8525; www.bpkids.org. This nonprofit organization is dedicated to educating the public about pediatric Bipolar Disorder. The Web site contains a message board, an online directory of mental health professionals, information about clinical trials, and numerous articles and essays about Bipolar Disorder in children.

Evans, Dwight L., and Linda Wasmer Andrews. *If Your Adolescent Has Depression or Bipolar Disorder: An Essential Resource for Parents.* New York: Oxford University Press, 2005. In clear, easy-to-understand language, this book provides a science-based explanation and analysis of childhood depression and Bipolar Disorder.

Faedda, Gianni, and Nancy Austin. *Parenting a Bipolar Child.* Oakland, CA: New Harbinger, 2006. Provides a comprehensive overview of the treatment options available for bipolar kids and gives practical parenting techniques for helping kids manage the disorder.

Juvenile Bipolar Research Foundation. 550 Ridgewood Road, Maplewood, NJ 07040; 1-866-275-0420; www.jbrf.org. The first charitable organization dedicated to supporting the study and research of Bipolar Disorder in children, its Web site has many downloadable articles reflecting the most current research on the topic.

Lederman, Judith, and Candida Fink. *The Ups and Downs of Raising a Bipolar Child.* New York: Fireside, 2003. First-hand stories from parents discuss the challenges of raising a bipolar child and offer advice on how to cope.

Lynn, George T. *Survival Strategies for Parenting Children with Bipolar Disorder.* Philadelphia: Jessica Kingsley Publishing, 2000. Drawing from psychiatric case studies and real-life examples, this book gives advice to parents on how to best support their bipolar child. Includes discussions about bipolar kids who have additional disorders like ADHD, Tourette Syndrome, and Asperger's Syndrome.

McGee, Caroline C. *Matt the Moody Hermit Crab: A Story for Children with Bipolar Disorder.* Nashville: McGee & Woods,

2002. A novel-length story for kids ages 8–12 who know someone with Bipolar Disorder or have the disorder themselves. Helps kids empathize with their bipolar friends and helps bipolar kids know that they are not alone.

Papolos, Demitri F., and Janice Papalos. *The Bipolar Child: The Definitive and Reassuring Guide to Childhood's Most Misunderstood Disorder.* New York: Broadway Books, 2006. Discusses the diagnosis, treatment methods, and long-term care of kids with Bipolar Disorder. Includes a discussion about the emotional challenges that parents face when raising a bipolar child.

Singer, Cindy, and Sheryl Gurrentz. *If Your Child Is Bipolar.* London, England: Perspective Publishing, 2003. With input from hundreds of parents and mental health professionals, this book provides practical strategies and advice on how to handle the day-to-day challenges of raising a bipolar child.

Waltz, Mitzi. *Bipolar Disorders: A Guide to Helping Children and Adolescents.* Cambridge, MA: O'Reilly Media, 2000. This book outlines diagnostic criteria, interventions, medications, and therapies for bipolar children. It discusses family life, answers insurance questions, and helps parents navigate the special education system.

Communication Disorders

ARTICULATION DISORDERS

The Childhood Apraxia of Speech Association of North America. 1151 Freeport Road, Suite 243, Pittsburgh, PA 15238; 412-767-6589; www.apraxia-kids.org. This nonprofit organization's goal is to strengthen the support systems in the lives of children with apraxia. The Web site contains many articles on all aspects of the topic, as well as information about support groups in the United States.

Dougherty, Dorothy P. *Teach Me How to Say It Right.* Oakland, CA: New Harbinger, 2005. Helps parents identify children's articulation problems and offers suggestions on how to create a positive language-learning environment.

RECEPTIVE AND EXPRESSIVE LANGUAGE DISORDERS

Bellis, Terri James. *When the Brain Can't Hear: Unraveling the Mystery of Auditory Processing Disorder.* New York: Atria Books, 2002. Explains the science behind receptive language problems. Includes information about how auditory processing problems are manifested in kids and adults.

STUTTERING

Lears, Lori. *Ben Has Something to Say: A Story About Stuttering.* Morton Grove, IL: Albert Whitman, 2000. A reassuring book about stuttering for kids ages 5–9.

Stuttering Foundation of America. 3100 Walnut Grove Road, Suite 603, P.O. Box 11749, Memphis, TN 38111; 1-800-992-9392; www.stutteringhelp.org. A nonprofit organization dedicated to providing the most up-to-date information about the prevention and treatment of stuttering. The Web site contains fact sheets, speech pathologist referrals, and sections especially for kids, teens, parents, and teachers.

PRAGMATIC LANGUAGE DISORDER

Michelle G. Winner's Center for Social Thinking. 3550 Stevens Creek Boulevard, Suite 200, San Jose, CA 95117; 408-557-8595; www.socialthinking.com. An organization dedicated to helping adults understand social-cognitive problems in children.

Social Stories™ Web site. www.thegraycenter.org/socialstories. A part of the Gray Center for Social Learning, this Web site provides information about Social Stories, a tool for helping kids with social and communication problems strengthen their understanding of social cues and expectations.

GENERAL RESOURCES

Agin, Marilyn C., Lisa Geng, and Malcolm Nicholl. *The Late Talker: What to Do If Your Child Isn't Talking Yet.* New York: St. Martin's Press, 2004. Explains the stages of language development in children and alerts parents to the warning signs of speech disorders.

American Speech-Language-Hearing Association. 10801 Rockville Pike, Rockville, MD 20852; 1-800-638-8255; www.asha.org. A professional and scientific association of speech-language pathologists, audiologists, and speech, language, and hearing scientists. The Web site contains research articles and a searchable database of speech-language professionals and programs in the United States.

Apel, Kenn, and Julie J. Masterson. *Beyond Baby Talk: From Sounds to Sentences, A Parent's Complete Guide to Language Development.* Roseville, CA: Prima Publishing, 2001. Outlines the stages of language development in children so that parents can track their child's progress. Includes a discussion on the effect of environmental and cultural factors on language acquisition and development.

Communication Connects. communicationconnects.com. Provides up-to-date information about speech and language disorders. Includes classroom and home activity ideas for teachers and parents.

Hall, Barbara J., Herbert J. Oyer, and William H. Haas. *Speech, Language, and Hearing Disorders: A Guide for the Teacher.* Boston: Allyn & Bacon, 2000. Information and advice for teachers on how to include and support students with speech, language, and hearing problems in their classrooms.

Hamaguchi, Patricia McAleer. *Childhood Speech, Language & Listening Problems: What Every Parent Should Know.* Oakland,

CA: New Harbinger, 2001. An overview of language problems found in children and advice on where to go for help.

Kaufman Children's Center for Speech, Language, Sensory-Motor, and Social Connections. 6625 Daly Road, West Bloomfield, MI 48322; 248-737-3430; www.kidspeech.com. The goal of this organization is to empower parents, caregivers, and families to help children become effective communicators. The Web site contains information about how to identify speech problems and how to find the best therapy.

Martin, Katherine L. *Does My Child Have a Speech Problem?* Chicago: Chicago Review Press, 1997. Helps parents identify potential language and speech problems in their children. Includes a helpful list of resources and organizations.

Voices Association. 11132 South Freeman Avenue, Suite C, Inglewood, CA 90304; 310-910-3555; www.4voices.org. A nonprofit organization committed to improving the lives of children with severe speech-language and communication disorders through community education, parental advocacy, and family support.

Learning Disorders

READING DISABILITY

Harvey, Stephanie, and Anne Goudvis. *Strategies That Work: Teaching Comprehension to Enhance Understanding.* Portland, ME: Stenhouse Publishers, 2000. An excellent presentation of specific strategies classroom teachers can use to improve reading comprehension.

Higgins, Judith, Kathleen McConnell, James R. Patton, and Gail R. Ryser. *Practical Ideas That Really Work for Students with Dyslexia and Other Reading Disorders.* Austin, TX: PRO-ED, 2003. Provides tools to identify and assess reading problems in the classroom and strategies to help struggling students succeed.

Hultquist, Alan M. *An Introduction to Dyslexia for Parents and Professionals.* London: Jessica Kingsley Publishers, 2006. Explains the causes of Dyslexia and outlines its various manifestations in children.

International Dyslexia Association of America. 8600 LaSalle Road, Baltimore, MD 21286; 410-296-0232; www.interdys.org. An international organization dedicated to the study and treatment of Dyslexia. In addition to Dyslexia, the Web site contains useful information about kids with general reading problems.

International Reading Association. 800 Barksdale Road, P.O. Box 8139, Newark, DE 19714; 1-800-366-7323; www.reading.org. They offer books, brochures, videos, and journals to support the teaching of reading and writing.

Nosek, Kathleen. *The Dyslexic Scholar: Helping Your Child Succeed in the School System.* Dallas: Taylor Publishing, 1995. Helps parents understand the education and special education system to ensure that their dyslexic child has a positive and successful school experience.

Partnership for Reading. www.partnershipforreading. This organization provides information on sound, research-based reading instruction. Visit the Web site to find many publications available for download, including "Put Reading First: The Research Building Blocks for Teaching Children to Read."

Reading Rockets. 2775 South Quincy Street, Arlington, VA 22206; 703-998-2001; www.readingrockets.org. A national multimedia project offering information on how kids learn to read, why some kids struggle with reading, and how adults can help.

Reid, Gavin. *Dyslexia: A Complete Guide for Parents.* New York: Wiley, 2005. Helps parents identify Dyslexia in their children, navigate the school system, and find the support they need.

Shaywitz, Sally. *Overcoming Dyslexia.* New York: Alfred A. Knopf, 2003. A leading authority and researcher on Dyslexia discusses the biology of this disability, gives tips on how to help struggling readers, and offers practical ways to help young people overcome the disability.

Simmons, Deborah C., and Edward J. Kameenui, eds. *What Reading Research Tells Us About Children with Diverse Learning Needs: Bases and Basics.* Mahwah, NJ: Lawrence Elbaum Associates, 1998. A comprehensive text on how to teach students with reading difficulties.

MATH DISABILITY

Burns, Marilyn. *About Teaching Mathematics: A K–8 Resource.* Sausalito, CA: Math Solutions Publications, 2000. Offers creative ways to teach math to reluctant students.

Cooper, Richard. *Alternative Math Techniques: When Nothing Else Seems to Work.* Longmont, CO: Sopris West Educational Services, 2005. Provides instructional concepts, techniques, and tips to teach math to struggling students. Includes a CD-ROM with 194 reproducible assignments.

FASTT Math. 100 Talcott Avenue, Watertown, MA 02472; 1-800-342-0236; www.tomsnyder.com. Research-validated methods help struggling students (grades 2 and up) develop fluency with basic math facts in addition, subtraction, multiplication, and division.

Ryser, Gail, Jamer R. Patton, Edward A. Polloway, and Kathleen McConnell. *Practical Ideas That Really Work for Teaching Math Problem Solving.* Austin, TX: PRO-ED, 2006. Helps teachers identify and assess math disabilities in their students and offers strategies to use with struggling students in the classroom.

What Works Clearinghouse (WWC). 2277 Research Boulevard, Rockville, MD 20850; 1-866-992-9799; www.w-w-c.org. A clearinghouse of math and reading interventions for teachers.

WRITING DISABILITY

Inspiration Software. 9400 SW Beaverton-Hillsdale Highway, Suite 300, Beaverton, OR 97005; 1-800-877-4292; www.inspiration.com. Inspiration (for older kids) and Kidspiration (for younger kids) create graphic organizers from student-entered text so kids can see what they are thinking. The programs help students transfer information from the graphic organizer to written documents.

Jones, Susan. "Dysgraphia Accommodations and Modifications." Arlington, VA: LD Online, 1999; www.ldonline.org/article/6202. An online article for teachers that outlines the symptoms of dysgraphia and offers suggestions on how to accommodate these students in the classroom.

Graham, Steven, and Karen R. Harris. *Writing Better: Effective Strategies for Teaching Students with Learning Difficulties.* Baltimore: Brookes Publishing Company, 2005. An invaluable resource for teachers that includes genre specific writing strategies, tips on brainstorming, goal-setting, and paragraph construction to help struggling students become better writers.

Richards, Regina G. "Strategies for Dealing with Dysgraphia." Arlington, VA: LD Online, 1999; www.ldonline.org/article/5890. An online article for teachers that offers practical classroom strategies for helping kids with dysgraphia.

NONVERBAL LEARNING DISABILITY

NLD on the Web. www.nldontheweb.org. Find links and articles on all aspects of Nonverbal Learning Disability including assessment, advocacy, and intervention.

NLDline. www.nldline.com. A Web site that educates the public about Nonverbal Learning Disability and provides a place for people to connect with others affected by the disorder.

Nonverbal Learning Disorders Association. 507 Hopmeadow Street, Simsbury, CT 06070; 860-658-5522; www.nlda.org. A nonprofit organization dedicated to the research, education, and advocacy for nonverbal learning disorders.

Stewart, Kathryn. *Helping a Child with Nonverbal Learning Disorder or Asperger's Syndrome.* Oakland, CA: New Harbinger Publications, 2002. Helps parents develop the skills they need to support their child with Nonverbal Learning Disability.

Tanguay, Pamela B. *Nonverbal Learning Disabilities at School.* London: Jessica Kingsley Publishers, 2002. Provides specific strategies teachers can use to motivate and support students with Nonverbal Learning Disability. Includes tips on modifying curriculum, creating cooperative learning environments, and teaching reading comprehension, writing, and math.

Thompson, Sue. "Neurobehavioral Characteristics Seen in the Classroom: Developing an Educational Plan for the Student with NLD." Arlington, VA: LD Online, 1998; www.ldonline.org/article/6119. Gives practical strategies to help NLD students function in the classroom.

Thompson, Sue. *The Source for Nonverbal Learning Disorders.* East Moline, IL: LinguiSystems, 1997. Summarizes research on Nonverbal Learning Disability in easy-to-understand language. Contains case study examples, developmental profiles, helpful checklists, and a list of resources.

GENERAL RESOURCES

Fisher, Gary, and Rhoda Cummings. *The Survival Guide for Kids with LD* (Learning Differences). Minneapolis: Free Spirit Publishing, 2002. Explains LD in terms kids ages 8 and up can understand, describes the different kinds of LD, and discusses LD programs. Includes resources for parents and teachers.

Harwell, Joan M. *Complete Learning Disabilities Handbook: Ready-to-Use Strategies & Activities for Teaching Students with Learning Disabilities.* San Francisco: Jossey-Bass, 2002. Provides helpful tips and strategies for teachers to use with struggling students. Includes diagnostic tools, intervention techniques, and an overview of the various learning disabilities teachers may encounter in their classroom.

Learning Disabilities Association of America. 4156 Library Road, Pittsburgh, PA 15234; 412-341-1515; www.ldanatl.org. The largest nonprofit volunteer organization advocating for people with learning disorders, their Web site contains a wealth of information for parents, teachers, and other professionals.

LD OnLine. www.ldonline.org. A great Web site that features hundreds of articles, monthly columns, first person stories, and a substantive list of LD resources. Includes sections especially for educators, parents, and kids.

Levine, Mel. *All Kinds of Minds: A Young Student's Book About Learning Abilities and Learning Disorders.* Cambridge, MA: Educators Publishing Service, 1992. Helps kids in grades 3–6 understand their learning strengths and weaknesses.

Levine, Mel. *A Mind at a Time.* New York: Simon & Schuster, 2002. Identifies eight mental abilities that contribute to learning and explains how parents and teachers can strengthen them in children.

Levine, Mel. *Keeping Ahead in School: A Student's Book About Learning Abilities and Learning Disorders.* Cambridge, MA: Educators Publishing Service, 1991. Helps students develop the skills they need to achieve better results in their schoolwork.

Reid, Robert, and Torri Ortiz Lienemann. *Strategy Instruction for Students with Learning Disabilities: What Works for Special-Needs Learners.* New York: Guilford Press, 2006. A practical, step-by-step guide for using instructional techniques to improve the cognitive development of students with learning disabilities.

SchwabLearning.org. This Web site provides parent-friendly, expert-approved information about learning disabilities.

Stern, Judith M., and Uzi Ben-Ami. *Many Ways to Learn: Young People's Guide to Learning Disabilities.* Washington, DC: Magination Press, 1996. Uses the analogy of mountain climbing to explain learning disabilities to kids ages 8–14.

Winebrenner, Susan. *Teaching Kids with Learning Difficulties in the Regular Classroom: Ways to Challenge & Motivate Struggling Students to Achieve Proficiency with Required Standards.* Minneapolis: Free Spirit Publishing, 2005. A goldmine of practical, easy-to-use teaching methods, strategies, and tips to help teachers differentiate the curriculum in all subject areas to meet the needs of all learners.

ADHD

ADD WareHouse. www.addwarehouse.com. A Web site features many resources for helping children with Attention Deficit Hyperactivity Disorder and related special needs. Find books, videos, and training programs for classroom use as well as resources for parents and students.

Attention Deficit Disorder Association. www.add.org. While this organization is for adults with attention deficits and impulsivity, the Web site is full of background information on diagnosis, coping strategies, and current research that can be useful in helping young people with ADHD.

Barkley, Russell A. *Taking Charge of ADHD: The Complete, Authoritative Guide for Parents.* New York: Guilford Press, 2000. A comprehensive resource on ADHD, this book includes a step-by-step plan for behavior management, information on the multitude of available treatments (including medication), and other practical advice for parents of children with ADHD.

Children and Adults with Attention Deficit/Hyperactivity Disorder (CHADD). 8181 Professional Place, Suite 150, Landover, MD 20785; 301-306-7070; www.chadd.org. CHADD is of the largest organizations in the United States serving individuals with ADHD. Chapters around the country allow parents, educators, professionals, and others interested in the disorder to connect and share insights into it. The Web site has lots of information on ADHD as well as membership and conference opportunities. Also available through the organization is the "CHADD Educator's Manual." Published in 2006, the resource is full of strategies for helping students in the classroom.

Dendy, Chris A. Ziegler, and Alex Ziegler. *A Bird's-Eye View of Life with ADD and ADHD: Advice from Young Survivors.* Cedar Bluff, AL: Cherish the Children, 2003. This book combines inspiration and practical information about attention deficits and impulsivity. Readers learn about the coping strategies and successes of other children and adolescents.

Dendy, Chris A. Ziegler, and Alex Ziegler. *Teenagers with ADD: A Parents' Guide.* Bethesda, MD: Woodbine, 1995. Including information on diagnosis, treatment methods, and advocacy efforts, this book is a handy guide for parents of young people with attention deficits.

Galvin, Matthew. *Otto Learns About His Medicine: A Story About Medication for Children with ADHD.* Washington, DC: Magination Press, 2001. This book for students ages 4–8 provides information on ADHD medications in a friendly, storybook format.

Jensen, Peter S. *Making the System Work for Your Child with ADHD: How to Cut Through Red Tape and Get What You Need from Doctors, Teachers, Schools, and Healthcare Plans.* New York: Guilford Press, 2004. Written for parents of all school-age children with ADHD, this book serves as a comprehensive guide to getting fair treatment for children at school and quality healthcare options. While specifically not for teachers, the book is full of great information on special education law and classroom accommodations.

Nadeau, Kathleen G. *Help4ADD@High School.* Altamonte Springs, FL: Advantage Press, 1998. A fun resource for high school students on all of the usual issues young people face—like difficulties at school, relationships, peer pressure, drugs, and more—all from the perspective of students with attention deficits or impulsivity.

Nadeau, Kathleen G., and Ellen B. Dixon. *Learning to Slow Down and Pay Attention: A Book for Kids About ADHD.* Washington, DC: Magination, 2004. A fun and accessible guide, this book might be considered a "first stop" for children who are diagnosed. An open, interactive format will help keep kids reading.

National Resource Center on ADHD. www.help4adhd.org. This Web collaboration between CHADD and the Centers for Disease Control and Prevention is a one-stop site for background information on ADHD, education issues, current research on treatment options (including medication), and much more.

Parker, Harvey C. *Problem Solver Guide for Students with ADHD: Ready-to-Use Interventions for Elementary and Secondary Students.* Plantation, FL: Specialty Press, 2001. This quick reference guide can help educators (and parents) develop study and organizational skills in students. Ideas for modifying difficult behaviors also are included.

Quinn, Patricia O., and Judith M. Stern. *Putting on the Brakes: Young People's Guide to Understanding Attention Deficit Hyperactivity Disorder.* Washington, DC: Magination Press, 2001. Concise information and an engaging format make this a valuable resource for children who have ADHD. Practical information and an upbeat tone make children with the disorder see that they can succeed with ADHD.

Rief, Sandra F. *The ADHD Book of Lists: A Practical Guide for Helping Children and Teens with Attention Deficit Disorders.* New York: Jossey-Bass, 2003. Full of strategies and interventions for helping children who have difficulties with attention, impulsivity, and hyperactivity, this book is a comprehensive resource for K–12 educators as well as parents. Reproducible forms, checklists, and tools make the book very easy to use.

Rief, Sandra F. *How to Reach and Teach ADD/ADHD Children: Practical Techniques, Strategies, and Intervention for Helping Children with Attention Problems and Hyperactivity.* New York: Wiley, 2005. This resource is full of practical strategies for educators interested in teaching to students' unique strengths and learning styles. Find recommendations for multiple-sensory approaches to academics, behavior management strategies, and more.

Rieff, Michael I. (editor), with Sherrill Tippins. *ADHD: A Complete and Authoritative Guide.* Elk Grove Village, IL: American Academy of Pediatrics, 2004. This book compiles information from a variety of authorities on the disorder to present a balanced view of diagnosis and treatment.

Ryser, Gail, and Kathleen McConnell. *Practical Ideas That Really Work for Students with ADHD Grades PreK–4* and *Practical Ideas That Really Work for Students with ADHD Grades 5–12.* Austin, TX: PRO-ED, 2005. These books include in-the-trenches information for helping students with ADHD. Also included is information for school psychologists, administrators, and others involved in the documentation of classroom interventions and student IEPs.

Taylor, John F. *The Survival Guide for Kids with ADD or ADHD.* Minneapolis: Free Spirit Publishing, 2006. For kids ages 8–12, this book features current information on ADHD and its treatment as well as advice young people can use in school, at home, and with friends. Fun illustrations and an interactive format keep kids reading.

U.S. Department of Education. "Teaching Children with Attention Deficit Hyperactivity Disorder: Instructional Strategies and Practices." Washington, DC: U.S. Office of Special Education Programs, 2004. www.ed.gov/teachers/needs/speced/adhd/adhd-resource-pt2.doc. This online document from the federal government has many ideas for accommodating the needs of students with ADHD in the classroom.

Ziegler, C. *Teaching Teens with ADD and ADHD: A Quick Reference Guide for Teachers and Parents.* Bethesda, MD: Woodbine, 2000. Pick up this book for concise information in key areas of helping students with ADHD to succeed at school. Includes brief information on IEPs and administrative issues related to educating students.

Disruptive Behavior Disorders

Agassi, Martine. *Hands Are Not for Hitting.* Minneapolis: Free Spirit Publishing, 2000. For ages 4–8, this book teaches children there are many positive, constructive ways to use their hands and that hurting others is never okay.

Barkley, Russell A., and Christine M. Benton. *Your Defiant Child: Eight Steps to Better Behavior.* New York: Guilford Press, 1998. This book for parents of defiant children offers a full program of positive, concrete strategies parents can use to promote positive behavior. Educators may also benefit from reading.

Bloomquist, Michael L. *Skills Training for Children with Behavior Problems: A Parent and Therapist Guidebook.* New York: Guilford Press, 2006. A comprehensive and practical resource, this book is for family therapists but includes information parents and educators will find helpful for addressing inappropriate behavior.

Carr, Tom. *131 Creative Strategies for Reaching Children with Anger.* Chapin, SC: Youthlight, 2000. With a focus on concrete strategies, this book provides educators and parents with ideas for different levels of anger in children—from mild to severe.

Crowder, Carolyn. *Eating, Sleeping, and Getting Up: How to Stop the Daily Battles with Your Child.* New York: Broadway, 2004. From a renowned parenting expert, this book offers advice on helping children through transitions and other difficult times throughout the course of the day. The approach is positive and emphasizes building skills in children (as opposed to punishing misbehavior).

Greene, Ross W. *The Explosive Child: A New Approach for Understanding and Parenting Easily Frustrated, Chronically Inflexible Children.* New York: Harper, 2005. This resource from a pediatric psychologist offers insight about angry and defiant children and provides parents with advice they can use to diminish volatile behaviors.

Greene, Ross W., and J. Stuart Ablon. *Treating Explosive Kids: The Collaborative Problem-Solving Approach.* New York: Guilford Press, 2006. While this book is primarily for therapists working with defiant children, detailed interventions for diffusing anger also make it a good resource for classroom use.

Jacobsen, Mary-Elaine. *The Brat Stops Here! 5 Weeks (or Less) to No More Tantrums, Arguing, or Bad Behavior.* New York: St. Martin's Griffin, 2006. This book offers parents and caregivers advice on setting clear behavior expectations and adjusting privileges to encourage positive behavior.

Levy, Ray, and Bill O'Hanlon. *Try and Make Me! Simple Strategies That Turn Off Tantrums and Create Cooperation.* New York: Rodale, 2001. This book is written to parents but includes straightforward information that teachers also will find helpful in handling challenging students.

MacKenzie, Robert J. *Setting Limits in the Classroom: How to Move Beyond the Classroom Dance of Discipline.* Roseville, CA: Prima Publishing, 1996. This guide to classroom management is positive and pro-student. Find many strategies for helping students understand and follow behavior expectations.

McConnell, Kathleen, Gail Ryser, and James R. Patton. *Practical Ideas That Really Work for Students with Disruptive, Defiant, or Difficult Behaviors: Grades 5–12.* Austin, TX: PRO-ED, 2002. Easy-to-implement strategies for the regular classroom and information relevant for guidance settings.

McFadden, Anna T., and Kathy Cooper. *Leave No Angry Child Behind: The ABCs of Anger Management.* Manassas Park, VA: Impact Publication, 2004. This resource for educators features basic strategies for helping students handle anger at school.

Pantley, Elizabeth. *Kid Cooperation: How to Stop Yelling, Nagging, and Pleading and Get Kids to Cooperate.* Oakland: New Harbinger, 2006. The primary focus of this book is to help parents foster cooperation in the family. Many of the concepts, however, can be useful in the classroom.

Phelan, Thomas W., and Sarah Jane Schonour. *1-2-3 Magic for Teachers: Effective Classroom Discipline PreK Through Grade 8.* Glen Ellyn, IL: Parent Magic, 2004. This no-nonsense approach to behavior helps teachers stay in charge of the classroom and promote positive student involvement.

Shore, Kenneth. *Elementary Teacher's Discipline Problem Solver: A Practical A–Z Approach for Managing Classroom Behavior Problems.* San Francisco: Jossey-Bass, 2003. This ready-to-use resource includes information on a wide variety of classroom behaviors—from spitting to complaining and backtalk to bullying. The emphasis throughout is on staying positive and trying to redirect negative behaviors while respecting students.

Spelman, C. *When I Feel Angry.* Morton Grove, IL: Albert Whitman and Company, 2000. For young children, this story features a rabbit that has learned how to deal with anger in constructive ways.

Taylor, John F. *From Defiance to Cooperation: Real Solutions for Transforming the Angry, Defiant, Discouraged Child.* Roseville, CA. Prima Publishing, 2001. Frustrated parents will find plenty of useful advice for addressing children's misbehavior. Featuring a positive approach, the book offers strategies for supporting children while at the same time diminishing defiance.

Thompson, Julia G. *Discipline Survival Kit for the Secondary Teacher.* San Francisco: Jossey-Bass, 1998. This resource offers teachers of grades 7–12 practical, easy-to-use information helpful toward addressing poor behavior in individual students as well as groups.

Verdick, Elizabeth, and Marjorie Lisovskis. *How to Take the Grrrr Out of Anger.* Minneapolis: Free Spirit Publishing, 2002. For ages 8–13, this book gives kids tools they can use to handle strong emotions in a constructive way that doesn't harm others.

Whitehouse, Eliane, and Warwick Pudney. *A Volcano in My Tummy: Helping Children to Handle Anger.* Gabriola Island, BC: New Society Publishers, 1996. Activities, stories, and games make this a lively resource for teaching kids ages 6–13 constructive ways to manage anger. Background information for teachers, parents, and caregivers also included.

Asperger's Syndrome

Asperger's Disorder Homepage; www.aspergers.com. This online resource maintained by Dr. R. Kaan Ozbayrak answers frequently asked questions about Asperger's.

Attwood, Tony. *The Complete Guide to Asperger's Syndrome.* London: Jessica Kingsley Publishers, 2006. A comprehensive resource full of cutting-edge information on Asperger's Syndrome and its treatment. The author, an authority on the disorder, also has a Web site (www.tonyattwood.com) where more information is available.

Autism Asperger Publishing Company. 15490 Quivira Road, P.O. Box 23173, Shawnee, KS 66283; 913-897-1004; www.asperger.net. An independent publisher, this company provides hands-on, practical information about autistic spectrum disorders to parents and educators.

Bashe, Patricia Romanowski, and Barbara L. Kirby. *The OASIS Guide to Asperger Syndrome: Advice, Support, Insight, and Inspiration.* New York: Crown Publishers, 2005. With survey input from thousands of parents, the author offers practical information, true stories, and support to anyone raising a child with Asperger's Syndrome.

Borba, Michele. *Nobody Likes Me, Everybody Hates Me: The Top 25 Friendship Problems and How to Solve Them.* San Francisco: Jossey-Bass, 2005. A great resource for parents and educators looking to help children improve peer relationships, this book also includes information on exclusion tactics, gossip, cyber-bullying, and other forms of social abuse.

Cumine, Val, Julia Leach, and Gill Stevenson. *Asperger Syndrome: A Practical Guide for Teachers.* London: D. Fulton Publishers, 1998. Provides effective strategies for teaching children with Asperger's Syndrome in regular classes.

Duke, Marshall P., Stephen Nowicki Jr., and Elisabeth Martin. *Teaching Your Child the Language of Social Success.* New York: Back Bay Books, 1996. Helps parents develop their child's nonverbal communication skills so they can interact more effectively with others.

Etlinger, Rebecca. *To Be Me: Understanding What It's Like to Have Asperger's Syndrome.* Los Angeles: Creative Therapy Store, 2005. A colorfully illustrated book for children ages 9–12 who are affected by or know someone who has Asperger's Syndrome.

Faherty, Catherine. *What Does It Mean to Me? A Workbook Explaining Self-Awareness and Life Lessons to the Child or Youth with High Functioning Autism or Asperger's.* Arlington,

TX: Future Horizons, 2000. Activities help kids with Asperger's Syndrome ages 9–12 understand their differences.

Frankel, Fred. *Good Friends Are Hard to Find.* Los Angeles: Perspective Publishing, 1996. A step-by-step guide helps parents help their children make friends and deal with other kids. Based on UCLA Children's Social Skills Program.

Future Horizons, Inc. 721 West Abram Street, Arlington, TX 76013; 1-800-489-0727; www.futurehorizons-autism.com. This leading publisher of books about Asperger's Syndrome has titles for individuals, families, and professionals.

Gagnon, Elisa, and Brenda Smith Myles. *This Is Asperger Syndrome.* Shawnee Mission, KS: Autism Asperger Publishing, 1999. Explains Asperger's Syndrome to kids ages 9–12 who have siblings, friends, or classmates with the disorder.

Jackson, Luke. *Freaks, Geeks, & Asperger Syndrome: A User Guide to Adolescence.* Philadelphia: Jessica Kingsley Publishers, 2002. A thirteen-year-old boy with Asperger's Syndrome explains how he understands his disorder. A helpful book for adolescents with Asperger's Syndrome as well as those who would like to understand the disorder from a personal perspective.

Jessica Kingsley Publishers. 400 Market Street, Suite 400, Philadelphia, PA 19106; 1-866-416-1078; www.jkp.com. This well-known publisher of books on autistic spectrum disorders offers resources for adults and kids.

Madorsky Elman, Natalie, and Eileen Kennedy-Moore. *The Unwritten Rules of Friendship: Simple Strategies to Help Your Child Make Friends.* New York: Little, Brown, 2003. This is a comprehensive resource on the social interactions of children. While the book is for parents, educators will also benefit from the insight into students' social lives.

McConnell, Kathleen, and Gail R. Ryser. *Practical Ideas That Really Work for Students with Asperger's Syndrome.* Austin, TX: Pro-Ed, 2005. Provides 34 instructional strategies for teachers to use with students who have Asperger's Syndrome.

Michelle G. Winner's Center for Social Thinking. 3550 Stevens Creek Boulevard, Suite 200, San Jose, CA 95117; 408-557-8595; www.socialthinking.com. This organization is dedicated to helping adults understand social-cognitive problems in children.

Moyes, Rebecca A. *Addressing the Challenging Behavior of Children with High-Functioning Autism/Asperger Syndrome in the Classroom: A Guide for Teachers and Parents.* Philadelphia: Jessica Kingsley Publishers, 2002. Explains the behavior of children with Asperger's Syndrome and helps teachers create a classroom environment that supports and nurtures affected children.

Moyes, Rebecca A. *Incorporating Social Goals in the Classroom: A Guide for Teachers and Parents of Children with High-Functioning Autism and Asperger Syndrome.* Philadelphia: Jessica Kingsley Publishers, 2001. Gives strategies for teaching social skills to kids with Autism or Asperger's Syndrome. Includes clear descriptions of the behavior commonly exhibited by these students in the classroom.

Myles, Brenda Smith, Diane Adreon, and Dena Gitlitz. *Simple Strategies That Work! Helpful Hints for All Educators of Students with Asperger Syndrome, High-Functioning Autism, and Related Disabilities.* Shawnee Mission, KS: Autism Asperger Publishing, 2006. Tells how to accommodate and nurture students with Asperger's Syndrome in the classroom without disrupting established classroom routines.

Myles, Brenda Smith, and Richard L. Simpson. *Asperger Syndrome: A Guide for Educators & Parents.* Austin, TX: Pro-Ed, 2003. Explains the symptoms and causes of Asperger's Syndrome in easy-to-understand language. Contains personal stories and practical strategies, useful for parents and teachers.

Online Asperger Syndrome Information & Support (OASIS). www.udel.edu/bkirby/asperger. This Web site contains information, articles, and a message board for parents who have kids with Asperger's Syndrome.

Ozonoff, Sally, Geraldine Dawson, and James McPartland. *A Parent's Guide to Asperger Syndrome & High Functioning Autism: How to Meet the Challenges and Help Your Child Thrive.* New York: Guilford Press, 2002. Provides advice for parents from leading psychologists about how to foster the strengths of children with Asperger's and cope with the challenges. Contains strategies for helping affected children interact with peers and understand the expectations of appropriate behavior.

Prior, Margo, editor. *Learning and Behavior Problems in Asperger Syndrome.* New York: Guilford Press, 2003. Offers information on how to diagnose, assess, and teach students with Asperger's Syndrome.

Sheridan, Susan M. *Why Don't They Like Me?* Longmont, CO: Sopris West, 1998. Helps kids ages 5–12 develop the social skills they need to make friends. Contains tear-out social skill cards to reinforce the messages of the book.

Social Stories™ Web site. www.thegraycenter.org/socialstories. A part of the Gray Center for Social Learning, this Web site provides information about Social Stories, a tool for helping kids with social and communication problems strengthen their understanding of social cues and expectations.

The Source for Autism, Asperger's Syndrome, and Pervasive Developmental Disorders. www.maapservices.org. This nonprofit organization is dedicated to providing information and advice to families of individuals with autistic spectrum disorders. The Web site contains a substantive collection of new and archived articles on the topic.

Stewart, Kathryn. *Helping a Child with Nonverbal Learning Disorder or Asperger's Syndrome.* Oakland: New Harbinger Publications, 2002. Helps parents develop the skills they need to support their child with Asperger's Syndrome.

Welton, Jude. *Can I Tell You About Asperger Syndrome? A Guide for Family and Friends.* Philadelphia: Jessica Kingsley Publishers, 2003. An illustrated book in which a young narrator explains Asperger's Syndrome and its symptoms, for kids ages 7–15.

Tic Disorders

Buehrens, Adam. *Hi, I'm Adam: A Child's Book About Tourette Syndrome.* Duarte, CA: Hope Press, 1990. Written from the perspective of a boy with Tourette Syndrome, this story helps kids realize they're not alone and teaches them to celebrate treatment successes.

Byalick, Marcia. *Quit It.* New York: Yearling, 2004. This book for middle grade readers tells the story of Carrie, a girl who is diagnosed with Tourette Syndrome before beginning seventh grade. Many of Carrie's friends turn on her and she experiences other difficulties in this tale of acceptance.

Chowdhury, Uttum. *Tics and Tourette Syndrome: A Handbook for Parents and Professionals.* Philadelphia: Jessica Kingsley, 2004. A comprehensive resource on tics and Tourette Syndrome, this book discusses how these disorders affect behavior in the classroom and at home. This great resource for both teachers and parents offers many strategies for helping children.

Cohen, Brad, with Lisa Wysocky. *Front of the Class: How Tourette Syndrome Made Me the Teacher I Never Had.* Acton, MA: VanderWyk and Burnham, 2005. A real-life tale of a teacher with Tourette Syndrome, this inspiring book helps readers understand the effects of the disorder and empathize with those affected by it.

Haerle, Tracy Lynne (editor). *Children with Tourette Syndrome: A Parent's Guide.* Bethesda, MD: Woodbine, 2007. The book is full of coping strategies parents (and teachers) will find useful in helping children with Tourette Syndrome.

Krueger, Tira. *Taking Tourette Syndrome to School.* Plainview, NY: Jayjo Books, 2002. For ages 9–12, this story features a girl with Tourette Syndrome. Children learn basic information about the disorder and are encouraged to accept themselves.

Niner, Holly. *I Can't Stop! A Story About Tourette Syndrome.* Morton Grove, IL: Albert Whitman and Company, 2005. For children in elementary school, this story about Adam—who has Tourette Syndrome—is a nonthreatening approach to sharing information about the disorder with young people.

Tourette Syndrome Association. www.tsa-usa.org. This national organization devoted to informing and advocating for people with Tourette Syndrome offers information on current research and treatment options at its Web site. It is a useful resource for educators, parents, and others involved in the care of students with the disorder.

Tourette's Syndrome Plus. www.tourettesyndrome.net. This Web site is full of information on Tourette Syndrome for parents and educators. Find downloadable brochures and handouts that are helpful in teaching students with the disorder and promoting an atmosphere of acceptance.

Tourette-Syndrome.com. www.tourette-syndrome.com. For families, this fun and interactive Web site features many options for students with Tourette Syndrome. They learn more about the disorder, connect with others affected, and much more.

Eating Disorders

Alliance for Eating Disorders Awareness. www.eatingdisorderinfo.org. This Web site is a great source of information on eating disorders and their treatment. Also find resources and contacts for getting students and families help.

Anorexia Nervosa and Related Eating Disorders. www.anred.com. With dozens of articles and documents, this Web site provides primer information on eating disorders, their prevalence, and tips for helping people who are affected by them. Resources point the way to additional information.

Costin, Carolyn. *Eating Disorder Sourcebook: A Comprehensive Guide to the Causes, Treatments, and Prevention of Eating Disorders.* Los Angeles: Lowell House, 1999. This book is a one-stop resource for all kinds of information on eating disorders—from counseling techniques to nutrition information and media factors to advocacy efforts.

Gurze Books. www.bulimia.com. A cataloger and online retailer, this company specializes in books on eating disorders for both adults and young people.

Heaton, Jeanne Albronda, and Claudia J. Strauss. *Talking to Eating Disorders: Simple Ways to Support Someone with Anorexia, Bulimia, Binge Eating, or Body Image Issues.* New York: Penguin, 2005. Impulsive responses to those with eating disorders are insensitive and can make a problem worse. This book offers ideas for effectively communictaing with those who have eating disorders.

Lock, James, and Daniel le Grange. *Help Your Child Beat an Eating Disorder.* New York: Guilford Press, 2005. Featuring current research, this resource for parents will also be helpful for educators looking to help children and adolescents with eating disorders.

Natenshon, Abigail H. *When Your Child Has an Eating Disorder: A Step-by-Step Workbook for Parents and Other Caregivers.* San Francisco: Jossey-Bass, 1999. This is a great resource for helping children overcome eating disorders.

National Association of Anorexia Nervosa and Associated Disorders (ANAD). www.anad.org. The Web site of this national organization is a great source of information on eating disorders and treatment options. It provides links to many other support groups and resources.

National Eating Disorders Association (NEDA). www.nationaleatingdisorders.org. The largest nonprofit company in the United States with a focus on eating disorders, NEDA is a clearinghouse for information on anorexia, bulima, binge-eating disorder, and other topics related to body image. Find referral options and links in your area for adolescents with these disorders.

Neumark-Sztainer, Dianne. *I'm Like, So Fat! Helping Your Teen Make Healthy Choices About Eating and Exercise in a Weight-Obsessed World.* New York: Guilford Press, 2005. While this resource is for parents of teens, teachers also benefit from reading this book. It explains how popular culture affects the body image of students and provides sound information on the right way to talk about weight and body image issues.

Something Fishy. www.something-fishy.org. This popular Web site is for people interested in learning more about eating disorders and national advocacy efforts. Referrals for treatment and current research on disorders are available.

Teachman, Bethany A., Marlene B. Schwartz, Bonnie S. Gordic, and Brenda S. Coyle. *Helping Your Child Overcome an Eating Disorder: What You Can Do at Home.* Oakland: New Harbinger, 2003. From researchers and therapists at the Yale Center for Eating and Weight Disorders, this book is a great introduction for parents of a child with an eating disorder.

Self-Injury

Alderman, Tracy. *The Scarred Soul: Understanding and Ending Self-Inflicted Violence.* Oakland: New Harbinger, 2006. This book provides information on cutting (and other self-harming behaviors) as well as available treatment options.

Bowman, Susan. *See My Pain! Creative Strategies and Activities for Helping Young People Who Self-Injure.* Chapin, SC: YouthLight, 2004. With a focus on therapy through the creative arts, this book can be used in classroom or guidance settings. The emphasis is on helping young people express the feelings that can cause them to cut or otherwise injure themselves.

Levenkron, Steven. *Cutting: Understanding and Overcoming Self-Mutilation.* New York: W.W. Norton and Company, 1999. This book includes general information about cutting and self-mutilation, stories from cutters, and recommendations for treatment and healing.

McVey-Noble, Merry E., Sony Khemlani-Patel, and Fogen Neziroglu. *When Your Child Is Cutting: A Parent's Guide to Helping Children Overcome Self-Injury.* Oakland: New Harbinger, 2006. Written for parents, this book also is a great source of information on cutting for teachers and counselors. It includes a straightforward discussion of the reasons behind self-injury, treatment options, and where to go for more information.

Self-Injury: A Struggle. www.self-injury.net. Seeking to help those who self-injure realize they are not alone, this Web site features stories from people who engage in cutting (and other forms of self-mutilation), an online support network, and information on getting help.

Strong, Marilee. *A Bright Red Scream: Self-Mutilation and the Language of Pain.* New York: Penguin Group, 1999. A look at self-injury through profiles of individuals who have lived through periods of self-mutilation. This book provides background information on why some young people choose to become cutters.

Note: For books and Web sites on suicide, see the resources section for mood disorders on pages 184–186.

Notes

The following "Notes" cite references that have been used throughout this book. Included here are the page numbers on which referenced material appears, the opening few words of the cited fact or statistic, and the original resources from which the information came.

INTRODUCTION

2. Only about 25 percent of children: Center for Health and Health Care in Schools. "Children's Mental Health Needs, Disparities and School-Based Services: A Fact Sheet." Retrieved February 7, 2007, from www.healthinschools.org/cfk/mentfact.asp.

2. Up to 10 percent of students: Mash, E., and Wolfe, D. *Abnormal Child Psychology (Second Edition)*. Belmont, CA: Wadsworth, 2002.

2. Add these numbers and you have: U.S. Census Bureau. "Statistical Abstract of the US 2004" (2006). Retrieved February 7, 2007, from www.census.gov/compendia/statab/files/pop.html.

PART I: THE ROLE OF SCHOOLS IN ADDRESSING MENTAL HEALTH AND LEARNING DISORDERS

8. Many other students—including those: U.S. Department of Health and Human Services. "Report of the Surgeon General's Conference on Children's Mental Health: A National Action Agenda" (2000). Retrieved February 7, 2007, from www.surgeongeneral.gov/topics/cmh/default.htm.

8. Many private schools (sectarian and nonsectarian): Carrico, M. "The Rehabilitation Act of 1973 (Section 504) as Applied to Private Schools" (2000). Retrieved February 7, 2007, from www.modrall.com/articles/article_51.html.

8. Defining Learning Disabilities: Silver, A., and Hagen, R. *Disorders of Learning in Childhood (Second Edition)*. New York: Wiley, 2002.

9. The model may over-identify students: National Joint Committee on Learning Disabilities. "Responsiveness to Intervention and Learning Disabilities" (2005). Retrieved on February 7, 2007, from www.ldaamerica.us/pdf/rti2005.pdf.

10. Research indicates that a student's IQ: Fletcher, J., Foorman, B., Boudousquie, A., Barnes, M., Schatschneider, C., and French, D. "Assessment of Reading and Learning Disabilities: A Research-Based Intervention-Oriented Approach." *Journal of School Psychology*, 40, 27–63 (2002).

10. In 2000–2001, almost one-half of public school students: Dybvik, A. "Autism and the Inclusion Mandate" (2004). Retrieved February 7, 2007, from www.educationnext.org/20041/42.html.

11. Some researchers have predicted: National Joint Committee on Learning Disabilities. "Responsiveness to Intervention and Learning Disabilities" (2005). Retrieved February 7, 2007, from www.ldonline.org/article/11498?theme=print.

24. Student Coping Plan: Adapted from a document used by Groves Academy (St. Louis Park, MN). Used with permission.

24. Ross Greene, in *The Explosive Child:* Greene, R. *The Explosive Child.* New York: Harper, 2001.

PART II. MENTAL HEALTH AND LEARNING DISORDERS

Anxiety Disorders

43. About 13% of young people: U.S. Department of Health and Human Services. "Mental Health: A Report of the Surgeon General" (1999). Electronic version retrieved February 7, 2007, from www.surgeongeneral.gov/library/mentalhealth.

45. About 3% of children and adolescents: U.S. Department of Health and Human Services. "Mental Health: A Report of the Surgeon General" (1999). Electronic version retrieved February 7, 2007, from www.surgeongeneral.gov/library/mentalhealth.

45. Younger children with GAD: Mash, E., and Wolfe, D. *Abnormal Child Psychology (Second Edition)*. Belmont, CA: Wadsworth, 2002.

50. Between 1% and 3% of children: Rilva, R., Gallagher, R., and Minami, H. "Cognitive-Behavioral Treatments for Anxiety Disorders in Children and Adolescents." *Primary Psychiatry,* 13 (5), 68–76 (2006). Electronic version retrieved February 7, 2007, from www.primarypsychiatry.com/aspx/article_pf.aspx?articleid=393.

50. Those with OCD are more likely: Mash, E., and Wolfe, D. *Abnormal Child Psychology (Second Edition)*. Belmont, CA: Wadsworth, 2002.

54. Between 1% and 4% of people: Mansueto, C., Ninan, P., Rothbaum, B., and Reeve, E. "Trichotillomania and Its Treatment in Children and Adolescents: A Guide for Clinicians" (2001). Retrieved March 6, 2007, from www.trich.org/articles/view_default.asp?aid=27. Ellis, C., and Roberts, H. "Anxiety Disorder: Trichotillomania" (2006). Retrieved March 6, 2007, from www.emedicine.com/PED/topic2298.htm.

57. Social Anxiety Disorder (SAD) affects: Kashdan, T., and Herbert, J. "Social Anxiety Disorder in Childhood and Adolescence: Current Status and Future Directions." *Clinical Child and Family Psychology Review,* 4, 37–61 (2001).

57. Up to 60% of these young people: Beidel, D., Turner, S., and Morris, T. "Psychopathology of Childhood Social Phobia." *Journal of American Academy of Child and Adolescent Psychiatry,* 38, 643–650 (1999).

57. Most commonly these disorders include: Mash, E., and Wolfe, D. *Abnormal Child Psychology (Second Edition)*. Belmont, CA: Wadsworth, 2002.

58. Assessing Young Children's Social Competence. McClellan, D., and Katz, G. "Assessing Young Children's Social Competence." Champaign, IL: ERIC Clearinghouse on Elementary and Early Childhood Education, 2001.

62. Fifty percent of these young people: Rilva, R., Gallagher, R., and Minami, H. "Cognitive-Behavioral Treatments for Anxiety Disorders in Children and Adolscents." *Primary Psychiatry,* 13 (5), 68–76 (2006). Electronic version retrieved February 7, 2007, from www.primarypsychiatry.com/aspx/article_pf.aspx?articleid=393.

62. Risk and Resiliency Factors for Post-Traumatic Stress Disorder: King, D., Vogt, D., and King, L. "Risk and Resilience Factors in the Etiology of Chronic Post-Traumatic Stress Disorder." In Litz, B. (editor) *Early Intervention for Trauma and Traumatic Loss.* New York: Guilford, 2006.

67. Between 1% and 5% of adolescents: Mash, E., and Wolfe, D. *Abnormal Child Psychology (Second Edition)*. Belmont, CA: Wadsworth, 2002.

70. Between 1% and 5% of children and adolescents: Fremont, W. "School Refusal in Children and Adolescents." *American Family Physician,* 68, 1555–60 (2003).

70. Ultimately, about 10% of students: Child Trends DataBand. "High School Dropout Rates" (2003). Retrieved February 7, 2007, from www.childtrendsdatabank.org/indicators/1HighSchoolDropout.cfm.

70. Up to 75 percent of students: Rilva, R., Gallagher, R., and Minami, H. "Cognitive-Behavioral Treatments for Anxiety Disorders in Children and Adolscents." *Primary Psychiatry,* 13 (5), 68–76 (2006). Electronic version retrieved February 7, 2007, from www.primarypsychiatry.com/aspx/article_pf.aspx?articleid=393.

70. Up to 40 percent of elementary school students: Beidel, D., and Turner, S. *Shy Children, Phobic Adults.* Washington, DC: American Psychological Association, 1998.

70. It's estimated that 160,000 students: National Education Association. "Youth Risk Behavior Survey" (1995).

72. Separation Anxiety Disorder (SAD) is one: U.S. Department of Health and Human Services. "Mental Health: A Report of the Surgeon General" (1999). Electronic version retrieved February 7, 2007, from www.surgeongeneral.gov/library/mentalhealth.

Mood Disorders

77. About 5% of children: Mash, E., and Wolfe, D. *Abnormal Child Psychology (Second Edition)*. Belmont, CA: Wadsworth, 2002.

77. Up to two-thirds of these young people: Virginia Commission on Youth. "Mood Disorders" (2003). Retrieved February 7, 2007, from coy.state.va.us/Modalities/mood.htm.

78. In the United States, a young person: Watkins, C. "Suicide in Youth" (2004). Retrieved February 7, 2007, from www.baltimorepsych.com/Suicide.htm.

79. Approximately 1% of children: Rogers, E., and Spalding, S. "Mood Disorder: Dysthymic Disorder" (2006). Retrieved February 7, 2007, from www.emedicine.com/ped/topic640.htm.

79. About 3% of children: Mash, E., and Wolfe, D. *Abnormal Child Psychology (Second Edition).* Belmont, CA: Wadsworth, 2002.

79. Between one-half to two-thirds: Harvard Health Publications. "Depression in Children—Part 1" (2002). Retrieved February 7, 2007, from www.health.harvard.edu/newsweek/Depression_in_Children_Part_I.htm. U.S. Department of Health and Human Services. "Mental Health: A Report of the Surgeon General" (1999). Electronic version retrieved February 7, 2007, from www.surgeongeneral.gov/library/mentalhealth.

80. Children with Dysthymia: U.S. Department of Health and Human Services. "Mental Health: A Report of the Surgeon General" (1999). Electronic version retrieved February 7, 2007, from www.surgeongeneral.gov/library/mentalhealth.

80. Up to 40 percent of children: U.S. Department of Health and Human Services. "Mental Health: A Report of the Surgeon General" (1999). Electronic version retrieved February 7, 2007, from www.surgeongeneral.gov/library/mentalhealth.

80. Symptoms of depression can vary: Harvard Health Publications. "Depression in Children—Part 1" (2002). Retrieved February 7, 2007, from www.health.harvard.edu/newsweek/Depression_in_Children_Part_I.htm.

83. Recent evidence shows that increased: Gibbons, R., Hur, K., Bhaumik, D., and Mann, J. *American Journal of Psychiatry,* 163: 1898–1904 (2006).

85. Estimates suggest that up to 1% of young people: U.S. Department of Health and Human Services. "Mental Health: A Report of the Surgeon General" (1999). Electronic version retrieved February 7, 2007, from www.surgeongeneral.gov/library/mentalhealth.

Communication Disorders

89. Approximately 3% of children: U.S. Department of Health and Human Services. "Mental Health: A Report of the Surgeon General" (1999). Electronic version retrieved February 7, 2007, from www.surgeongeneral.gov/library/mentalhealth.

89. About half of these children: Mash, E., and Wolfe, D. *Abnormal Child Psychology (Third Edition).* New York: Wadsworth, 2004.

89. A small percentage of students: American Speech-Language-Hearing Association. "Frequently Asked Questions" (2005). Retrieved February 7, 2007, from http://asha.org/public/speech/development/schools_faq.htm.

91. About 10% of all children: Mash, E., and Wolfe, D. *Abnormal Child Psychology (Third Edition).* New York: Wadsworth, 2004.

94. Between 3% and 5% of preschool: Medical Encyclopedia. "Mixed Receptive and Expressive Language Disorder" (2006). Retrieved February 7, 2007, from www.nlm.nih.gov/medlineplus/ency/article/001545.htm.

94. Receptive Language Disorder and Expressive Language Disorder are not caused: Mash, E., and Wolfe, D. *Abnormal Child Psychology (Third Edition).* New York: Wadsworth, 2004.

94. Children with Receptive Language Disorders may: "Speech and/or Language Exceptionality Definition." Retrieved February 7, 2007, from www.edu.gov.nf.ca/special/speech.htm.

95. Children with an Expressive Language Disorder may: Medical Encyclopedia. "Mixed Receptive and Expressive Language Disorder" (2006). Retrieved February 7, 2007, from www.nlm.nih.gov/medlineplus/ency/article/001545.htm.

100. About 1% of young people: Medical Encyclopedia. "Stuttering" (2006). Retrieved September 5, 2004, from www.nlm.nih.gov/medlineplus/ency/article/001427.htm.

100. The most obvious difficulty in school: Pediatric Speech Pathology. "Stuttering." Retrieved February 7, 2007, from www.stronghealth.com/services/speechpathology/conditions/stuttering.cfm.

104. The majority of students with the disorder: Ozonoff, S., Dawson, G., and McPartland, J. *A Parent's Guide to Asperger Syndrome and High-Functioning Autism.* New York: Guilford, 2002. Center for Disease Control and Prevention. "Mental Health in the United States: Parental Report of Diagnosed Autism in Children Aged 4–17 Years—United States, 2003–2004." In "Morbidity and Mortality Weekly Report," 55 (17), 481–486 (2006). Retrieved February 7, 2007, from www.cdc.gov/mmwr/preview/mmwrhtml/mm5517a3.htm.

Learning Disabilities

109. School districts consider only about 5% of students: Lyon, G., and Fletcher, J. "Early Warning System" (2001). Retrieved February 7, 2007, from www.educationnext.org/20012/22.html. LD Online. "About Learning Disabilities." Retrieved February 7, 2007, from www.ldonline.org/questions/aboutld#5063.

109. Young people with learning disabilities: Friedman, M., Chabildas, N., Budhiraja, N., Willcutt, E., and Pennington, B. "Etiology of the Comorbidity Between RD and ADHD: Exploration of the Non-Random Mating Hypothesis." American Journal of Medical Genetics, 120, 4 (2003).

110. Special Education Today: Fletcher, J., Lyon, G. R., Fuchs, L., and Barnes, M. *Learning Disabilities: From Identification to Intervention.* New York: Guilford, 2007.

111. Between 10% and 15% of all students: Fletcher, J., Lyon, G. R., Fuchs, L., and Barnes, M. *Learning Disabilities: From Identification to Intervention.* New York: Guilford, 2007.

111. The brain of a person with Dyslexia: Fletcher, J., Lyon, G. R., Fuchs, L., and Barnes, M. *Learning Disabilities: From Identification to Intervention.* New York: Guilford, 2007.

115. Vocabulary development using computer-based instruction: National Reading Panel. "Teaching Children to Read: An Evidence-Based Assessment of the Scientific Research Literature on Reading and Its Implications for Reading Instruction." Jessup, MD: National Institute for Literacy, 2001.

118. Elements of Classroom Reading Instruction: Torgeson, J. "Avoiding the Devastating Downward Spiral." *American Educator,* 6–45 (2004).

119. About 6% of students: Shalev, R. "Developmental Dyscalculia." *Journal of Child Neurology,* 19, 765–771 (2004).

124. At least 10% of students: Fletcher, J., Lyon, G. R., Fuchs, L., and Barnes, M. *Learning Disabilities: From Identification to Intervention.* New York: Guilford, 2007.

124. It is the most common learning disability: Mayes, S., Calhoun, S., and Crowell, E. "Learning Disabilities and ADHD: Overlapping Spectrum Disorders." *Journal of Learning Disabilities,* 33, 417–424 (2000).

129. Less than 1% of the population: Thompson, S. "Nonverbal Learning Disorders" (1996). Retrieved February 7, 2007, from www.ldonline.org/article/6114.

ADHD

135. About 8% of young people: "Mental Health in the United States: Prevalence of Diagnosis and Medication for Attention-Deficit/Hyperactivity Disorder—United States, 2003." In "Morbidity and Mortality Weekly Report" (54), 842–847 (2003). Retrieved February 7, 2007, from www.cdc.gov/mmwr/preview/mmwrhtml/mm5434a2.htm.

138. Something to Think About . . .: Harris, Ruth E. "An ADD Child's Bill of Rights." Eau Claire, WI: Northwest Reading Clinic, 1997. Used with permission.

142. Use classroom management techniques: Barkley, R. *Attention Deficit Hyperactivity Disorder (Third Edition).* New York: Guilford, 2006.

144. The Ideal Teacher (and Parent) for an ADHD Child: Gordon, M. *ADHD/Hyperactivity: A Consumer's Guide.* DeWitt, NY: Gordon Systems Inc., 1991. Used with permission.

Disruptive Behavior Disorders

147. About 10% of children and adolescents: Tynan, W. "Oppositional Defiant Disorder" (2003). Retrieved February 7, 2007, from www.emedicine.com/PED/topic2791.htm.

153. Tips for Avoiding Power Struggles: Levy, R., and O'Hanlon, B. *Try and Make Me!* New York: Rodale, 2001. Used with permission.

154. Residential programs and "boot camps": Tynan, W. "Conduct Disorder" (2003). Retrieved February 7, 2007, from www.emedicine.com/ped/topic2793.htm.

Asperger's Syndrome

155. Asperger's Syndrome occurs in about: Centers for Disease Control and Prevention. "How Common are Autistic Spectrum Disorders (ASD)?" (2006). Retrieved February 7, 2007, from www.cdc.gov/ncbddd/autism/asd_common.htm.

155. It is much more common in boys: Ozonoff, S., Dawson, G., and McPartland, J. *A Parent's Guide to Asperger Syndrome and High-Functioning Autism.* New York: Guilford, 2002.

155. Up to 40% of children: Attwood, T. *The Complete Guide to Asperger's Syndrome.* Philadelphia: Jessica Kingsley, 2006.

161. What It's Like . . .: Jackson, L. *Freaks, Geeks and Asperger Syndrome.* Philadelphia: Jessica Kingsley, 2002. Used with permission.

Tic Disorders

163. Between 1% and 2% of people experience: Pennington, B. *The Development of Psychopathology.* New York: Guilford, 2002.

166. What It's Like . . .: Pillen, G. "He Can't Stop It." *South Florida Sun-Sentinel.* August 27, 1991, E 1,6. Used with permission.

Eating Disorders

167. While exact figures are not known: National Institute of Mental Health. "Eating Disorders: Facts About Eating Disorders and Their Solutions" (2001). Retrieved February 7, 2007, from www.nimh.nih.gov/publicat/eatingdisorders.cfm.

167. While these percentages reflect: U.S. Department of Health and Human Services. "Eating Disorders" (2003). Retrieved February 7, 2007, from www.mentalhealth.org/publications/allpubs/ken98-0047/default.asp.

167. One-third of people with eating disorders: National Association of Anorexia Nervosa and Associated Disorders. "Facts About Eating Disorders" (2000). Retrieved February 7, 2007, from http://anad.org/site/anadweb/content.php?type=1&id=6982#facts.

167. Underlying issues of eating disorders: Mash, E., and Wolfe, D. *Abnormal Child Psychology (Second Edition)*. Belmont, CA: Wadsworth, 2002.

168. In truth, eating disorders are potentially: Alliance for Eating Disorders Awareness. "Eating Disorders" (2005). Retrieved February 7, 2007, from www.eatingdisorderinfo.org/4.html.

Self-Injury

173. Estimates suggest that between: Focus Adolescent Services. "What is Self-Injury?" (2000). Retrieved February 7, 2007, from www.focusas.com/SelfInjury.html.

173. They are a response to overwhelming: Alderman, T. *Scarred Soul*. Oakland: New Harbinger Publications, 1997.

174. Recent research suggests that certain abnormalities: Crowell, S., Beauchaine, T., McCauley, E., Smith, C., Stevens, A., and Sylvers, P. "Psychological, Autonomic, and Serotonergic Correlates of Parasuicide Among Adolescent Girls." *Development and Psychopathology* (17), 1–23 (2005).

176. It is the third-leading cause of death: National Institute of Mental Health. "Suicide in the U.S.: Statistics and Prevention" (2003). Retrieved February 7, 2007, from www.nimh.nih.gov/publicat/harmsway.cfm#children.

179. "I have come to the frightening conclusion." Ginott, Haim. *Teacher and Child: A Book for Parents and Teachers*. New York: Collier, 1993. Used with permission.

Index

Note: Page numbers in italics indicate sample pages. Page numbers in boldface indicate reproducible forms.

A

B

C

D

E

F

G

M

N

O

P

Q

R

S

T

U

V

W

Y

About the Author

Myles L. Cooley, Ph.D., ABPP, is a Board Certified Clinical Psychologist who has had a private practice in psychology for over 30 years. For the second half of his career, he has specialized in learning, behavioral, and developmental disorders in children and adolescents. He has provided training on these topics to physicians, educators, school psychologists, parents, and mental health professionals. He has served as a consultant to several public and private schools and has published several articles on ADHD and learning disabilities.

Myles and his wife live in Palm Beach Gardens, Florida, where they enjoy the beautiful weather in winter and try to avoid hurricanes in the summer. Myles enjoys tennis, piano, choral singing, and lecturing on cruises. For more information on speaking engagements, consultation, or training, you can contact him at www.drmylescooley.com.

Other Great Books from Free Spirit

The Survival Guide for Kids with ADD or ADHD
by John F. Taylor, Ph.D.
In kid-friendly language and a format that welcomes easily distracted readers, this book helps kids diagnosed with ADD or ADHD succeed in school, get along better at home, and form healthy, enjoyable relationships with peers. Kids learn to sit still when it's time to be still, pay attention, make decisions, stay calm, and deal (when needed) with doctors, counselors, and medication. Includes a special message for parents.
$13.95; 112 pp., 2-color illust., softcover; 6" x 9"

The Survival Guide for Kids with LD*
*Learning Differences
by Gary Fisher, Ph.D., and Rhoda Cummings, Ed.D.
Kids need to know they're smart and can learn—they just learn differently. This book answers the many questions they have; explains what LD means (and doesn't mean); defines different kinds of LD; describes what happens in LD programs; helps kids deal with feelings; and inspires young people to set goals and plan for the future.
$10.95; 112 pp., illust., softcover; 6" x 9"

What to Do When You're Scared & Worried
A Guide for Kids
by James J. Crist, Ph.D.
From a dread of spiders to panic attacks, kids have worries and fears, just like adults. This is a book kids can turn to when they need advice, reassurance, and ideas. They'll find out where fears and worries come from, practice Fear Chasers and Worry Erasers, and learn to seek help for hard-to-handle fears they can't manage on their own.
$9.95; 128 pp., 2-color illust., softcover; $5\frac{3}{8}$" x $8\frac{3}{8}$"

What to Do When You're Sad & Lonely
A Guide for Kids
by James J. Crist, Ph.D.
All kids feel sad and lonely sometimes. Growing numbers of children are living with depression, a disease often mistaken for sadness. This reassuring book offers strategies and tips kids can use to beat the blues and blahs, get a handle on their feelings, make and keep friends, and enjoy their time alone. The second part focuses on depression, bipolar disorder, grief, and other problems too big for kids to handle on their own, and describes what it's like to go to counseling. Includes a note to grown-ups and a list of resources.
$9.95; 128 pp., 2-color illust., softcover; $5\frac{3}{8}$" x $8\frac{3}{8}$"

The Behavior Survival Guide for Kids
How to Make Good Choices and Stay Out of Trouble
by Thomas McIntyre, Ph.D. (also known as Dr. Mac)
Up-to-date information, practical strategies, and sound advice for kids with diagnosed behavior problems (BD, ED, EBD) and those with general behavior problems so they can help themselves. Resources for parents and teachers are available as a *free download* at our Web site.
$14.95; 176 pp., illust., softcover; 7" x 9"

Teaching Beyond the Test (Book and CD-ROM)
Differentiated Project-Based Learning in a Standards-Based Age, Grades 6 & Up
by Phil Schlemmer, M.Ed., and Dori Schlemmer
Transforming students into confident, self-directed, lifelong learners requires differentiated instruction and project-based learning. This practical classroom resource presents 28 strategies for differentiation among learners (flexible grouping, choice boards, tiered assignments, and more) and 15 fully developed content-focused projects, each modeling one or more differentiation strategies. All projects are aligned with rigorous, comprehensive content standards in the areas of English/language arts, math, social studies, and science. Designed for use by any teacher, in any classroom, in any school. Includes reproducibles.
$29.95; 240 pp.; softcover; 8½" x 11"

The Essential Guide to Talking with Teens
Ready-to-Use Discussions for School and Youth Groups
by Jean Sunde Peterson, Ph.D.
Tested with thousands of teens in many kinds of schools (plus community centers, churches, and workshops), these guided discussions are proven ways to reach out to young people and address their social and emotional needs. Teens gain self-awareness and self-esteem, practice problem-solving and goal-setting, feel more in control of their lives, and learn they have much in common with each other—they are not alone. Each session is self-contained and step-by-step. Many include reproducible handouts. Introductory and background materials help even less-experienced group leaders feel prepared and secure in their role. For advising teachers, counselors, and youth workers in all kinds of school and group settings.
$29.95; 288 pp.; softcover; 8½" x 11"

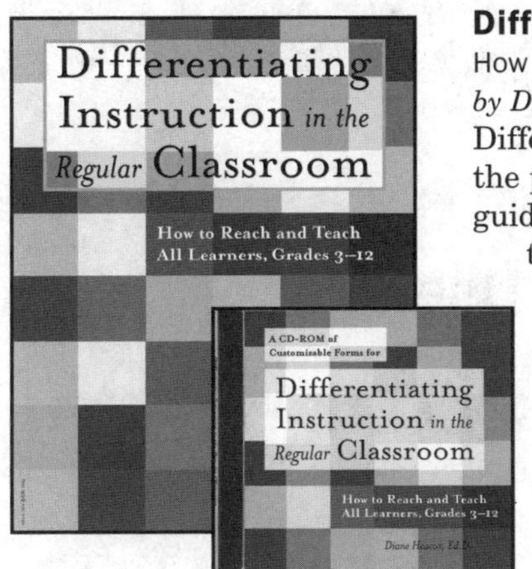

Differentiating Instruction in the Regular Classroom
How to Reach and Teach All Learners, Grades 3–12
by Diane Heacox, Ed.D.
Differentiation—one of the hottest topics in education today—means changing the pace, level, or kind of instruction to fit the learner. This timely, practical guide is a menu of strategies, examples, templates, and tools teachers can use to differentiate instruction in any curriculum, even a standard or mandated curriculum, and ensure that every child has opportunities to learn and develop his or her talents. Includes dozens of reproducible handout masters.
$29.95; 176 pp.; softcover; 8½" x 11"

Differentiating Instruction in the Regular Classroom CD-ROM
All of the forms from the book, plus additional materials and more examples of curriculum maps and matrix plans, ready to customize and print out.
$17.95; Macintosh and PC compatible, 5" CD-ROM, 63 reproducible handout masters.

Teaching Kids with Learning Difficulties in the Regular Classroom
Strategies and Techniques Every Teacher Can Use to Challenge & Motivate Struggling Students
by Susan Winebrenner
From the relentless pressure to make sure all students score at the proficient level on high-stakes tests, to the rigorous requirements of "No Child Left Behind," teachers are being held more accountable than ever before—making this book more important than ever before. A gold mine of practical, easy-to-use teaching methods, strategies, and tips, it helps teachers differentiate the curriculum in all subject areas to meet the needs of all learners—including those labeled "slow," "remedial," or "LD," students of poverty, English Language Learners, and others who struggle to learn. An essential resource for every educator. Includes reproducibles.
$29.95; 248 pp.; softcover; 8½" x 11"